FROTH & SCUM

FROTH & SCUM

TRUTH,
BEAUTY,
GOODNESS,
AND THE
AX MURDER
IN AMERICA'S
FIRST
MASS
MEDIUM

SCUM

ANDIE TUCHER

THE
UNIVERSITY
OF NORTH
CAROLINA
PRESS
CHAPEL HILL
AND
LONDON

Grateful acknowledgment is made to the following: Manuscripts and Archives Section, The New York Public Library, Astor, Lenox and Tilden Foundations, for its approval of my use of excerpts from the Horace Greeley Papers and the James Gordon Bennett Papers. The Special Collections Library, Duke University, for permission to quote from the Gallaher Family Papers and the Bedinger-Dandridge Family Papers. The American Antiquarian Society, The New-York Historical Society, and the Library of Congress, for permission to reproduce illustrations from their collections.

© 1994 The University of North Carolina Press

Manufactured in the United States of America

The paper in this book meets the guidelines for permanence and durability of the Committee on Production Guidelines for Book Longevity of the Council on Library Resources.

Library of Congress Cataloging-in-Publication Data

Tucher, Andie.

Froth and scum: truth, beauty, goodness, and the ax murder in America's first mass medium / Andie Tucher.

p. cm.

Includes bibliographical references and index.

ISBN 0-8078-2162-4 (cloth). — ISBN 0-8078-4472-1 (pbk.)

1. Press — United States — Objectivity. 2. Journalistic ethics — United States. I. Title.

PN4888.O25T83   1994

071'.3 — dc20 94-4238

CIP

98 97 96 95 94   5 4 3 2 1

I know 2 species of men.

The vast majority are men of society.

They live on the surface, they are interested

in the transient & fleeting — they are

like drift wood on the flood — They ask forever

& only the news — the froth & scum of

the eternal sea.

— Thoreau, Journal

CONTENTS

ACKNOWLEDGMENTS

Thanks to many friends, supporters, colleagues, and champions, this project only *seemed* interminable.

Aid from several generous sources helped me complete the earliest incarnation of this work. A travel grant from the Bibliographical Society of America put me aboard buses to do crucial field research. A fellowship at the American Antiquarian Society gave me access to a rich collection and a congenial community of scholars and staff, as well as to the counsel and friendship of the late Stephen Botein, an invaluable gift. The Kaltenborn Foundation revived me splendidly in a bleak hour, and later a Dean's Dissertation Fellowship from New York University gave me the luxury of carefree time. I am thankful to all for their interest, their support, and certainly their patience.

For assistance, advice, and encouragement, I am also grateful to Paul Baker and Michael O'Malley at NYU, to Kenneth T. Jackson and Ene Sirvet of the Society of American Historians, and to Lewis Bateman and Pamela Upton, my astute and vigilant editor, at the University of North Carolina Press.

Meg Fagan, my old and dear friend, ensured that one graduate student starved a lot less than she had any right to expect. My current and previous colleagues at the ABC News Twentieth Century Project and at Public Affairs Television were generous with their cheer and understanding, and Bill Moyers took on the duty — now, at last, no longer thankless — of inspiring, heartening, and prodding me to finish. And my family, who warmed me all along the way with their love, encouragement, and pride, proved there is one *other* thing besides education that no one can ever take from me. Rob Tucher merits a special thanks for his photographic work.

I am deeply grateful to Thomas Bender, not just for guiding my work from the very beginning, but also for inspiring me with his vision, his enthusiasm, and his example. Daniel J. Czitrom read the manuscript with care and offered many perceptive and canny suggestions. And Dan Bischoff made everything better, including the manuscript.

Any error or misinterpretation I claim as my just deserts, and mine alone.

FROTH & SCUM

PROLOGUE

Routed from her bed at three o'clock one Sunday morning in 1836 by a late customer's knock, Rosina Townsend, the keeper of a stylish house of prostitution on Thomas Street in Manhattan, was surprised to find a lamp burning unattended in the parlor and the back door standing open. She picked up the lamp and made the rounds of the house. When an ominous smell led her to open the door to Helen Jewett's second-floor room, she was instantly enveloped in a thick cloud of smoke.

Townsend's screams aroused the entire house and brought the city watchmen rushing in to find Jewett lying dead in her smoldering bed. The killer, however, was not the fire. The blaze had been set in an unsuccessful attempt to hide the real cause of death: the victim's head had been deeply gashed three times by a sharp weapon. Police immediately arrested the young woman's favorite admirer, a drygoods clerk who had paid her a visit that night in celebration of his nineteenth birthday.

American journalism set out to discover the truth. It ended by unearthing an array of different truths that frequently were untrammeled by fact.

Five years later, on a warm September day in 1841, the mysterious week-old disappearance of a respectable New York printer was finally explained when his naked and decomposing body was found bundled in an awning and jammed into a crate in the cargo hold of a ship bound for New Orleans. The victim's head had been hacked and mangled by a sharp weapon.

The prime suspect, a teacher of bookkeeping who owed money to the dead man, soon confessed his guilt, but at the trial his attorneys contended that he had been forced to kill the printer in self-defense when an argument over the amount of the debt took a violent turn. Their legal arguments were overwhelmed, however, by courtroom theatrics ranging from the exhumation and exhibition of the victim's mutilated head to a demonstration by the defendant's brother, Samuel Colt, of how well his new revolving pistol could shoot.

American journalism set out to discover the facts. It ended by unearthing an array of facts in support of a single incomplete truth.

In the 1830s an entirely new kind of newspaper, the urban penny press, introduced American readers to a novel idea of what their relationship with news ought to be. Common wisdom has held ever since that the great achievement of the penny press was its development of the ideal of objectivity: the premise that the duty of a reporter — operating free of bias, preconception, outside pressure, or personal agenda — is to marshal the facts that will reproduce as far as possible the world as it really is.

Yet a curious problem has warped most recent thinking about the growth of objectivity in the penny press. It is a slippery concept, hard to define and harder to recognize, and a careless presumption in its favor can make impossible its own objective verification. Modern historians, however, have done just that. Having already decided that objectivity was the great contribution of the penny press, they accept everything in such papers as objective and base their arguments entirely on the sandy foundation of yellowing newsprint. Having already decided that penny editors embraced fact, they assume the consummation of that embrace and trust without verifying.[1]

Objectivity is not the same as truthfulness, however; facts do not necessarily add up to reality, and although journalists have often been guided by noble ideals, they have also been shaped by their need to present facts and truths that make sense to the community of consumers they are trying to lure and that accommodate their vision of the way the world works.

The penny press, like every institution ever nurtured by the human mind, grew sloppily, capriciously, along convoluted paths that often surprised its own progenitors. It was devised in a time of rapid and often blind change, by newspapermen who were unsure exactly what they were creating. They did not set out to invent a mass medium; they did not sit down and create an ideal called objective journalism. They *did* invent a medium that was appealing enough to grow massive, a medium whose continuing commercial success was often abetted by a developing stratagem that has come to be known as objectivity.

And in these complicated, ambiguous relationships among journalism, truth, the market, and the public that began in the embryonic years of the New York penny press lie the roots of many of the problems — from the suspicion and cynicism of their readers to the fragmentation of their public — that bedevil journalists to this day.

The bloodlines of these relationships, along with an inkling of the complexities that would arise in the future, can best be explored in the penny press's treatment of the two murders that easily provided the most notorious, most intricate, and most spellbinding stories of its first years. The charge that journalists — and their readers — are overly preoccupied with the unseemly, with apparently trivial sensations of the moment, is, of course, neither new nor startling. Within a generation of the birth of the penny press, Henry David Thoreau would voice a sentiment more eloquent than rare when he complained that the vast majority of people are merely "men of society. They live on the surface, they are interested in the transient & fleeting — they are like drift wood on the flood — They ask forever & only the news — the froth & scum of the eternal sea."[2]

Yet because the unseemly is also so unsettling, so threatening to personal security as well as to the social order, the way this kind of news is presented and the way the public reacts to it can be immensely revealing, resonant with the fears, hopes, and anxieties of society at large and sensitive to gusts and currents of change. Because a murder is so often a mystery, too, a puzzle that may or may not be solved, a story that may well defy any definitive resolution, it permits — even invites — readers to shop around for the explanation that best fits their views of the world. A battle for the hearts and minds of readers between explanations that are gravely contradictory can offer invaluable clues to the roots and ramifications of social conflict.

To comprehend what really happened during the infancy of the world's first mass medium, we must reexamine the facts of each murder in turn, reconsider the significance of each in its social milieu, and reimagine the very meaning of such familiar concepts as truth, reality, deception, class, community, and the public good. We must discover and explore the unspoken assumptions, presumptions, observations, and beliefs shared by the readers of the penny press. We must rove far afield to places like Arkansas and Virginia and investigate whether readers who did not share the same observations and beliefs could nonetheless agree on any universal truths.

We will discover that the story of the dead harlot and the depraved teenager, as covered by the penny press, was not entirely froth or scum. Rather it became a public exploration of some of the hardest, most critical, most eternal questions a people must face together. It was about the possibility of justice, the privileges of power, the inequities of class, the consequences of sin, and the nature of evil; it was about the need to figure out who one was and where one fit into a community riven by change. It was an odyssey in search of some great Truth — but it ended in the triumph of the truth most useful and congenial to society's most powerful citizens, a truth that let an obvious criminal go free.

That idea of the duty of the press became so successful as to ensure its own swift demise. Just half a decade later, in the case of the importunate printer and the truculent bookkeeper, the consequences of success conspired to convince journalists and their readers that the Truth could best be found through the accumulation and investigation of a host of plain facts. The penny-press coverage of the printer's murder seemed to approach much closer to objectivity, to the ideal that came to define the practice of modern journalism. And it entirely missed the single fact that could have kept a secret criminal from going free.

I

FIGHTING FOR THE TRUTH

1

THE PENNY PRESS IS BORN

      In the spring of 1836, the penny press was most distinctive for its fierce spirit of competition and rivalry. At that point Benjamin Day of the *Sun*, the dean of the fraternity with two and a half years of business behind him, was reveling in a circulation of at least twenty-two thousand, a loyal coterie of advertisers, and a yearly profit well in excess of twenty thousand dollars.[1] His success had inspired many imitators, most of whose journalistic acumen was worth little more than the coin they occasionally managed to winkle out of the passing pocket. Hopeful new penny papers soon began sprouting, blooming, and usually drooping in Philadelphia and Boston as well as New York.

    A few of the new papers, however, did seem capable of threatening the

Sun's hegemony. In 1834, two former colleagues of Day's, Willoughby Lynde and William J. Stanley, started their own paper, the *Transcript.* Soon it was selling nearly as well as the *Sun* in New York City and even better in the nearby cities and towns. Then in 1835 James Gordon Bennett, a squint-eyed Scottish immigrant who had spent the previous fifteen years working for, leaving, establishing, and failing in newspapers up and down the East Coast, sank his last five hundred dollars into a new venture, the *Morning Herald* (soon known simply as the *Herald*), with the determination that this time he would succeed.

In the spring of 1836, however, all this frantic editorial competition more closely resembled a cock fight than a horse race. The editors had no particular desire other than winning and no clear goalpost to reach. They were still struggling to decide just what a cheap paper ought to be and what readership it ought to attract.

They did know what it wasn't. It wasn't anything like the newspapers Americans already knew. It was no ragamuffin hometown weekly retailing stale national and international news for a tiny local community. Nor was it one of those huge, somber, expensive urban dailies known as "sixpenny" sheets. Those were devoted chiefly to politics and financial news, were expected to serve the interests of politicians, businessmen, merchants, and the local gentry, and, like the small-town papers, were usually under the patronage — and therefore the thumb — of a particular political party.

Party journalism did confer certain advantages on both the party and the journalist. Because no party could flourish without a mouthpiece to rally its troops and harry its opponents, political operatives valued the help of editors skilled in the ways of rhetorical warfare. And because few individuals could afford the heavy expenses of paper, ink, labor, and printing equipment without aid, aspiring editors welcomed the patronage of a political party.

Yet because that patronage required the editor's devotion to party interests and his persecution of its enemies, candor often suffered, and the penny editors explicitly rejected this constraint. Often and vigorously they criticized party papers as mere tools of the establishment. "Depending more than we do," the *Transcript* proclaimed on 14 June 1836, "upon the approbation and support of particular sects, parties, or *claques,* [the sixpenny paper] may bow obsequiously to the suggestions, or bend submissively to the will, of any subscriber who may feel offended at the articles which they publish."[2]

The new editors had very different labels for themselves. *Fearless* was a favorite, as were *candid, honest,* and *independent.* Rather than seeking the dubious and cramping support of stalwarts, zealots, or nabobs, the penny editors financed their operations solely through advertising and sales revenues, and they developed new, aggressive selling ploys to push those revenues as high as possible.

No longer did the urban reader have to seek out the newspaper office and produce ten dollars on the spot for a yearly subscription; it became harder to resist a paper than to buy one from the ubiquitous legions of ragged boys who hawked copies in the streets and earned more money the more papers they sold. The penny editors left the ponderous articles about world and national affairs to the Wall Street sheets while they concentrated on snappy, even sensational stories of more human interest and more local relevance.

Benjamin Day did these stories the best, even though he frequently did them by accident. Experimentation, serendipity, and even logistical and financial constraint were just as important as design in the *Sun's* development. If indeed Day's readers seemed to love lively stories about happenings in their own city — fires, theatrical performances, elephants escaping from circus caravans, women trampled in the street by hogs run amok — these stories were also easier and cheaper to report. If Day could not, in the early days, get the Washington news as fast as the *Journal of Commerce* with its twenty-four-horse express relays, he could still afford to pay the unemployed printer George Wisner four dollars a week to rise before dawn and record the tiny dramas of the police court. And if the sixpenny papers did cover elections, financial affairs, and overseas imbroglios more thoroughly, New Yorkers soon learned that the penny papers were the best place to read all about how Daniel Sullivan beat and choked his wife to death in a drunken rage or to verify the rumor that the Reverend Joseph Carter had been arrested for rape.

Chronicles of crime were not a particularly new phenomenon in America, but *news* of crime was. Newspapers had traditionally paid very little attention to lawbreakers and wrongdoers. Their reticence sprang in part from logistics: hard-pressed local weeklies could rarely spare precious space to report on events that most townspeople would already have heard about, clucked over, and dissected for every nuance of meaning as they went about their daily business in the town square, the shops, or the taverns.

But many newspaper editors were also constrained by a high sense of delicacy and civic responsibility. Along with their readers, they preferred not to publicize matters that could only embarrass their community, tarnish their image, and perhaps even corrupt weak-minded readers into taking up a life of crime themselves. The eminent Philadelphia physician Benjamin Rush had made the case eloquently in 1786. "In order to preserve the vigour of the moral faculty," he wrote, "it is of the utmost consequence to keep young people as ignorant as possible of those crimes that are generally thought most disgraceful to human nature. Suicide, I believe, is often propagated by means of newspapers. For this reason, I should be glad to see the proceedings of our courts kept from the public eye, when they expose or punish monstrous vices." In another essay he urged newspaper editors never to publish anything "that you would not wish your wife or daughter (if you have any) should read or understand."[3]

Americans who wished to indulge in colorful accounts of the evil deeds, confessions, and executions of malefactors and ne'er-do-wells did, however, have another resource: cheap, hastily printed, crudely illustrated pamphlets and broadsides produced by job printers who were as nonchalant about accuracy as they were about local honor. Although these accounts presented themselves as true, they usually relied for their details more on tradition, legend, and formula than on fact.

Many included such creative and melodramatic accompaniments as a "genuine" interview with the condemned prisoner in his cell, "authentic" letters or diaries documenting a life gone awry, and the criminal's own poignant "dying words," which were often composed in advance by the shrewd publisher who was hawking them at the foot of the scaffold even before the body stopped swinging. One Philadelphia pamphleteer, determined to remove any possible doubt about the authenticity of his wares, festooned the title page of an 1824 account of a murderous burglar with protestations of truth. Apparently dissatisfied with the stalwart conviction displayed by his title, *The Only Copy of the Life, and the Testimony That Convicted Michl. Monroe Alias James Wellington . . . for the Murder of Wm. Bonsall . . . Containing the Testimony of Mary Warner, Phoebe Bonsall, Dr. Morris C. Sealcross, &c. . . . Together with a List of the Jury*, he added another line at the bottom of the page. "This is the Only Original Copy," it read. "All others are Spurious."

This ephemeral crime literature had taken early root in Puritan-dominated colonial New England. Partly as a didactic device and partly as an excuse for indulging in sensationalism, authors and printers had accompanied their tales of the sordid with some sort of pious lesson or stern warning about the consequences of sin — with a sermon delivered at a murderer's execution or a description of an infanticide's conversion and redemption through the love of Christ. As society grew increasingly secular, however, the sensationalism began to outstrip the moralism, and a particularly audacious or clever rogue could find himself celebrated rather than condemned. Luridly imaginative crime pamphlets soon became a popular pastime for many American readers as well as a lucrative product for printers who found them a cheap, quick, easy, and highly saleable way to get more use out of their presses.

Not until the 1820s did crime news noticeably begin to creep into journalism. That was when a number of novelty-seeking papers in London began running a regular column reporting on amusing cases of petty crime — public drunkenness, audacious minor larcenies, lewd behavior — brought before the Bow Street police court. American city papers soon followed suit. Although most were content merely to copy the London reports, a few — notably James Watson Webb's *Courier and Enquirer* — went so far as to add the occasional funny or newsworthy note from their own police courts. It was Webb who in 1830 sent his associate editor, James Gordon Bennett, all the way to Salem, Massachusetts, to cover a notorious criminal trial in which Senator Daniel Webster himself joined the team prosecuting three young men accused of murdering a retired sea captain for his money. The unprecedented press attention so distressed the judges that they vainly attempted to forbid the publication of any and all news about the trial.[4]

Yet crime reporting remained a diffident and sporadic presence in the press until the penny papers burst onto the scene. For them, crime news became an immediate and natural staple: it was easy and inexpensive to gather; it was pleasant and familiar to readers already conversant with street literature; it provided New Yorkers with useful and important information about the way their city worked; and it would meet no serious competition from the established press. Its other advantages as an extraordinarily sensitive social barometer would soon become apparent as well.

For all the penny editors' apparent boldness and conviction as they went about inventing this new kind of newspaper, however, they were still somewhat ambivalent about who their new audience was and who they wanted it to be. In New York the editors certainly recognized the potential of a vast and unserved market, the growing working class — artisans, laborers, domestic servants, journeymen — who saw themselves as a distinct group within the city's social and economic hierarchy, a group with different interests and expectations from those of the traditional newspaper buyers of the professional class.

These readers were literate enough to enjoy light reading, solvent enough to spare a penny a day for entertainment, and buoyed by the egalitarian sense that they deserved every civilized accessory the "better sort" did. They were fascinated by their city — vast, swarming, fabulous, and bizarre. They were ripe for a literature of their own, a press that would accompany and perhaps even guide them as they strove to clarify the environment in which they lived and the terms of their own distinctiveness.

Many of the new penny editors were themselves members of this working class. Several had recently been active in the Working Men's movement, Jacksonian New York's first, confused, and abortive encounter with radical popular politics. A few years earlier, Day, Lynde, and Stanley had all worked to some extent on the short-lived *Daily Sentinel*, a champion of the freethinking republicanism of Thomas Paine and a darling of reformers and egalitarians like Robert Dale Owen and Fanny Wright. Lynde, moreover, was serving as the printers' delegate to the General Trades' Union, an umbrella group that would be responsible for organizing more than fifty craft unions and some forty strikes in just four years.[5]

Not surprisingly, therefore, the editors' sympathies inclined toward the laboring class, often explicitly. According to the *Sun's* prospectus, its objective was to give all the news of the day "at a price within the means of every one." Two months later, on 9 November 1833, Benjamin Day proclaimed that the penny press was "effecting the march of intelligence" by "diffusing useful knowledge among the operative classes of society."

Despite their declarations of nonpartisanship, the early penny editors all tended to support Democratic party candidates and the Democratic side of public questions — from choice this time, and not, as the party papers did, for survival. The penny editors firmly defended territorial expansionism, for instance, and tended to criticize abolitionist agitators while remaining ambivalent on slavery itself. Most of them made a point of sympathetically covering workingmen's issues such as the wave of strikes in the spring of 1836 and the subsequent trial of twenty journeyman tailors for conspiracy when they attempted to resist reduction of their wages. They were, in short, slowly developing America's first successful alternative press.

Still, for all their working-class roots and sympathies, the penny editors were also businessmen. As businessmen, they must have seen clearly an unsettling truth: no enterprise could long survive that depended solely on the working class for its sustenance. The *Daily Sentinel* and the other Working Men's papers had, after all, lived only briefly. Indeed the whole Working Men's movement had fared no better. The movement had been organized in the hard winter of 1829 by a disparate collection of journeymen, artisans, small masters and merchants, reformers, and radicals. It was the culmination of four or five years of haphazard, mostly ineffectual labor agitation as well as a growing conviction among poorer New Yorkers that the recently empowered Tammany Democrats were becoming just as aristocratic, autocratic, and corrupt as the old political machine they had managed to replace.

Among the Workies' specific demands were the ten-hour workday, free republican schools for all, the election of working men to city offices, an end to compulsory militia service, and the abolition of private banks, chartered monopolies, the hereditary transmission of property, and imprisonment for debt.[6] Their impressive showing in the 1829 election for state assembly seemed to augur a promising climate for radical reform.

By the spring of 1830, however, this dangerously seditious movement had been co-opted and the Working Men's party itself taken over by its own conservative wing, led by Noah Cook, a canny commission merchant who had campaigned for the patrician John Quincy Adams in the election of 1828. This faction "included far more men who listed themselves in the city directory as large-scale manufacturers and employers; its craftsmen included an unusually high percentage of master carpenters and builders, and at least some men of great wealth. . . . [T]he Cookites included twice as many men from the 'aristocratic' First Ward . . . [and] all those 'workingmen' known as leading proponents of evangelical temperance reform."[7] The conservative coup left the reformers homeless, powerless, and largely disillusioned with the political system as an agent of change.

The gloomy memory of this failed sedition colored the penny editors' next attempt at journalism and forced them into a state of delicate schizophrenia as they pursued their new audience. It was dangerous, they realized, to be too flagrantly alternative; it was futile, they feared, to be too stubbornly political. Thus these former rebels and Working Men learned a careful temperance. Instead of attacking and excoriating the wealthy and the master class, they began to send out conciliatory signals that any class was welcome to enjoy their new kind of newspaper. Even as Day promised in his prospectus to produce a newspaper within the means of everyone, he added that it would "at the same time afford an advantageous medium for advertising." Even as he dedicated himself to furthering the intelligence of the operative classes, he went on to remark that his paper was "of a character (we hope) deserving the encouragement of all classes of society."

Gone now was the aggressively rebellious tone of the Working Men's papers. The urgent calls for social justice and economic revolution had been almost entirely replaced by the low babble of the street, the theater, and the police court. The reckless demands for equal rights had been elbowed aside by the piquancies of rampaging elephants and dissolute clergymen. Devoting their columns to the small tragedies and comedies of daily life, the editors recognized, was a safe choice as well as a practical one. Not only was reporting on such incidents cheap and easy; it also avoided the dangers of overt warfare against well-armed and seasoned opponents.

Yet the old radical spirit was not entirely extinct. The new penny press had rescued, refurbished, and hoisted as its banner one tattered memento of the Working Men's movement. It must have seemed a relatively innocent relic to the masters and entrepreneurs who were still trembling over their brush with egalitarianism. It posed no overt menace to property or capital or free enterprise. It directly threatened no banks, no inheritance laws, none of the established institutions so vital to the maintenance of the capitalist order. Yet it had been especially precious to the Working Men, the "pole star," as the now-defunct *Sentinel and Working Man's Advocate* had proclaimed on 23 June 1830, "to which our efforts point." The Working Men, and their successors of the penny press, wanted knowledge.

What the Working Men had actually demanded, to be more accurate, was as much practical knowledge and education as the master classes had, and they boldly declared their entitlement to it as free and equal citizens. As Fanny Wright herself put it, "Is this a republic — a country whose affairs are governed by the public voice — when the public mind is unequally enlightened? Is this a republic, where the interest of the many keep in check those of the few — while the few hold possession of the courts of knowledge and the many stand as suitors at the door?"[8]

When all the schools, libraries, and newspapers were created, directed, and priced for the use of the moneyed elite alone, that elite could monopolize access to information as greedily as it monopolized property and power. And in an era of breathtaking progress in science and technology, gaining a monopoly on the sources of information guaranteed the continued control of property and power as well. Only by breaking those strangleholds could the working classes participate as fully as they deserved in the economic and political life of the republic.

The penny editors practiced care in their new campaign for workers' enlightenment and self-improvement. Rather than larding their columns with incendiary words like *monopoly*, they emphasized the practical benefits of learning. "Diffusing useful knowledge among the operative classes of society," as Day had put it early on, was certainly much more socially acceptable than calling for state-run schools for every child in America.

Yet the penny editors also presented as a given, not even open to argument, the proposition that their readers were intellectually equal to the elite. It was "obvious," Day would assert, that "the public have as good an opportunity of forming as correct an opinion" on public matters as the jury or the authorities. They therefore had a "right to express that opinion, whatever it may be." Nor was the judgment of the authorities necessarily infallible. Official decisions on public matters, the *Transcript* would point out, were insufficient without the approbation of the "Court of Public Opinion" as well.

Merchants and businessmen seemed just as ambivalent about the penny papers' direction as were the editors at this point. Many did believe that a reasonably knowledgeable work force was better than an ignorant one. While some, however, saw enlightenment as a social and spiritual benefit in itself and applauded workers' efforts at self-improvement, others preferred the improvement without the prefix. They believed that education, properly administered, would afford them an opportunity to control the "disorderly" classes and to improve the behavior, discipline, and productivity of their own workers.[9]

Although many of the elite denounced the cheap press for pandering to the innate vulgarity of the mob, moreover, they were also coming to recognize that Day was right: his "vulgar" medium was indeed highly advantageous for advertising. Businessmen of all sorts soon decided that no mild lingering strains of artisanal radicalism should prevent their exploiting so promising an advantage for their wares. Those wares included many that must have been well beyond the means or even the experience of the typical "operative" Day and the other editors had in mind.

The close-set gray advertising columns always included scores of calls for cooks, maids, coachmen, bricklayers, and men to open oysters in restaurant kitchens; they trumpeted dozens of opportunities for the poor but industrious who wished to relocate in Texas. But they also directed the less straitened browser to everything from life insurance to "respectable" room and board establishments, lessons in fencing and French, and firms that exchanged gold and notes. Obviously, both the oyster opener and the oyster eater were regular readers of at least a couple of pages in the new cheap papers.

Thus the early penny press did indeed pithily symbolize the social and economic turmoil of the Jacksonian age, the clashing of the interests of the rising classes with those of the entrenched elite, as many commentators have suggested. The cheap press was undoubtedly a popular, often populist organ dedicated chiefly to the interests of people who had never before considered a daily newspaper important to their well-being. Yet it also symbolized the turmoil and conflict going on *within* both the working class and the gentry as they struggled to define their own places in a tumultuous society and to decide how intimately to cohabit with each other.

James Gordon Bennett was different from the other penny editors. *He* cohabited with any reader who would pay him. Wracked with none of the class ambivalence of his colleagues, serenely untroubled by ideological rigor, and free of the guidance as well as the trammels of tradition, he was unhampered by any conviction save one: that a newspaper editor ought to make a great deal of money.

Whereas Day and the others were first of all working men who found profit in becoming businessmen, Bennett was wholly a businessman in ardent search of what would make the most profit. Born in rural Scotland of a comfortable Catholic farm family, educated at a small Aberdeen college, an emigrant to America at the age of twenty-four, he had no ties to the metropolitan laboring class and no particular interest in its welfare.[10] While Day, Lynde, and Stanley were throwing themselves into the Working Men's press, Bennett was beginning his reporting career on a series of very bourgeois sixpenny papers.

He did, like the other penny editors, profess himself free of all party alliances. He had, like the others, developed his professedly independent stand after an unhappy experience with partisan politics. But unlike them, he had no objection to abandoning his convictions when trouble arose. The personal wounds ran too deep, the economic risks too high, and, quite probably, the convictions themselves too shallow for him to do otherwise.

Bennett had spent most of his early New York career on papers controlled by the Tammany Democrats — precisely the faction that soon thereafter exasperated the Working Men into open rebellion. Later, in 1833, after his boss James Watson Webb of the *Courier and Enquirer* dropped Andrew Jackson and turned Whig, Bennett left that paper and bought a small Philadelphia daily, hoping to step into Webb's place and become the Democrats' great new spokesman.

He was, however, either too naive, too rebellious, or too perverse to acknowledge that if one represents oneself as a party spokesman, one ought to accurately present the views of the party leaders on whose behalf one is claiming to speak. Even after Bennett infuriated such high-level Democrats as Amos Kendall by prematurely printing news of Jackson's removal of the bank deposits, even after he contentiously opposed a Pennsylvania Senate candidate supported by the influential national Democratic organ, the *Washington Globe*, he professed himself surprised and embittered that Martin Van Buren and the local party men declined to lend his little *Pennsylvanian* their financial support. He carefully fostered the impression ever after that he had been martyred by his political steadfastness — that after sacrificing all to leave Webb in righteous indignation over the editor's defection to the Whigs, he found himself spurned and ignored by the ungrateful Democrats. Yet though his contemporaries did in fact agree that Bennett had been a valuable and talented reporter for Webb, many considered him ambitious and opportunistic as well.

In 1829, before leaving Webb and moving to the *Pennsylvanian*, Bennett had suggested that Webb merge his *Courier* with M. M. Noah's *Enquirer*, a rival Democratic paper. The suggestion was obviously a bid for power, but less obvious was the intended beneficiary: neither the party nor the editors but Bennett himself. He "believed that the new paper would be unacceptable to the local leadership at Tammany Hall, where Webb was disliked and distrusted. Then, the Scotsman hoped, Tammany would call upon him to start a new party organ in Manhattan." This attempt, along with the *Pennsylvanian* debacle, suggest that what Bennett really wanted was not mere political independence; he preferred an absolute and aggressive autarky.[11]

The experiences also left him with a deep understanding that partisanship of any sort, whether political, economic, or social, whether acknowledged or underground, was simply too limiting for a businessman who wanted to sell to all comers. He left the *Pennsylvanian* in November 1833 and returned to New York just in time to witness the smashing success of Day's independent and unfettered *Sun*. But after both the *Sun* and the *Transcript* declined to hire him, Bennett struck out on his own with a paper he envisioned as even more unlimited than theirs. His prospectus in the first issue of the *Herald*, dated 6 May 1835, was neither equivocal nor subtle: he straightforwardly and plainly sought the largest possible market for his paper. The *Herald*, he declared grandly, was "equally intended for the great masses of the community — the merchant, mechanic, working people — the private family as well as the public hotel — the journeyman and his employer — the clerk and his principal." His paper would "openly disclaim all steel-traps, all principle, as it is called — all party — all politics."

Bennett labored hard to provide something for everyone, regardless of class. The low price of his paper, the police reports and theatrical columns, the bright local news bits, the advertisements for work, were all tried-and-true working-class favorites. Yet he also set a variety of baits to lure more elite readers. Sometimes he tried frontal assault: from the very beginning, the *Herald* included financial reports directed squarely toward Wall Street merchants. Sometimes he tried ingratiation with the merchant class: he frequently taunted Day as a "Fanny Wright infidel," an epithet guaranteed to warm the hearts of any who feared working-class agitation even as it disturbed the old Working Men themselves. Sometimes he tried simple omission. The fraught rhetoric of intellectual egalitarianism so prominent in the other papers was scarcely discernible in the *Herald*.

Most important of all, he learned to be supple. He had avidly defended the striking journeyman tailors in the weeks before their trial on conspiracy charges. Yet on 14 June 1836, as soon as their sentence had been announced, he solemnly proclaimed in his *Herald* that "all the evils and disasters of which mechanics of all classes have to complain of during the last two years, have arisen entirely from the precipitate measures of their own — listening to agitators — running into strikes — neglecting their work." The blame for the whole mess actually lay with the "incendiary" editors of the *Sun* and the *Transcript*, he said, who incited agitation by "pretending to be the friends of the mechanics interests." Bennett actively cultivated this rare facility for coming out on the side of the winner in any story — the minute he figured out who the winner was.

Although his enemies accused him of having no principles at all, Bennett did possess at least one: he ridiculed all potential readers almost equally. Unlike the other penny editors, whose cautious sedition was always directed against the same target, Bennett ruffled anyone who might pay attention. Beginning with the first issue of the *Herald*, his single favorite device was the attack — without discrimination, without fear, and often without discernible reason. In his first few years alone he assaulted the Catholic Church and the Protestants, Free Love and prudery, the abolitionists and the police, banks, beggars, high society, low society, extremes of fashion, failures in etiquette, the sixpenny press, and the penny press as conducted by anyone other than Bennett himself. Perhaps Bennett was a little harder on the rich and lofty, but they did present a larger and more interesting target than the lowly, the poor, and the ordinary. Then again, he did compensate those rich and lofty with darts at Fanny Wright and with Wall Street reports of their very own.

Tactically a Bennett attack was the journalistic equivalent of the Charge of the Light Brigade, all noise and commotion and vainglory that excited the onlooker but just barely covered up its incompetence to cripple the enemy. It was also highly creative, composed of half-truths, pointed innuendo, fabricated evidence, and unproven accusation.

His attentions to the other penny editors, especially the circulation leader, Day, were particularly inspired. On 16 February 1836, Bennett smugly unveiled what he called a scandal. Day, he said, had accepted five hundred dollars to destroy a planned exposé about a storekeeper named Mackie.

The resourceful Bennett went on to report that he had managed in some unexplained manner to salvage three copies of the "suppressed" issue and was prepared to fulfill the painful "duty" of disclosing an "instance of unmanly and detestable villainy, unequalled and unrivalled in the peculiar loathsomeness of its character." The wretched Mackie, *Herald* readers learned, had allegedly drilled holes in the floor of his fashionable dry-goods shop so he could sneak into the cellar and look up ladies' skirts. Although the truth of Bennett's exposé is now impossible to judge, the consequences are more clear. Mackie, listed as a merchant in the 1834−35 volume of *Longworth's New York Directory*, was described in 1835−36 as "escaped!" He did not appear at all in 1836−37.

So Bennett struggled to make his new *Herald* a success. As hungry for attention as a child prodigy's sibling, as defensive toward his critics as a parvenu caught misusing his fish fork, he expended half his energy in sniping and smearing all comers and the other half in loudly proclaiming himself the avatar of morality, the arbiter of literary taste, and the tireless advocate of whoever happened to be reading his pages.

His own evaluation survives to this day. Bennett's admirers have hailed him as the most influential journalist ever born, as the first true investigative reporter ever hatched, as the staunchest upholder of the rights of man ever to blaze into print. Not even a genuine American icon like Washington, Jefferson, or Lincoln has been so reverently and uncritically granted the freedom to write his own eulogy as this ornery and strabismic Scotsman.

Bennett was indeed something of an innovator in the newspaper world, as the following pages will show. He often did manage to divine and satisfy deep needs and unarticulated desires in his audience, and he well deserves his reputation as one of the most influential journalists of his century. But Bennett was also frequently a scoundrel, sometimes a failure, and almost always on the lookout for the main chance. Like all the penny editors, he was experimenting, finding his way, driven by a multitude of ideas, motives, passions, and misapprehensions; it was the peculiar nature of the journalist's job that his failures and successes alike were indiscriminately enshrined in print to survive together for generations to come. But we must not allow ourselves to be so seduced by our reverence for the sovereign vestments of newsprint that we fail to notice when those clothes have no emperor.

ON PUBLIC DUTY

The young man who celebrated the ninth of April, 1836, with a birthday visit to the prostitute Helen Jewett had been a favorite of hers. Richard P. Robinson, who used the alias Frank Rivers for his frequent visits to the house, was a "prepossessing" youth from a "highly respectable," old-line Connecticut family; his character had hitherto been "unimpeachable." He was employed as a clerk by his cousin's former partner, the dry-goods merchant Joseph Hoxie of Maiden Lane.[1]

According to the madam, Rosina Townsend, Robinson had recently announced his engagement to a young woman of good family and was anxious to retrieve the letters and gifts he had sent to Jewett. He was last seen in bed in Jewett's room around eleven o'clock, when Townsend brought the two of them a bottle of champagne.

As soon as the young woman's body was discovered, more watchmen were called in, but the six "gentlemen" who were visiting other boarders at the house that night fled unmolested through the front door. A search of the backyards turned up a blue cloth cloak and an ax damp with something that may or may not have been dew. Officials surmised that both articles had been dropped during a scramble over the nine-foot-high whitewashed fences.

Officers were sent to arrest the clerk at his lodging house, where they found him tucked up in the double bed he shared with his roommate. He rose immediately at their request, seeming quite calm and composed, but when he put on his pantaloons, the garment displayed suspicious white smears that might have been lime — an ingredient in whitewash. Also sinister was his possession of a miniature portrait that had been seen in Jewett's room the previous day. To the expressed satisfaction of most of the city newspapers, Robinson was charged with murder and imprisoned in Bellevue. To defend him, Hoxie hired three of the most celebrated attorneys in the city: Ogden Hoffman, William Price, and Hugh Maxwell.

The five-day trial in early June turned into a vast citywide carouse. Even on the second morning, when a fierce rainstorm lashed the streets, some five or six thousand would-be spectators were already jammed into a sodden mass in front of City Hall by the time the high constable arrived to open the court. The judges refused to enter the courtroom until the sheriff arrived with his deputies and thirty special constables, and at one point the mayor contemplated calling in the militia to restore order. Inside the courtroom each day, Robinson was continually cheered and applauded by an obstreperous crowd of youthful fellow clerks who seemed, in the words of one scandalized onlooker, "thoroughly initiated into the arcana of such houses as Mrs. Rosanna [sic] Townsend's."[2]

District Attorney J. P. Phoenix and his colleague, Robert Hunter Morris, presented the case for the People. Their evidence against Robinson was circumstantial but plentiful. Townsend and several of her boarders firmly identified Robinson as Jewett's visitor that night. One of the women linked the cloak to the accused man through the braided black silk tassel she had once repaired for him. Hoxie's porter recognized the ax, with its dark markings and distinctive pattern of blunting, as the one he had always used for chopping wood, and he told the court it had been missing from the shop on the Monday after the murder. Jewett's black maid told the court that the miniature found in Robinson's room upon his arrest was the same one Jewett had handed her two days earlier to clean and dust. After she had cleaned it, Sarah Dunscombe said, she had returned it to a drawer in Jewett's room.

Two public porters testified that they had carried letters between Robinson and the victim. Robinson's roommate said that his friend had been out late on the murder night and had returned home some time after one or two o'clock. Finally, a clerk for Chabert the Fire King, a nearby druggist, swore that Robinson had come to their shop just a week or so before the murder. Giving his name as Douglas, the accused had asked for some arsenic with which to kill rats. "We are always in the habit," said the clerk, "of refusing to sell arsenic to strangers and others."

Robinson's counsel, however, was able to produce a silk handkerchief belonging to another man that had been found in Jewett's room that night and, even better, a respectable grocer named Furlong who insisted that the accused had been tranquilly smoking cigars and reading the papers in his shop a mile and a half from the house on Thomas Street for the entire evening in question. Hoxie's nephew testified that on the Saturday morning before the murder their shop had been painted, and both he and the accused had gotten white paint on their clothes. Young Robinson's private diary, which according to rumor betrayed evidence of a black and vicious character, was ruled inadmissible as evidence when his employer professed himself unable to swear that every single page was in the prisoner's handwriting. Finally, after several rounds of legal wrangling, only one of the fifteen or so letters from Robinson found in Jewett's room was actually read aloud in court.

The prosecution's case was also hurt by the sudden and mysterious death of a potential witness. Maria Stevens, whose room at Thomas Street was divided from Jewett's only by a thin lath-and-plaster wall, allegedly caught a severe cold on the day of the murder. She moved to another brothel, kept by a Mrs. Gallagher, and died there just days before the trial began.

The lawyers' final arguments were both eloquent and expansive: all five took the opportunity to address the jury, District Attorney Phoenix for two hours, defense counsel Hoffman for three. Price, also speaking for the defense, reminded his hearers of Townsend's "infamous and abandoned" life, of how she had profited from "the prostitution of young and tender females, whom she had inveigled into her toils, to vegetate in vice of the most abominable kind, to wear out their lives in her odious service, and to die in misery and disgrace." Such a woman, he said, was too corrupt and rotten ever to speak the truth. When he suggested that Townsend might even have been capable of the murder herself, the courtroom rang with a round of applause.

In his summation, Judge Ogden Edwards informed the jury that a prostitute's testimony was likely to be as corrupt as her way of life. "When persons are brought forward who led such profligate lives," he warned, "their testimony is not to be credited unless corroborated by testimony drawn from more creditable sources." After less than ten minutes of deliberation, the jury returned a verdict of not guilty.[3]

Richard Robinson fled New York soon afterward to join the fighting in Texas. Rosina Townsend, whose house had been closed since the murder, reportedly moved to Philadelphia, at least temporarily. No other suspects were ever tried.

A month after Robinson's acquittal, a friend of his, one William Gray, was arrested for shoplifting. Gray had originally been scheduled to testify at Robinson's trial but had never been called. In his possession when he was arrested were some letters Robinson had written him at the time of the trial. On and around 13 July, many of the city papers published the letters, which proposed a sordid bargain between the two friends. The accused murderer promised that if Gray "went easy" on him in court, he would then happily seduce Gray's wife, thus giving the disgruntled husband the grounds for the divorce he wanted.

Much of New York found the whole episode distasteful. The sixpenny editors, doubtless reflecting the feelings of their upper-crust clientele, treated the case with a circumspect coolness, positively ignoring it whenever they could. William Cullen Bryant seemed to speak for most of them when, upon publishing the verdict in his august *Evening Post* on 8 June, he declared himself "glad that our columns are relieved from this disagreeable subject."

But the juicy story galvanized the penny papers. For the first time ever, a popular press aiming for a large circulation was competing for a hot local story loaded with moral and meaning, full of sex, gore, intrigue, and sin. In their struggle to outsell one another, the rival editors mounted nothing short of internecine journalistic war, using without scruple or treaty any weapon they could devise, commission, or steal.

The "horrible and melancholy affair," the "cold-blooded, atrocious" way in which the young woman was "horribly butchered," inspired page after page of baroque prose, luridly melodramatic scenes, dark innuendoes, blatant partisanship, obvious inconsistencies, vicious personal attacks on other editors as well as suspects in the crime, and accusations of blackmail against virtually everyone involved. From paper to paper and from day to day, the "facts" varied wildly, and the whole story was fraught with exaggeration, inconsistency, illogic, speculation, and bias. Any attempt to discover, from the penny papers alone, exactly what happened in Thomas Street snarls into an insoluble knot of contradictions and confusions.

James Gordon Bennett had a name for what he and the other penny editors were doing. On the Monday morning after the body was found, the editor of the *New York Herald* laid out for his readers the precise terms under which the penny press would be covering the dramatic story. "Yesterday afternoon, about 4 o'clock, the sun broke out for a moment in splendor. I started on a visit to the scene at 41 Thomas-street," wrote Bennett. "A large crowd of young men stood around the door, No. 41, and several groups along the street in various directions. The excitement among the young men throughout the city was beginning to spread in all directions."

He knocked at the door of the elegant house, identified himself, and was promptly admitted by the police officer in attendance.

"'Mr. B. you can enter,' said he, with great politeness. The crowds rushed from behind seeking also an entrance.

"'No more comes in,' said the Police Officer.

"'Why do you let that man in?' asked one of the crowd.

"'He is an editor — he is on public duty.'"[4]

Bennett may well have been fabricating the police officer's words, as we shall see. But he was not fabricating the kind of public role he other editors were playing. He was inventing and defining it.

WHO WAS ASPASIA?

Throughout the Jewett affair, the penny editors assured their readers again and again that they printed nothing but the truth and cared for nothing but the good of the public. They declared that "the public press of a country [is] the best guardian of its institutions and laws, when faithfully and independently devoted to the public good." They asserted their conviction that the new cheap press was one of the "most powerful elements of civilization and refinement" in the world. They proclaimed repeatedly that the press, by presenting the people with the unadorned facts they needed to understand public questions for themselves, was encouraging democracy, advancing civilization, and fulfilling a civic duty.[1]

Let no one think, they frequently cautioned their readers, that it was anything but a formidable and sometimes thankless job. A case in point was the arrest of a black prostitute for picking a customer's pocket while the two were engaged in an alley. Upon examination the prisoner turned out to be a man who used "ingenious artificial devices" to "gratify without detection, the debased appetites of the beastly lechers." The editors of the *Transcript* reported that they had been tempted to suppress so "disgraceful" a story. But, as they explained on 17 June 1836, they nerved themselves to publish by recalling that the exposure of criminal practices was "a painful part of our duty as public journalists, and the silence, in such cases, would only encourage the perpetrators to fresh enormities."

Yet the penny papers could not all have been telling the truth when they proclaimed absolute fidelity to the truth. Immediately after Jewett's murder, the *Sun*, the *Transcript*, and the *Herald* all hurried to publish eyewitness reports on the background and life of the murdered woman. And each account, touted as true, was different from the others.

The papers did agree on a few minor points. In the first two days after the murder, each presented a dazzling résumé of Jewett's preternatural accomplishments, allegedly gathered from precise and observant but mostly unnamed witnesses. According to the *Sun's* information from a "respectable source," she was "one of the most intelligent, beautiful and accomplished women to be found in her class of life"; she spoke French and Italian "with great elegance and fluency," and "aside from her disreputable calling, was deemed a high minded and honorable woman." A "first-rate source" told the *Herald* that her letters showed "great talent, power, pathos, and brilliancy," and that her "great intellectual passion" was reading Byron.

The *Transcript* implicitly named its source when it proudly claimed a retroactive scoop: two years earlier, on 30 June 1834, it had published an account of Jewett's life written by its own police reporter, William Attree. At that time Jewett had gone to the police court to lodge a complaint against one John Laverty, son of a partner in the Pearl Street firm Laverty and Gantley, who had accosted and kicked her in the theater, then run away laughing. Attree's report of that episode, entitled "Fruits of Seduction," had included a "brief sketch of the history of this young girl" in order to "convince our readers of the misery resulting from the villainous artifices of those whose sole aim in life seems to be the seduction of a young and innocent girl, and then abandon her to the sneers and insults of the heartless and despicable."

On 12 April 1836, the *Transcript* reprinted Attree's two-year-old piece whole except for the delicate substitution of dashes for the perpetrator's name. In this version, too, Jewett was "very genteel and pretty" and, despite her profession, managed to distinguish herself by her "quiet and genteel deportment."

Yet while all three editors concurred that Jewett was a paragon of gentility, beauty, honor, and elegance, they could not agree on so simple a point as the spelling of her first name. The *Herald* usually called her Ellen, the *Transcript* most often spelled the name Helen, and the *Sun* hovered indecisively between the two. And the sources were curiously and uniformly deficient on one critical point. Because woodcut illustrations were too expensive and too time-consuming an indulgence for a daily newspaper, editors had to rely on words alone to convey an idea of Jewett's appearance. Yet though all three papers agreed that Jewett was as beautiful as she was accomplished, for all the painstaking detail about what she *did*, not one editor included a single precise detail about how she *looked*. What shade was her hair? What color were her eyes? Was she tall or short? How many of the mostly anonymous witnesses had ever actually seen the young woman they were describing?

The outlines of Jewett's early life sketched by all three papers were similar enough to suggest some common basis, either in fact or in fantasy. Both the *Sun* and the *Transcript* had the young girl growing up in a quiet country town in New England. Sent to boarding school at a tender age, far from a mother's careful supervision, she had been pursued, seduced, and abandoned by a charming but callous rogue. "In consequence of his heartless perfidy," as the *Sun* put it — or as the *Transcript* would have it, "in order to escape from scenes that only served to remind her, with a soul-harrowing power, of what she was and what she had been," she fled to the anonymity and degradation of the big city. There, the *Transcript* continued, her "accomplishments, beauty, and attractions" revealed themselves clearly superior to "those ordinarily possessed by the common herd of unfortunates."

Yet the two papers battled vigorously over details. Was she born in Massachusetts or in Maine? Was her seducer a bank cashier or a merchant's son? Was her father Major General Spaulding or nameless and long dead? Did her family disown her or try to forgive her? The discrepancies were never resolved.

Bennett was bolder. In a scoop both daring and dramatic, the editor reported that he had visited the scene of the crime and had entered the

The Thomas Street TRAGEDY.

TRIAL OF ROBINSON!

Murder of Ellen Jewett.

INTERESTING PARTICULARS

Connected with the APPALLING TRAGEDY, and

Trial of the Prisoner;

AN IMPRESSIVE WARNING

To Youth ; affording striking Evidence of the Misery resulting from Licentiousness, and that Sin, and Shame, and Sorrow, await the Frequenters of

DENS OF INFAMY!

" Remember thy Creator in the days of thy youth "

NEW-YORK:
PRINTED FOR AND SOLD BY THE BOOKSELLERS
1836.

Cheap murder pamphlets like this one offered
graphic embellishments the penny papers lacked.
(*Courtesy of the New-York Historical Society*)

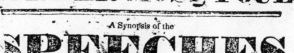

This cheap pamphlet makes it plain who seduced whom.
(*Courtesy of the American Antiquarian Society*)

murdered prostitute's very bedroom. Not only did this personal account run counter to a decades-old tradition of reportorial invisibility; it also allowed him to indulge in some memorable description. In his article of 11 April he remarked on the costly furnishings and splendid paintings inside Townsend's mansion, but he reserved his most lavish prose for a description of Jewett's room. It was "elegant, but wild and extravagant in its ornaments." He examined her fancy sketches, novels, and literary periodicals and noted a portrait of Byron as "the presiding genius of the place." The large mahogany double bed was heaped with linens burned "black as cinders." And there on the floor, covered with a sheet, lay the body.

"Slowly I began to discover the lineaments of the corpse as one would the beauties of a statue of marble," Bennett reported. " 'My God,' exclaimed I, 'how like a statue! I can scarce conceive that form to be a corpse.' Not a vein was to be seen. The body looked as white, as full, as polished as the purest Parian marble. The perfect figure — the exquisite limbs — the fine face — the full arms — the beautiful bust — all — all surpassed in every respect the Venus de Medicis according to the casts generally given of her."

Bennett was not content with merely reinforcing other papers' version of Jewett's life. On 12 April he delivered a long, detailed, and florid tale, recounting not a young girl's pathetic mistake but a flawed woman's tragic fall. In the pages of the *Herald*, Jewett was no innocent victim, but rather a headstrong coquette who destroyed herself through her own folly and willfulness. Bennett described in detail her childhood in Augusta, Maine, where she had been born Dorcas Dorrance. She was orphaned very young and was taken into the home of one Judge Western as "a *chere-amie* of his daughters — a companion and a playmate." Then, "just as her mind was budding," she was sent to a noted Female Academy in nearby Coney, where she became "the pride of her teachers . . . beloved of her school mates . . . obliging, good-tempered, intellectual and refined."

All this, however, soon changed. By the time she was sixteen, she was giving indications of a "wild, imaginative mind — without fixed principles. . . . Her passions began to control her life." While on a visit to another town, Dorcas met a young bank cashier whose name Bennett gave coyly as H— Sp—y, and soon "all was gone that constitutes the honor and ornament of the female character." After a quarrel with the judge, she fled Augusta to become a "regular Aspasia" in ever bigger cities, progressing from Portland to Boston to New York. She used to promenade in a green dress on Broadway, looking brokers boldly in the eye, and she particularly delighted in seducing young men, for she had a "mortal antipathy" to them. "You have ruined me," she would say, "I'll ruin you — I delight in your ruin."

It was a lurid tale, not the sort of reading one was accustomed to find in a newspaper, but in printing it Bennett had, he said, only the best interests of his readers at heart. He was doing it to inspire a wholesale reform of public and private morals. He was doing it for New York's own good. It was an editor's public duty.

"We are all guilty alike," he wailed on 13 April.

> The courts of law have not alone a right to investigate this crime — this red-blooded atrocity. The whole community have an interest — the present generation are both court, jury, witness[,] culprit, and execu-tioner. It has sprung from a state of society, that we men, and ye women also, of this age have permitted to grow up among us, without let or hindrance. Suppose Robinson is guilty . . . suppose he is carried out to Bellevue, and privately executed accordingly to our bloody law. . . . Will that take away the awful guilt of the present age — of this city — of our leaders in society — of our whole frame of morals and manners in permitting such a state of things to exist in a respectable, moral, and Christian city?

Any attempt to rate and rank the truthfulness of the various versions of this story swiftly becomes maddening. The *Transcript*'s report is appealing because it had initially appeared in print long before the spur of instant notoriety might have warped it, and it was written by a reporter who presumably had seen the young woman in court alive. Yet the *Transcript* was the only paper in the city to set Jewett's origins not in Maine but in Boston — clearly in error.

Nor can we assume that Attree got any of his information from Jewett herself; he never actually claimed he did. Pressed by an approaching dead-line, overeager to make his moral point, or simply confident that his version would ring true enough for any practical purposes, he may well have fabricated the story or at least patched something together from whatever clues, rumors, and secondhand information he already knew. And even if he had spoken directly to the young woman, we still have no reason to believe she gave him an accurate version. Shame or delicacy or mischief would all have been understandable reactions from a woman in her situa-tion confronted with personal questions.[2]

While the penny papers sparred and contended with each other, however, respectable journals both in New York and outside the city were unanimous. They asserted that absolutely none of what the penny papers said was true. The *New York Courier and Enquirer* warned solemnly on 18 April that the cheap press was stirring up a tremendous public excitement with "reports which are utterly destitute of truth, and which are indented [*sic*] and propagated only for catchpenny purposes."

Notably distressed by the falsehoods were readers and editors around Jewett's alleged hometown in Maine. The town of Portland, in particular, was understandably sensitive about being cast as a breeding ground of prostitutes: many residents still recalled the shameful year 1825, when rioting mobs attacked and burned waterfront whorehouses on no fewer than three occasions. They leaped to defend their reputation.

The Portland press agreed, stiffly, with other local papers that Dorcas had been no Aspasia but rather a decidedly ordinary girl, the daughter of a drunkard, who had worked for the judge as a mere domestic; according to one paper she had been chiefly remarkable for her "obtuseness of moral perception," her "natural depravity and reckless disposition," and her propensity to sneak thievery. Yet notwithstanding her already unappealing character, all these out-of-town papers agreed it was the desperate state of morals in New York that was finally responsible for her tragedy.[3]

Although the editors of the *Sun* and the *Transcript* soon withdrew from the debate over Jewett's early life, Bennett refused to abandon the issue. He set out to substantiate his version with a tactic that seemed authoritative, reporting that he had commissioned his assistant, William Wilder, to write directly to the person most likely to know the truth about the young woman's childhood and subsequent disgrace. Jewett's purported mentor was, conveniently enough, the most trustworthy man in all of Maine: Nathan Weston (not "Western," as first reported) was chief justice of the state.

Three weeks after the murder, the *Herald* published what it called the judge's reply to Wilder's letter. "Some intimations in the papers," Weston wrote, induced him to believe the murder victim was indeed Dorcas Doyen. He went on to explain that the girl, at age thirteen, had become a servant in his own family at the request of her widowed father, a mechanic whose intemperance had long before reduced him to poverty. She had been sent to the common schools and to Sunday school and was allowed to indulge her taste for reading. But after five years of satisfactory service, "reports to her prejudice" became so general that, notwithstanding her protestations of innocence, she was dismissed. "I have reason to believe," the judge continued, "that she has misrepresented the condition in which she resided in my family." He did not know, he said, who her seducer had been.

The judge himself may have been obfuscating a bit on the last point. Seeing that his own daughter had recently sued her husband for divorce on the grounds of an adultery committed in 1830, the same year Weston sent Dorcas away, he may have known perfectly well who had seduced the girl. Nevertheless, Dorcas — whose father, a shoemaker, was still alive and married to his second or third wife — was clearly not an abandoned orphan, had clearly been a servant, though perhaps a petted and privileged one, and had clearly not been a cherished favorite at a noted boarding school.[4]

Thus the letter that was supposed to reveal the truth confirmed the Maine papers' version of events more closely than it did the *Herald*'s. The very contrariness of the response is in fact the best evidence that it was genuine: if Bennett had invented the reply he would certainly have supported his own story more generously. Yet with a remarkable nonchalance he presented Judge Weston's communication as a complete validation of his own story. "Every material fact we have published of this unfortunate creature," he boasted in his own preface to the letter, "is thus clearly substantiated by the highest legal authority in Maine."

It is a curious episode. The accusations of mendacity obviously pricked Bennett; he was concerned enough about his credibility to write a letter seeking verification of what he had claimed was true. This well-publicized appeal to a higher authority also advanced the image of authenticity and validity that was obviously important to him. Yet after scorning the simple stratagem of falsifying a letter, Bennett did go on to lie, brazenly and transparently, about what his higher authority's real letter implied about his own truthfulness — as if the judge's corroboration were the just reward for Bennett's good faith and enterprise in seeking it at all.

Other aspects of Bennett's reporting display a similarly ambiguous relationship with fact. His bold and celebrated "visit to the scene," first reported on 11 April, was quite likely another fiction. A comparative reading of the other accounts of the day, penny and sixpenny alike, shows up much of Bennett's coverage as sketchy and inaccurate. He was wrong about many particulars, such as where Robinson's cloak was found, who identified it for the police, and how many stories Townsend's house had. He missed other details completely, including most of the dramatic ones so lovingly presented by other editors. Not until the following day — after he had had a chance to read the other penny papers — did Bennett manage to catch up with descriptions of Robinson's recent engagement, his use of an alias, the call for champagne, the late-night knock, the mysterious lamp, the incriminating whitewash on the pantaloons. The struggling editor with his skeleton staff was plainly ill equipped to cover the story adequately.

Whatever he lacked in furnishings, however, Bennett made up for in imagination and audacity. Many of the details he did include (among them a few that the other papers shared) are more picturesque than credible. A mechanic's daughter who had attended a common school in the country between her other duties would have been hard pressed to learn painting, music, and the art of elegant correspondence. The scandalous Byron, dead just a dozen years, was exactly the sort of "presiding genius" any good high-class prostitute ought to have. Marmoreal beauty would have been surprising in any murder victim's corpse, let alone one that had been found lying in a heap of blackened cinders. And the policeman's respectful admittance of Bennett — only Bennett — to perform his public duty was impressive and convenient, but a porter named William Van Nest testified later at the trial that he had twice gotten in to see the corpse himself.[5]

On one point we actually have documentary evidence of Bennett's preference for art over realism. Five days after his first report, he claimed to have made a second visit to the scene, during which he allegedly interviewed Townsend herself. The notorious madam, he told his fascinated readers, "has an eye — a pair of them — and they are the eyes of the devil. We looked at them — we looked through them — we caught as we believed a glimpse of the very soul within. It is passion and malevolence. That hollow cheek — that deep-set eye — that perturbed spirit we did not like. When I cross-examined her, she could hardly look me in the face. She scowled, and averted her flashing eye."

The *Sun*, however, reported that Townsend denied ever having talked with Bennett; she "unhesitatingly pronounced the whole to be a base and utter forgery, and declared that she never spoke a syllable to any man, of all that was there set forth, and had never in her life exchanged a word, with its depraved inventor!" And though the *Sun* had every reason to try to discredit its rival paper, Bennett's version of Townsend's story is indeed suspect, conflicting in several particulars with the testimony given by Townsend herself at the inquest and the trial. They are minor details —

who owned the only other lamp in the house that matched Jewett's, for instance — and they serve to cast doubt more on the directness of the author's source than on anyone's guilt or innocence.

Even more convincing is the rather more private record made by an observant young college student of his own encounter with the monstrous Rosina. A few days before Bennett's "interview," young George Templeton Strong, the future lawyer and public servant, went to take a look at the infamous house for himself. In the doorway he saw "an old lady, dressed in black," he told his diary, "with a very good-natured, mild countenance whom I should never have suspected of being such a character as she is."[6]

4

WHO KILLED HELEN JEWETT?

The penny papers' handling of a second crucial aspect of the Jewett story — the issue of the accused man's guilt — was for the most part just as exhaustive and just as murky to the critical eye as their coverage of Jewett's life. In degree of vituperation it was even worse. At times, in fact, readers might well have questioned whether it was Robinson's atrocities or those of Bennett or Lynde, Day or Stanley that concerned the rival editors most.

Throughout the entire course of the affair, up until the delivery of the verdict, the reporting proceeded along predictable lines. Once again, the *Sun* and the *Transcript* agreed on the obvious interpretation of the affair: that Robinson and only Robinson was clearly and atrociously guilty of the "foul assassination" of the poor girl. "He alone," the *Transcript* reported on 14 April, "is the guilty individual, and . . . his hands only are stained with the blood of Helen Jewett."

The *Sun* was equally positive. "Everything which has as yet transpired in relation to this strange and unnatural case," it noted on 13 April, "goes so strong against the unfortunate young man, that it seems impossible a loop can be found whereon to hang a doubt that the life of Miss Jewett was taken by another hand than his. If he is the guilty one — and who can doubt it? — the artificial appearance of ease and confidence which he has thus far assumed, must ere long give way to that powerful and unerring monitor within, his conscience."

Once again, Bennett stood alone on the other side of the issue, arguing a more controversial case with more passion and bile than logic. On 13 April, two days after he had called Robinson "a villain of too black a die [*sic*] for mortal," the editor of the *Herald* seized the spotlight for himself with an abrupt, belligerent announcement that Robinson was innocent.

Bennett came to this conclusion so quickly that several days later he was still working out the details. As his "evidence" he called on the theory of probability. So young and promising a man, who had lived thus far "without a stain, except falling a victim to the fascination of Ellen Jewett," could not, Bennett insisted, have jumped "at once from the heights of virtue to the depths of vice," nor could "a man in any respect . . . act so terribly towards lovely woman." The use of an ax rather than poison or a dagger and the deliberate firing of the house were more characteristic of "the vengeance of female wickedness — the burning of female revenge" than anything a male would do.

At first Bennett professed himself convinced that one of the other inhabitants at Townsend's, jealous of Jewett's superior attractions, had done the deed — possibly, he said, inspired by a large portrait in the Thomas Street parlor that showed a pair of Indians about to scalp a beautiful young woman *with a hatchet.* Next he suggested that Rosina Townsend herself — who, he claimed, was in debt to Jewett — might be the culprit. And then, within a day, Bennett was printing an obviously faked letter, immediately branded as such by the other papers and never again mentioned by Bennett, purporting to be a confession from the real but anonymous killer. This elusive character was supposed to have been a jealous rival of Robinson's who had murdered his beloved in order to incriminate her other suitor and who now, according to his letter, was suffering bitter pangs of remorse.

Soon, however, Bennett settled on a favored theory. Without accusing anyone by name, he branded the whole affair as a "bloody and unnatural conspiracy . . . a most wicked and atrocious conspiracy, in violation of law — in violation of truth — in violation of all virtue and honesty, to take away the life of a young, amiable, and innocent youth." The plot was devised by "the licentious inmates of a fashionable brothel," he claimed, aided and abetted by "part of the police establishment, which is rotten to the heart," and by "an indicted thief and editor of a daily paper" — that is, Benjamin Day of the *Sun*.[1]

Bennett worked tirelessly to prove that a conspiracy was afoot. In the disputed interview he claimed to have had with the "devil-eyed" Rosina, he found proof that she and the police were deeply implicated. "The whole story — the very cue to the arrest, was given to the Police by Rosina," he fulminated. "She alone saw [Robinson] come in — she alone saw him in bed . . . she alone gave the Police the number of his boarding house in Dey street — she alone is the only direct evidence in the whole investigation. . . . She is the author and finisher of the mystery. . . . Who is Rosina Townsend? She is a common woman, who has lived several years in this city, kept the house in Thomas street, and is reported to have been kept by an *attache* of that very police who have this affair in their hands." And after the verdict, on 20 June, Bennett reported that Townsend had driven in her carriage to the *Sun* office, spent half an hour there, and "civilized" the editor with a hundred-dollar bill.

Yet Bennett's assaults ranged well beyond the small circle of people directly involved in the murder investigation. In the juicy case he found plenty of opportunities to belabor his rival editors for personal as well as professional iniquities. No one could know, as he slyly reported on 15 April, that the editor of the *Transcript* was *not* a pimp for Townsend. Bennett's favorite target, however, was always the *Sun*, the most successful of the penny papers. "The attempt of the Sun to protect the character of the fashionables in Thomas street," he remarked on 18 April, "is all proper in him. An Infidel for many years standing, the printer and editor of Fanny Wright's infamous system of religion and morals — a seal breaker — an indicted thief not yet tried, he cannot help possessing a congeniality of of [*sic*] feeling towards the amiable syrens [*sic*] of St. Thomas Hotel. Their morals, are the morals of the editor of the Sun — their principals are alike — their purposes are alike."

Nor did the *Sun* and the *Transcript* restrain themselves from counterattacking. They assailed Bennett's integrity and his allegations with vigor and venom equal to his. On 14 April, the very day after Bennett "exonerated" Robinson, the *Transcript* commented:

> The excitement in the public mind in reference to this monstrous affair, continues to be unabated; and, notwithstanding the puny and purchased efforts of a ricketty [*sic*], tottering print — notorious only for its easy access to petit bribery, and as being the most corrupt, profligate, and contemptible concern that was ever yet palmed upon any community — to produce an impression that other persons than Robinson have been the perpetrators of the foul assassination; yet the general conviction, from the evidence before the public, is, (and we record it with regret,) that he alone is the guilty individual.

Both of Bennett's main rivals loftily laid claim to their own mysterious tidbits of inside knowledge as well. The *Transcript* had "some particulars in reference to this horrid affair," it gloated on 13 April, "which will electrify and appal [*sic*] a great part of this community; — particulars which, as far as we at present know, are known but to very few other persons besides ourselves." The promised particulars seem to have remained in the possession of those very few.

Day floated a conspiracy theory of his own. On 18 April, two days after Bennett published his alleged interview with Rosina Townsend, the *Sun* loosed a broadside attack on the *Herald*, the accused man, his friends, the legal system, and the course of justice in general. Day began his blast, more than a full column's worth, in one great breathless gallop of indignation.

"We should be doing violence," he roared,

> to our own sense of duty to the public as the conductors of the most extensively read paper in the country, to whom that public look for correct information on all matters of general concernment, were we to pass, unnoticed, the heartless and fiend-like attempts which are now in vigorous progress, made by the associates of the prisoner Robinson in his debaucheries and iniquities, through a supple tool whom they have found willing to prostrate his press to their diabolical purpose, to create in the public mind a prejudice against the unfortunate inmates of the house at which the murder occurred, and particularly against Mrs. Townsend, its proprietor.

Yet for all their invocations of journalistic principle, for all their proclamations of civic duty, these furious editors were making up their stories as they went along. Bennett's defense of the accused clerk may have been fervent, but it was also unwarranted. Robinson was guilty. Both the testimony at the trial and the surviving contemporary comments argue as much. The editors of the *Transcript* and the *Sun* admittedly had other motives for attacking Bennett's version of the facts. Virtually all the "respectable" editors of the sixpenny papers, however, were also clear-eyed or hardheaded or red-faced enough to acknowledge that Robinson was lucky — at least — to be acquitted.

The *Journal of Commerce* for 9 June was typically lukewarm: "The verdict of the Jury acquitting the prisoner, was of course founded upon the evidence before them; and however dark portions of it may have been . . . yet there were other portions which were of a different character, and which left upon the minds of the jury at least 'a reasonable doubt' . . . and 'it is better that ten guilty persons should go unpunished, than that one innocent man should suffer.' "

Other credible observers including George Templeton Strong, Philip Hone, and the visiting Englishman Frederick Marryat expressed private convictions of the guilt of the "wretched youth," as Hone called him. Strong professed himself convinced that "Furlong [the grocer] is a perjured man, and a man who has perjured himself for the sake of some of Mr. Hoxie's cash." Two and a half years later, the suicide of the "perjured man" who had provided Robinson's alibi would be widely reported throughout the city press.[2]

Even Bennett's future archrival, Horace Greeley, whose struggles to make a success of the intellectual weekly *New-Yorker* were just beginning to betray his shortcomings as a businessman, revealed no shortcomings as a shrewd observer of the case. That May he shared his opinion with a friend. "I believe the majority think with me," he wrote, "that he is unquestionably and atrociously guilty, and ought to walk up the ladder. And yet, if money, influence and splendid counsel (Ogden Hoffman and Hugh Maxwell) can save him, he will cheat the gallows, and I believe that will be the result. The great contest will be on disallowing Mrs. Townsend's testimony on account of her character."[3]

Robinson's acquittal in the face of this widespread opinion against him brought rejoicing from Bennett. He described the scene tenderly: "Mr. Hoxie was in tears; the kind, the noble, the eloquent Mr. Hoffman could not restrain his tears; Price, the hard-featured, imperturbable Price, did not attempt to stop his. . . . Robinson went with his father and uncle to Mr.

Hoxie's, where he might pour into their ears, and theirs alone, the feelings of his heart, and his deep and lasting gratitude to that jury who had not sacrificed an innocent victim on the altar of an abandoned woman."

Even while other papers in the city questioned the verdict, the conduct of the trial, and the *Herald* too, Bennett continued to stand firm. Not only did he cling to his story, he made a cudgel of it, warning portentously of further scandals to unfold. The case, he said, was not yet closed. Robinson's vindication still did not solve the question of who the real murderer was. "The first step in this great duty is the instant arrest of every man, married or single, who was caught in the arms of love and licentiousness in that house of infamy," thundered Bennett. "We know the name of him who luxuriated with lovely Emma French — we know the name of him who fondled on the thin lips of Rosina Townsend. . . . The murderer must be sought and discovered." He called for the Thomas Street "inmates, male and female," to be arrested en masse and demanded that Rosina Townsend be "caged at once." And he explicitly menaced evildoers with the power of his press. "We shall begin a general review of this whole subject," he warned, "this triple crime of murder, arson, and conspiracy. We have a fearful development to make. Some of the highest men in the city are in it. . . . We fear nothing but God and Eternity. Prepare people of New York for an awful *expose*."[4]

Then suddenly, without either explanation or exposé, the "innocent youth" lost his staunchest defender. In the most astonishing of the many journalistic inconsistencies that marked the entire case, Bennett began to suggest that Robinson was not entirely guiltless. And in occasional references to the case as months and years passed, the suggestion gradually gave way to repeated shrieks for vengeance — on Robinson.

Bennett gave no reason for his about-face; in fact, he never acknowledged changing his opinion at all. On 10 June he was still proclaiming emphatically, *"Robinson is innocent. We pronounce it openly and decidedly. Every piece of evidence against him can be explained, and will be explained."* Just five days later, however, Bennett conceded that "Robinson indeed may have murdered Ellen Jewett. The circumstances are against him. . . . But even in Paradise, when Cain killed his brother Abel, and Jehovah was witness, judge, and jury, the criminal was permitted to go at large with a mark for men to avoid him. Robinson like Cain, has mingled with wickedness, and will wander like him, over the earth, an outcast and a wretch." By 21 November 1839, Bennett was reporting on "the singular and just dispensation of Providence" in having reached into Texas and arranged a paralyzing war wound for Robinson in "the arm, that in all probability committed the bloody deed."

His change of heart has several possible explanations. Most obvious was Bennett's habitual preference for conspicuousness over consistency. In the same spirit that would later move the explorer Roald Amundsen coolly to go off and conquer the South Pole upon hearing that Admiral Peary had just reached his own original goal to the north, Bennett deliberately pursued the visibility of the less-populated extremity — whichever that might be. The editor of the *Herald* had a mind too large for the hobgoblins of foolish consistency.

Years later, one of Bennett's more temperate critics remarked that this indifference to consistency was the secret to his success because it freed him "from the ordinary restraints that develop, but often hinder mortals." The editor, this critic said, "understands that a daily newspaper is emphatically a thing of to-day, and that the mass of people care very little for what it has said yesterday, or may say to-morrow. Consequently, he issues every number as if there never had been, and never would be another, and so prospers."[5]

The *Sun*, the *Transcript*, and other papers, however, had another explanation for the *Herald*'s change of heart: that Bennett was less an editor than an extortionist. He had, they said, been shaking down the men who were caught in other rooms at Townsend's when the cry of fire was raised. He was also taking money from Joseph Hoxie, Robinson's employer, to defend the youth. Bennett turned on Robinson, the theory went, because Hoxie fell into arrears after the acquittal.

Confirmation of these charges is, at this point, impossible. Bennett's contemporary biographer, Isaac Pray, heatedly denied them, as he heatedly denied any and all criticism of his principal. Yet Bennett apparently did resort to blackmail on other occasions. Frederick Marryat reported that during his visit to America, he received in the mail an issue of the *Herald* that included an article attacking him. "Send twenty dollars," ran a handwritten note in the margin, "and it shall be stopped."[6]

The blackmail theory would explain several curious circumstances of Bennett's reporting about the Jewett case. His deep interest in the involvement of rich, upper-class "fashionables," which his modern partisans ascribe so eagerly to his passionate crusade for equal rights and equal justice, had another equally likely explanation. The rich pay better. If one is interested in extortion, it is most profitable to extort from upper-class fashionables.

Blackmail would also explain the ebb and flow in Bennett's expressed interest in those rich men. *Before* the delivery of the verdict, he had laid the supposed "conspiracy" at the door of the police, the madam, and the *Sun*. Although he did at times indulge in a luxurious wallow over the awful "state of society, that we men, and ye women also, of this age have permitted to grow up among us," he never specifically implicated the other men caught at Townsend's. Apparently they were paying him well enough to ensure his silence — and at this point Bennett was scrupulously observing his obligations.

At one point during the trial, for example, police officer Brink was questioned on the witness stand about several previous complaints involving Jewett and the madam with whom she had formerly lived. A man implicated in the first complaint was identified in court by name, and Brink was pressed to name another "gentleman" who had supposedly paid him "for arranging a difference between two prostitutes, where one had torn the clothes of the other." When defense attorney Hoffman objected to that disclosure, the matter was dropped. But whereas most of the penny and sixpenny papers, as well as the official trial transcript, dutifully printed the entire exchange, the *Herald* did not include in its otherwise exhaustive account what must have been a painful and clear reminder of past scandal for the gentlemen in question.[7]

It was only *after* the acquittal, with his victims sensing liberty and his blackmail income threatening to dry up, that Bennett turned on the "highest men in the city." *That* was when he began his strident demands for the exposure of "every man, married and single," who was caught at Townsend's; that was when he thundered ominously of "fearful developments" and "awful *exposes.*" And apparently those wretched hostages, unlike Hoxie, continued to pay. For all Bennett's thunder, he never hurled any lightning bolts. No one was ever exposed by name in his columns.

Hoxie's case was different. In the aftermath of the trial, Bennett betrayed a deep and lasting animus against the merchant. When the Whigs nominated Hoxie for county clerk in October 1837, Bennett devoted the entire two-week campaign period to a savage, relentless, spiteful attack, not against the Whig ticket — he approved of the senatorial candidate, Gulian Verplanck — but against Hoxie alone. The editor composed heavily sarcastic letters supporting Hoxie and signed them with Robinson's alias,

Frank Rivers; he reminded his readers again and again of the merchant's "perverted conduct" in sitting "side by side with the felon hypocrite, . . . preventing the truth from coming to light, and [allowing] the final escape of the seducer, the murderer, the horrible reprobate." Hoxie won anyway.

The seducer and horrible reprobate won, too. Richard Robinson, who had, with Bennett's eager help, subjected the citizenry of New York to months of turmoil, discord, anger, and anguish, went on to discover that crime did indeed pay. In 1837, under the name Richard Parmalee, he settled in Nacogdoches County, Texas. Within ten years he had acquired a wealthy wife, an influential father-in-law, and twenty-one slaves; he had joined the local Masonic Lodge; and he had been elected by his fellow citizens to the clerkship of the district court. His chief professional responsibility was to compile, order, and preserve the records pertaining to every felony committed in the county.[8]

The end of the trial and the flight of Robinson were not, however, the end of the story of the Jewett murder. In mid-June 1836, after the cacophony and fantasy of the spring's reporting, after the delivery of the shady verdict, after Robinson was freed and gone, one editor *did* mount a close and reasoned analysis of the crime. As we shall see in detail later, his conclusion was unsparing: the trial was corrupt and farcical, rigged from the beginning and indefensible in the end. This editor's analysis was bold and perceptive. It also happened to be accurate. That, however, may well have been incidental.

TRUTH OR HUMBUGGERY

If the penny press of the 1830s was *not* presenting objective facts — was *not* giving an accurate picture of the world — then what on earth *was* it doing? What was its purpose? Was all its talk about "effecting the march of intelligence" and "editors on public duty" sheer bunkum?

That judgment does not at first sound too far wrong. Antebellum America was a jamboree of ballyhoo, exaggeration, chicanery, sham, and flimflam; antebellum America literally invented the word *bunkum*. As Edgar Allan Poe put it in 1845, a freewheeling deceptiveness seemed to be nothing less than man's "destiny . . . his aim — his object — his *end*." Man, he said, "is an animal that diddles, and there is *no* animal that diddles *but* man."[1] In fact, we cannot understand nineteenth-century culture, let alone nineteenth-century journalism, without understanding its complicated relationships with the truth.

The "diddles" Americans loved to perpetrate were not necessarily mean or evil. Many of them were purely recreational and undoubtedly ingenious, evidence more of high spirits than of low cunning. These were flush times for the tall tale, the object of which was to pile eccentricity on grotesquery on outlandishness until the imagination finally quailed. Such tales usually featured rowdy, violent, often superhuman exploits by boastful back-woodsmen: they rode the lightning; they hitched up a team of horses to move an island to a finer spot in the river; they melted the ice that had frozen the earth's axis into immobility by wringing the warm blood out of a bear. Some tales portrayed fictional heroes like Nimrod Wildfire; others cast real, flesh-and-blood people like Davy Crockett or Mike Fink in the main roles. The adventures of man and myth were completely indistinguishable and equally improbable.

In the heat of spontaneous composition, a teller of tales might well be forgiven for embroidering the truth, but not even an author's willingness to pickle a tale in the brine of print was any guarantee of pure intentions. Poe, for one, often combined a straight face with a crooked pen. One of his earliest efforts, a tale about a terrible storm at sea that bristled with authentic-sounding nautical detail and shivered with frissons of terror, unfolded in the first person. It ended on a note equally coy and thrilling: "Oh, horror upon horror! The ice opens suddenly to the right, and to the left, and we are whirling dizzily. . . . We are plunging madly within the grasp of the whirlpool — and amid a roaring, and bellowing, and thundering of ocean and tempest, the ship is quivering — oh God! and — going down!" The masterstroke of this epic was its suggestive title, "MS. Found in a Bottle."

Until the end of his brief life, Poe continued to tease readers with calculatedly credible tales of scientific discovery or high adventure. Americans discussed and debated the genuineness of his convincing stories of mesmerism, of alchemy, of transatlantic crossings by balloon. The U.S. Senate, for one, did not discuss and debate one episode quite enough; in 1840 the Select Committee on the Oregon Territory included in its official report a reference to "The Journal of Julius Rodman," an account of an expedition across the Rockies, noting solemnly that "nothing as yet appears, either in the journal or relating to it, calculated to excite suspicions with regard to its authenticity." When the Senate issued a second edition of the report four years later, however, the reference to Rodman was dropped — presumably because someone had finally discovered that Rodman and his entire expedition had been fabricated by Poe.

"The Narrative of Arthur Gordon Pym" — a bloodcurdling first-person compendium of massacres, starvation, mutiny, cannibalism, pirates, shipwreck, gory hand-to-hand combat, and storms at sea — appeared first as fiction under Poe's name in the *Southern Literary Messenger*. In the subsequent book version, however, a preface signed by "Pym" claimed that the adventures were real and the eponymous hero the tale's true author. "Pym" explained that although he had initially insisted on concealing himself behind Poe's name out of fear that no one would ever believe so incredible a story, he soon realized that the clever public had seen through the ruse. Some reviewers turned out to be not so clever: several believed the work to be a purposeful hoax, and others were completely confused about the extent of Poe's involvement.[2]

This was also the age that spawned and embraced the master of humbug, P. T. Barnum. In 1836, while the penny papers were occupying themselves with Helen Jewett and her lover, Barnum was touring the country with a blackface dancer, a venerable black crone whom he presented as George Washington's former nurse, and a couple of jugglers playing out a carefully choreographed rivalry. But the ambitious Barnum wanted more. By the early 1840s he had established a museum on Broadway in Manhattan and was busy filling it with the bizarre, the beguiling, and the delusory: dwarves, giants, ventriloquists, jugglers, orangutans, albinos, fat boys, automatons, magicians, musicians, dioramas, models of the Niagara Falls, Santa Anna's wooden leg captured on the battlefield (from, one must presume, the live and well Santa Anna himself), and the famous Fejee Mermaid, a blackened and desiccated little nonesuch with a fishtail, a head, and hands. "At the outset of my career," Barnum wrote later, "I saw that everything depended on getting the people to think, and talk, and become curious and excited." He did just that.[3]

Many of the exhibits people flocked to see were in some way counterfeit. The exotic mermaid had actually been deftly cobbled together from the cadavers of a fish and a monkey. The amazing chess-playing automaton had a man cleverly hidden inside. The beasts featured in the Grand Buffalo Hunt — staged across the river in Hoboken — were ancient, panicky, and frail. Yet though the showman relished his reputation as a master of humbug, he did not consider himself a charlatan.

To Barnum and his contemporaries, the label "humbug" was not necessarily an insult; it had not yet taken on its current odor of malicious deviousness, of cynical manipulation, of imposition without acquiescence. Barnum believed religiously that his humbugs must give his audiences *something* for their money, whether or not it was quite what they had expected. In a best-selling book written at the height of his career, he distinguished carefully between a mere swindle, in which the perpetrator "cheats or imposes on the public," and his own specialty.

A humbug, he said, "consists in putting on glittering appearances — outside show — novel expedients, by which to suddenly arrest public attention, and attract the public eye and ear." If a merchant attracts a crowd of customers by his "unique displays," for instance, and then "foolishly fails to give them full equivalent for their money," his customers properly denounce him as "a swindler, a cheat, an impostor; they do not, however, call him a 'humbug.'" But, Barnum continued, a man who simply "advertises his wares in an *outré* manner" can be termed a humbug "without by any means impeaching his integrity."[*]

As Barnum himself recognized, there was also a darker side to this American penchant for deception, and many of its practitioners deserved a sharper name than diddler — something like "fraud." These were flush times, too, for the chiseler, the swindler, and the confidence man. *Their* activities were much more insidious in intent and more mortifying in consequence than those of the showman or talespinner.

In the face of the wrenching social changes of Jacksonian America, the archetypal figures of the slick deceiver, the crafty peddler, the plausible rogue, were rapidly becoming national bogeymen as emblematic as the national bird. Vast growth in the cities, the disconcerting progress of mechanization in the workplace, a growing emphasis on becoming rich, greater personal mobility, the weakening of traditional social controls, all were sentencing the ordinary citizen to a growing conviction that everyone else was an alien, accountable to no one and quite probably on the lookout for opportunity wherever it might come. That opportunity could well come at the expense of the ordinary citizen's own life, home, or pocket.

In her study of mid-nineteenth-century personal-conduct manuals, Karen Halttunen found a widespread middle-class terror of two "archetypal hypocrites," the confidence man and the painted woman. "In what was believed to be a fluid social world where no one occupied a fixed social position, the question 'Who am I?' loomed large; and in an urban social world where many of the people who met face-to-face each day were strangers, the question 'Who are you really?' assumed even greater significance."[5] Not without reason did many Americans consider the practice of deception a threat to the health of the body politic, the sort of sin that might even warrant an expansion of the Decalogue.

Even the swindler, however, had his defenders. To some ambitious Americans, deceptiveness was a necessary economic and social tool. The slicker who talked his way onto a higher rung of society's ladder was only proving the unlimited promise of America. The crafty Yankee who sold a nutmeg carved from wood as the real article might even be admired for his hustle, his drive, his good old American determination to get ahead — and any bakers who let themselves be deluded out of their apple pandowdy deserved the comeuppance.

The English critic Mrs. Trollope was impressed by the phenomenon. "All agree in saying that [the New England states] present a spectacle of industry and prosperity delightful to behold," she recalled. ". . . [Y]et I never met a single individual in any part of the Union who did not paint these New Englanders as sly, grinding, selfish, and tricking. The Yankees (as the New Englanders are called) will avow these qualities themselves with a complacent smile, and boast that no people on the earth can match them at over-reaching in a bargain."

America's ambivalence about deceptiveness soon came to be epitomized by a notorious New York swindler of the 1840s who went by the name of William Thompson. Thompson was the world's first con man, literally: his striking modus operandi inspired the invention of the title "confidence man." He would ask strangers whether they had enough "confidence" in him to lend him their watches, with which, of course, he would immediately abscond.

It was a particularly invidious stratagem, manipulating people's simple decency and making a mockery of trust and faith. Yet public reaction to Thompson's exploits was not entirely critical. Many admired his enterprise, lauding him as an "original," even a "genius." His odd forte became the germ for Herman Melville's 1857 work *The Confidence Man: His Masquerade*, a meditation so cryptic in tone and message that to this day no one can decide for sure whether it was meant to be a comedy — or whether it succeeded as one.[6]

For all its noisy embrace of the truth, the cheap press offered no help in clarifying the obscure boundaries between humbugs and lies, swindles and jokes, high jinks and low blows. By the time of the Jewett murder, in fact, the penny editors had already earned a reputation among their fellow New Yorkers as either humbugs or liars: the distinction was each onlooker's to make.

Scholars have long acknowledged that the most popular and most notorious journalistic story of the day — the story that first riveted public attention on the new medium and launched its flourishing career — contained not a grain of truth. Most, however, have dismissed it as a cute aberration, an early false step that was quickly and eagerly corrected. They are wrong. There was nothing false about the Moon Hoax except its facts.

The hoax was one of many experiments undertaken in the early struggle to figure out exactly what a penny paper was and what its audience wanted. On 25 August 1835, Benjamin Day of the *Sun* began publishing a series of articles reportedly taken from a recent issue of an Edinburgh scientific journal. They described the astonishing astronomical discoveries made by Sir John Herschel with his telescope "of vast dimensions and an entirely new principle," which was set up at the Cape of Good Hope. With this new telescope, Sir John was able to see with pristine clarity the inhabitants and vegetation of the moon.

The public was enthralled with the astronomer's descriptions of amazing creatures: spherical amphibians that rolled instead of walking; blue goats with a single horn each; biped beavers that carried their young in their arms; short hairy men with bat wings. The *Sun's* articles were reprinted, published as pamphlets, translated, demanded, and fought for in cities throughout Europe and the United States. Scientists were delighted, religious ladies proposed sending missionaries aloft, and most sixpenny editors swallowed their chagrin at the cheap paper's scoop to praise the great achievement in their columns.

The whole affair was soon revealed to be a hoax. Day himself never actually confessed; when he finally commented about the affair on 16 September, he mischievously maintained the mystification. "Certain correspondents have been urging us to come out and confess the whole to be a hoax," he wrote, "but this we can by no means do, until we have the testimony of the English or Scotch papers to corroborate such a declaration. In the meantime, let every reader of the account examine it, and enjoy his own opinion. Many intelligent and scientific persons still believe it true, and will continue to do so to their lives' end; whilst the scepticism of others would not be removed though they were in Dr. Herschel's observatory itself."

But the series had actually been concocted and conceded by Day's prize reporter, Richard Adams Locke, perhaps aided and abetted, according to some accounts, by Lewis Gaylord Clark, the ultrarespectable editor of the sophisticated literary magazine *Knickerbocker*. The story succeeded in its primary purpose. It forced the sixpenny papers to acknowledge that their despised cheap rivals might also possess enterprise and talent.

It also had a second important consequence. During the run of the story the *Sun's* daily circulation reached nearly twenty thousand, four times that of the most successful sixpenny paper and more than that of the *London Times* — thus arguably taking over as the largest in the world.[7] So many advertisers clamored for inclusion in the bumptious little sheet that Day soon had to enlarge the size of his page to fit everything in. This success suggested to the onlooking fraternity of hungry would-be journalistic moguls that readers might well buy wildly if presented with a spectacular story, preferably one slow to unfold, in which a mere germ of plausibility and a great deal of excitement stood substitute for any amount of fact.

Thus, although the penny papers continued to deal realistically with actual events of the day, each editor also began to develop reserve strategies to compensate for a boring police court, a day without elephants on the lam, or simply a sagging circulation. No outward sign or clue distinguished the serious report from the fake. In the next column over from an earnest account of a drunken street fracas, the president's latest message, or the progress of the Astor Hotel, could be lurking any kind of straight-faced whopper.

Many of these would have passed P. T. Barnum's exacting standards. Some were so *outré* they barely deceived at all. Richard Adams Locke, the author of the Moon Hoax, left Day within a year to start a penny paper of his own, the *New Era*. When he began publishing the "lost manuscripts" of the Scottish explorer Mungo Park, who had vanished thirty years before on his way to Timbuktu, his experienced readers tumbled to the trick immediately.

Other humbugs featured expedients both novel and desperate. The scrappy little *Transcript*, struggling gamely to keep up with its rivals, perfected the hoax by innuendo. It regularly spiced stories of ordinary crimes with dark but safely vague hints of what scandals could be told if only solid proof were forthcoming, or the trial were over, or someone unnamed were not suppressing evidence. The *Transcript* never did come through with any of this promised scandal — just as it never hesitated to use whatever solid proof it did have, as the case of the ingenious transvestite prostitute made clear.

Part of the machinery of the humbug required constant scrutiny and eternal vigilance on the part of each penny editor lest his rivals actually succeed in duping *him*. When the *Sun* reported on 4 September 1835 that one Matthias the Prophet, a peripatetic religious quack whose recent prison term had earned him the new sobriquet "Impostor," had committed suicide by leaping off the Newark ferry, Day felt compelled to add that his information came from "a gentleman on whose veracity we can repose the most unbounded confidence."

Unimpressed, the *Transcript* immediately declared that the story, printed in "two or three of the 'moon-story' papers yesterday," was false. Undaunted, the *Sun* instantly retorted that "Our discontented little satellite [*sic*]" invariably questions the authenticity of "every article of news in which it is anticipated by its cotemporaries [*sic*]." Unrepentant, the *Transcript* responded at once that the *Sun*'s refusal to recant was a "commentary on the folly (to say the least of it) of our neighbors in obstinately asserting as a truth that which they know to be wrong." The *Transcript* did not address the question of whether, by choosing that same week to reprint Edgar Allan Poe's rival epic of lunar exploration, "Hans Pfaal" (an odd tale too fantastic to fool anyone as a hoax, yet too realistic in its technical detail to dismiss as merely a fantasy), it qualified itself as a "moon-story paper," too.

Sometimes, in fact, the public debate over a humbug could whirl the reader deep into a hall of mirrors. Such a case was that of Joice Heth, Barnum's prize hoax — the ancient, blind, and toothless slave billed as George Washington's 161-year-old former nurse. When Heth finally died, an autopsy was ordered, and Day unmasked Barnum's "precious humbug." He reported on 26 February 1836 that the autopsy showed her actual age to be barely half of what Barnum had claimed. Day's rival Bennett then tried to unmask as a humbug Day's unmasking of Barnum's humbug. *He* responded the next day that Heth was still alive and that the *Sun*'s autopsy was "a complete hoax from beginning to end," having actually been performed on the body of a perfectly ordinary and "respectable old negress called AUNT NELLY."

Yet some journalistic put-ons, like some diddles, were less than just good clean fun. Sometimes the editors' expedients for arresting public attention crossed over the line from the glittering to the tawdry. In early

1836, Day's disingenuous manipulation of the familiar rhetoric of journalistic obligation nearly caused a riot.

The editor had, he announced on 18 January, decided to reprint some excerpts from a new book, out of "our imperative sense of public duty, as conductors of a public journal, to expose crime to public abhorrence wherever it is detected, and to meet the just claims of our readers upon whatever subjects of interest that may be found in the columns of our cotemporaries [*sic*]." Yet he went on to confess that "we do not, and indeed cannot, vouch for the truth of the appalling disclosures which this remarkable work contains. They may be true or they may be false; they may be partially true, or partially false; and we have no better means than are possessed by every reader to decide upon their truth or falsehood."

Trumpeted abroad in the most widely read publication of the day, the "Awful Disclosures" did indeed attract the public eye and ear. A nun who went by the felicitous name of Maria Monk was claiming that the sisters at her former convent, the Hôtel Dieu in Montreal, were brutish and corrupt harpies who fornicated with monks and murdered their own bastards. Such inflammatory disclosures could only worsen the prevailing anti-immigrant and anti-Catholic climate. Panic and loathing gripped Protestants and Nativists, while Catholics seethed with indignation. And some New Yorkers were enraged at the splashy publication of so flimsy a story. The feisty Col. William L. Stone of the sixpenny *Commercial Advertiser* actually traveled all the way to Montreal to check out the tale himself and returned denouncing it as a fake.

As enthusiastically as they embraced humbugs and frauds, in fact, the penny editors themselves virtually conceded that they were dubious journalistic tactics. With unprecedented delicacy, they refused to claim credit for their ingenuity: although no editor ever missed an opportunity to accuse his rivals, in public and with unblushing indignation, of pulling off another hoax, not one ever openly confessed to having engineered one himself. Obviously they understood that spreading false information in a newspaper — with whatever good or bad intention — was not entirely orthodox. Thus "trash" was a humbug perpetrated by the *other* guy. Truth was the property of *this* fine and upright fellow.

THE TRUTH ABOUT HUMBUG

P. T. Barnum's conscientious semantic distinctions and Benjamin Day's stunningly successful lunar fantasy together suggest a solution to the question of just what the cheap New York newspapers were doing with their coverage of the Jewett affair. The penny press was not publishing bunkum; it was not perpetrating fraud; it was not swindling readers when it claimed to be performing a public duty. The penny press was, instead, launching a humbug, whose readers were governed by two unspoken but clearly understood presumptions. An untruth that does not deceive is not a lie. And a truth that does not satisfy is no better than a lie.

We can best begin to understand the first of these presumptions by looking again at how Barnum explained himself for posterity. In his careful discrimination between a humbug and a swindle, the showman was actually making his own use of an ancient ethical and philosophical principle. Deception, according to the traditional argument, is wrong principally because it denies to the deceived their individual freedom.

"To the extent that knowledge gives power," as one modern moral philosopher puts it, "to that extent do lies affect the distribution of power; they add to that of the liar, and diminish that of the deceived, altering his choices at different levels. . . . [People who learn they have been deceived] see that they were manipulated, that the deceit made them unable to make choices for themselves according to the most adequate information available, unable to act as they would have wanted to act had they known all along."[1]

People do not choose to grate up splinters instead of spices or to cede a penny at a footbridge to a tolltaker whose sole authority is his own audacity. People do not go out and purposefully select confidence men as their sons-in-law. Frauds like those succeed precisely because their victims are not given the option of just saying no. When they succeed, they destroy the tissue of trust essential to the health and progress of any society.

Yet Barnum built his career on the knowledge that a humbug differs vastly from a lie. A successful humbug is not a power play by one side only; it involves the participation, the consent, and even the pleasure of *both* parties. Where a swindle deprives one of choice, a humbug demands it. Where a fraud squelches freedom, a humbug bestows it. Where a scam imposes limits, a humbug explodes them. And where a lie destroys social bonds, a humbug cements them.

When Barnum presented an ancient crone who *might* have rocked the Father of Our Country in her skinny arms or a shriveled little grotesque that *might* have been a fabulous mermaid, he did not insist they were real. He accompanied the show with a nudge-and-wink that nearly bruised his visitors' ribs. Make your own choice, he was saying. You are free to do so. You don't need an expert to tell you the answer. You have the power. And his visitors would nudge and wink right back.

It was all a great game. Barnum understood that controversy was the best publicity. He understood it so well, in fact, that he saw no reason to wait for controversy to strike on its own and became a master of his own publicity. He would himself start rumors that his own exhibits were frauds, write angry anonymous letters to local editors, and hire people to prosecute him for imposture. The curious would inevitably flock to his hall to ask whether the disputed showpiece were real or humbug. "That's just the question," Barnum always replied; "persons who pay their money at the door have a right to form their own opinions after they have got up stairs."

Barnum intended his various escapades and stratagems above all to entertain people. Yet he knew that the special brand of entertainment he offered was also, as the showman's recent biographer has pointed out, a "peculiarly patriotic" recreation for its times. In an age when the pursuit of useful and scientific knowledge was becoming a national religion, participating in a scientific debate about the existence of mermaids was a genuflection at the public shrine. In an age when technological progress was promising to conquer time, space, adversity, and ill, scrutinizing a mechanical chess player was a panegyric to American ingenuity. And in an age when many Americans were claiming for the first time their republican right to form their own opinions just like anybody else, forming an opinion about a wizened old crone was a vote for civic responsibility. Working through and solving a hoax, in short, demanded from every citizen the democratic duty of judgment. It offered to every citizen the democratic delight of choice. It allowed to every citizen the democratic satisfaction of participating in public life.

"Experiencing a complicated hoax," Barnum's biographer points out, "was pleasurable because of the competition between victim and hoaxer, each seeking to outmaneuver the other, to catch him off-balance and detect the critical weakness. Barnum, Poe, Locke and other hoaxers didn't fear public suspicion; they invited it. They understood, most particularly Barnum understood, that the opportunity to debate the *issue* of falsity, to discover how deception had been practiced, was even more exciting than the discovery of fraud itself. The manipulation of a prank, after all, was as interesting a technique in its own right as the presentation of genuine curiosities."[2]

In one important sense, however, a humbug does resemble a lie. There *are* victims. They are not actively injured; they pay no penny, ruin no dessert. Often they do not even know they are casualties. Yet without them there would be no humbug. They are the ones who do not catch on.

A humbug, by definition, is an in-joke that not everybody gets. It naturally divides its beholders into two separate and unequal camps: the "ins" and the "outs," those who understand and those who do not. Museum visitors, to be sure, did enjoy debating the issue of falsity. They did find satisfaction in seeing through the hoax and discovering how the deception had been practiced. Adding immeasurably to their pleasure, however, was their knowledge that *other* people were not smart enough to figure it all out.

Those who managed to solve the puzzle — who understood that the untruth in question was not a lie — could rightfully consider themselves select and special. They could pride themselves on possessing sharper perceptions and keener insights than those ordinary mortals who had been taken in and claim fellowship in a select and enviable community. They could share in the just and proper reward of any good humbug: a smirk at the expense of those who were oblivious. Without the near presence of the duped, the deluded, and the dim, the smarter would have felt merely smart.

Humbugs were not Barnum's only contribution to popular culture, of course, and falsity was not the only topic he proffered for public debate. Perhaps his most famous feat was bringing the beloved European singer Jenny Lind to America in 1850. In a press campaign as dazzling and flamboyant as it was ubiquitous, Barnum presented the young woman as more than a mere musical genius: she was also a paragon of piety, delicacy, and taste. Yet Barnum's real coup was his success in making this paragon a heroine for the masses, living proof that even the most ordinary American could display an artistic taste as refined as any European. Rather than confining her appearances to private recitals for the rich and well connected, Barnum sent Lind on a ninety-five-concert tour across the nation, often staging an auction of opening-night tickets to send the message that everyone had an equal chance to obtain admittance. It looked like culture as democracy: like visitors to Barnum's museum, anyone who could pay money at the door had a right to partake in the entertainment.

In the end, Barnum's signal achievement among some that were rather more dubious was that he "created a public. He cajoled, humbugged, and marshaled an audience into being, using the new technologies of communication, and therefore of power, available in the Nineteenth century city; indeed, he created a sense of 'the public' that is most recognizable today."[3]

It was the penny editors, however, who pioneered the use of those new technologies, and their contributions to the creation of "the public" were not inconsiderable — many of them deriving directly from the humbug. The Moon Hoax had set the guidelines: "facts" were not necessarily true. Untrue facts were thus no longer lies. The stories of the moon voyage, the lost African explorer, and Aunt Nelly's corpse were not swindles imposed on gullible readers, but rather recreations in which readers joined fully and gleefully.

For these New Yorkers, reading a penny newspaper required much more than merely moving their eyes across cheap newsprint. It meant flinging themselves wholeheartedly into competition with the editors and reveling in the heady thrill of choosing for themselves whether or not to believe. A generation after the birth of the penny press, the great editor Charles A. Dana is supposed to have defined news as anything that made people talk. But for the first penny editors and their readers, news was the thing that *required* people to talk.

This was precisely the kind of talk, in fact, that Thoreau would later scornfully dismiss as chasing froth and scum. But the ascetic philosopher, who would also dismiss the great push to stretch telegraph lines all the way from Maine to Texas because "Maine and Texas, it may be, have nothing important to communicate," never did understand why people like talking to each other.[4] The man who used solitude with such eloquence displayed a much weaker grasp of the imperatives, the uses, the vitality, and indeed the eloquence of the *sharing* of information. He did not understand that sharing information is the truest way to build a community, to form a population into a public.

Historians and theoreticians of journalism have long argued that this was originally the newspaper's most fundamental role. "The public was activated into a social relation by the news," as one put it, "and, in turn, the primary subject of the news was the public, the opinions being expressed in public by merchants, traders, citizens, and political activists of the time. . . . [The press's] function was not one of informing the public or educating the public as those terms are commonly employed today in an era of professionalism. It furnished materials for argument, information in the narrow sense, but the value of the press was predicated on the existence of the public, not the reverse."[5]

During the Jewett affair, the penny press activated its public as never before. "For the last ten days," the *Herald* reported on 20 April 1836, "this tragedy and the accused have occupied every tongue — been the leading topic of every conversation — is [*sic*] discussed in every drawing room and gin shop throughout the extent of New York. . . . No point of interest — no event — no contingency ever took place in New York, which has so completely divided public opinion, and created a general debate. . . . A general investigation has taken place — extra-judicial and extra-ordinary."

The reverberations of this investigation, however, were gravely different from anything emanating from Barnum's hall of freaks. The showman's humbugs involved nothing more momentous than fat boys and mermaids; his visitors split into groups of no deeper or more lasting significance than a schoolyard apportionment into Reds and Blues. The penny press, however, dealt not only with wondrous telescopes and lost African explorers. It also addressed questions of serious social and political import, and it carried those questions to a readership that was growing increasingly restless with its traditional ostracism as an "out" group in a society long dominated by powerful "ins." That is what brought into play the second tacit but ironclad rule of penny journalism: a truth that does not satisfy is no better than a lie.

There was, as we have seen, no journalistic bright line dividing the conscious, lighthearted humbug from the story based on more authentic happenings. Readers scrutinized all penny-press stories with the same wary skepticism — and the same eager self-confidence. Turning their pennies over to the newsboys earned them more than the permission to decide the genuineness of Aunt Nelly's corpse or of the charlatan's leap off the ferry boat. Along with it, they were also claiming the power to determine the credibility of the debauched nun and the freedom to express their own opinions on the trustworthiness of Helen Jewett's accused murderer.

For the New Yorkers who read the penny press, taking part in this extraordinary investigation was revolutionary. Striking enough was their casual assumption, salvaged and nursed along from the wreckage of the Working Men's press, that their opinions were just as valid and important as those of their "betters." Even more insurrectionary, however, was the corollary: these readers of normally humble status, smirking together at the "outs" from the sanctity of the new *inner* circle they had made for themselves, were also at liberty to express the opinions and choose the truths that made the most sense to that particular inner circle.

The Jewett affair was nasty. Murder is one of the most cataclysmic of social events, prostitution one of the most subversive, and injustice one of the most heart-wrenching. Plenty of true facts about the crime were indeed available: the accused worked for a merchant; the victim lived in a house of prostitution; the grocer provided an alibi. Yet such unadorned facts were no help to a New Yorker trying to understand and cope with a world in which so ugly a crime could happen and its author — whoever he was — escape justice. The facts explained nothing about tragedy or violence or suffering or fairness. They clarified nothing about how a promising young man could go so wrong, a blooming young girl so bad, or a judicial system so rotten.

The penny-press coverage of the murder, although it frequently wandered away from objective, verifiable fact, never strayed far from Truth.[6] Readers and editors alike made full use of their liberty to devise their own explanations. Those explanations were more supple, more versatile, more illuminating than fact; they were truer to the messiness, the confusion, the meanness, and the glister of daily life.

Large, universal truths concerning death and sex and evil illuminated the penny-press reporting of Helen Jewett's life. Subterranean, parochial truths involving class, privilege, ambition, and resentment informed the debate over Robinson's guilt. New Yorkers who chose to buy one penny paper instead of another were doing more than enriching one shrill little street urchin rather than his fellow. They were choosing an identity, a community, and a truth they could understand and accept.

MURDEROUS CONVENTIONS

The penny editors and their readers did not have to search far for the most compelling truths behind why Helen Jewett died. They had heard them all before. In fact, her story made sense to the New Yorkers reading the cheap press precisely *because* they had heard it all before.

Robinson's inamorata was not really a city streetwalker in a green dress who met an unfortunate end. She was an archetype, a symbol, a myth, a heroine of popular tradition; she was the latest incarnation of a painfully tragic and appallingly familiar figure, the frail, flawed female undone by sex. As the spiritual sister of Helen of Troy, of Clytemnestra, of Messalina, of Guenevere, of Faust's Gretchen, of Clarissa Harlowe, Jewett transcended her sordid little death. She entered instead the realm of the universal and the metaphorical, giving up her life to the perennial human attempt to fathom why evil happened and who should pay for it.

Popular tradition becomes traditional because it *is* popular — because it explains the curious, confusing, or troubling matters of everyday life in straightforward ways that satisfy people. These traditional explanations are resonant, familiar, intelligible. They make sense of difficult matters. They carry the weight of custom and the stamp of authority. They account for strangeness and change in calm, everyday terms. They offer the comforting assurance that everything necessary is known; everything possible is understood. For the readers of the cheap press, precise, accurate, and consistent particulars about the life Jewett actually lived were irrelevant, even dangerous, to the usefulness of a story that popular tradition already had well under control.[1]

Yet even though off-key details like the undereducation of a prostitute are inevitably edited out of the retelling of popular myth, some choices and controversies always do remain even for those who seek their solace in the tried and true. Like other emotionally wrenching themes, the motif of death by sex has generated a variety of perfectly satisfying and complete mythic traditions that differ radically from each other in tone, style, and lesson.

By the time of Helen Jewett's death, the popular literature of seduction and debauchery was enormous, its conventions fixed and immutable, and its heroines divided into two equally traditional camps. The Poor Unfortunate was a victim, a trusting innocent from the country betrayed and abandoned by a slick city rake to the tardy realization of how precious and irreplaceable was her honor. The Siren, on the other hand, was a predator, the gleeful incarnation of Original Sin who perversely sought the destruction of the social order.

The real "news" about Jewett's death has more to do with these traditions than with facts. Just because the stories in the penny press were ready-made does not mean they were merely expedient. A myth works for the members of a community only if it illuminates a truth important to them in a way they find congenial. By exercising their freedom to choose different myths, the various penny editors and the readers who supported them were embracing different truths and perspectives about the way things were. They were manifesting two very distinct ways of thinking about sin and justice, men and women, masters and mastered, rightness and rights. They were unrolling two opposing visions of New York, of

America, and of the world. They were fulfilling the public duty of the press in quite disparate ways. And they were learning to recognize the volatile and slippery boundaries of class in the Age of Jackson.

Murder and prostitution are rarely socially acceptable. Yet to the American of 1836 the killing of a harlot — the ultimate combustion of sex and death — was a particularly grave and painful matter, bringing with it special anxieties, seductions, and conflicts. This was a time of swift change that challenged not just traditional economic and social organization, but also the most basic assumptions about family and personal life. On such prime institutions as the bank, the factory, and the city slum, the marks left by the strains and upheavals accompanying America's difficult metamorphosis from a simple agrarian society to a complex industrial economy were obvious. But the changes also rippled much wider than that, crossing the thresholds of the family home and finding a place at the family hearth. The increasing complexity of economic and social relations was also forcing a "thoroughgoing transformation of the gender system ... that is ... all those arrangements of work, sexuality, parental responsibilities, psychological life, assigned social traits and internalized emotions through which the sexes defined themselves respectively as men and women."

In anxious response to these changes, the United States and in fact much of the Western world were experiencing nothing less than "a sexual explosion — not of acts, licit or illicit, but of words, images, fantasies, fears." Among the images — some might even call it a fantasy — specifically created to counter and contain the pervasive anxieties was what has been labeled the "Cult of True Womanhood." This was born of the attempt by many middle-class men, along with some of their wives, sisters, and mothers, to clarify and cement a dominant social position for the male by carving out one for the bourgeois woman that was distinctly separate, subordinate, supportive, and "female." Woman must be the embodiment of purity and piety, the guardian of morality and culture, an anchor of stability in the domestic sphere, and a paragon of respectability — a condition that included sexlessness.[2]

Small wonder, then, that among the era's greatest fears — and, again, fantasies — was the specter of a "fallen woman" like Helen Jewett, the absolute opposite of everything the True Woman stood for.

Some men fled the prostitute as a temptress; others turned to her for passionate, uninhibited pleasures they could not expect from their wives. Many women, reformers, and moral leaders feared the prostitute as a barbaric threat to home stability; others pitied her as the victim of every-thing that was bestial and domineering about the male. Some impover-ished women, struggling to support themselves or their families, lived in fear of having to make the terrible choice between death and a fate even worse. Others embraced that fate as a way to assert independence, find adventure, or earn more than they ever could in the harsh world of domes-tic service and piecework labor. As the *Advocate of Moral Reform* reported in 1848, many women resorted to "houses of infamy for food and shelter" because they "can't live by plain sewing in New York."[3]

The career of Rosina Townsend, as she described it to the court from the witness stand, was not at all unusual. Abandoned by her husband in Cincinnati when she was twenty-eight, she returned briefly to her father's house but apparently found the situation untenable. By herself, knowing no one, and never having visited the city before, she came to New York in 1825, where she took in sewing until "my head became so affected that my sight was injured, and applied to Dr. David L. Rogers who operated on me." A brief stint as chambermaid followed, but soon Townsend "went to live at a house kept by a woman named Maria Piercy; that was a house of assignation . . . and since then have either been a boarder at or the keeper of a house of prostitution." Between the lines of this bare résumé can be read the poignant story of a woman struggling to survive and surmount deser-tion, illness, and poverty with no resources but her own.[4]

America's potent and contradictory reactions to sexuality were magni-fied in New York. It was a city full of Rosina Townsends and Richard Robinsons — a place where the young, the desperate, the adventurous, and the solitary clustered most thickly and most free from the oversight of friends and relatives. No social problem could have seemed more threaten-ing — or more available.

The crusading evangelist John McDowall had recently stunned and outraged the good citizens of New York with his estimate that some ten thousand prostitutes were working in their midst. The possibility that one-twentieth of the city's population was soliciting in the streets shocked the respectable even as it beckoned the thrill seeker.[5] Thus, in the nation's largest urban settlement, the fallen woman was coming to embody ulti-mate fears as well as deep desires, freedom as well as enslavement, all that was exotic and alluring about the city as well as everything that was sordid and criminal.

Citizens responded in various ways to this crisis. Some expressed themselves inarticulately, violently, and personally. Not at all uncommon in this era were reports of men abusing prostitutes in the street, raising a mob to burn down a brothel, or breaking into bawdy houses on a furious rampage of terrorism, assault, destruction, and rape. Nor was murder itself an aberration. Shortly after Jewett died, a reform group surveyed a single Manhattan block lined with twenty-two brothels and turned up a death toll of no fewer than twenty young women in the past three months alone. Several of them had died violently.

Some attacks were mounted as revenge for advances spurned; others were intended as acts of vigilante justice, a long and familiar American tradition. Prompted by civic embarrassment or moral distaste, indignant citizens often banded together to punish crimes or retaliate against offenses that local authorities would not or could not handle. Throughout the eighteenth and nineteenth centuries, brothels, which outraged many citizens even as they enjoyed the patronage and protection of many others, were a frequent focus of vigilante action in cities from Portland and St. Louis to Boston and Detroit.

Often, however, the "brothel bullies," usually but not exclusively of the working class, were men capping off their evening of heavy communal drinking with an anarchic spree against a target fraught with the symbolism of their frustrations and resentments. Troubled by their low status, low pay, and low expectations, these men vented their rage against a group of women who, even though "weak" and "helpless," often enjoyed an enviable measure of independence and economic success. Beating up a prostitute could have been a showy way for these marginalized men to reassert the supremacy of the male sex.

Tearing up a prostitute's home, furthermore, could have been an equally showy way for marginalized men to challenge the supremacy of the *privileged* male. A great gulf separated most of the rioters from the men who patronized elegant private brothels like Townsend's — men who had wealth and standing, who could purchase access to a select world of luxurious parlors, fine food and drink, and attentive courtesans, and who could count on the proper authorities to offer no inconvenient opposition to their pleasures. The rioters' brutal, rum-soaked rampages "offered an illusion of power to powerless men . . . a moment of independence, autonomy, and honor."[6]

Other citizens took a more benevolent approach to the problem. John McDowall's own Magdalen Society for the redemption of prostitutes was short-lived, a victim of its founder's indulgence in overblown rhetoric that in the eyes of many bordered upon the obscene. But in 1834 a group of women founded the New York Female Moral Reform Society to combat male licentiousness and redeem its victims. They published a weekly newspaper, distributed Bibles in almshouses and jails, held prayer vigils in front of notorious brothels, and called for a great female crusade to hold men to the same standards of sexual propriety that bound women. And when a group of male evangelicals, having formed themselves into the Seventh Commandment Society, brashly informed the ladies they could henceforth leave the work of moral reform to practitioners more fit for the task, the women firmly refused. It was a women's issue, they said, not one for men.[7]

Many New Yorkers, however, did more reading than either rioting *or* reforming, and much of their reading featured the Poor Unfortunate. Her sad story embodied stock conflicts and characters already well known to most readers: preyed-upon female versus brutal male, country innocence versus city guile, virtue versus pleasure. The inevitable denouement, while tragic, also reaffirmed an age-old lesson: if you sin, you pay.

Even better, the Poor Unfortunate had already undergone cultural legitimization. Samuel Richardson, Daniel Defoe, Hannah Foster, and other inventors and refiners of the art of the novel had accomplished the deed as part of their fight for the good name of their literary creation. These pioneer novelists of the eighteenth century had found themselves struggling to refute outraged claims that novels planted false ideas in ignorant heads and distracted readers from more important duties. Works of fiction, critics charged, were frivolous toys that did nothing to improve either minds or morals. Some argued an even more extreme case. An article published in London in 1797, "Novel Reading a Cause of Female Depravity," was reprinted several times in America.

The novelists responded to this criticism by making their novels useful. The detailed story of a wretched female's descent into infamy did provide a sort of shivery entertainment, but it could also be taken — or at least presented — as a moral lesson especially directed at the most dedicated class of novel readers, young ladies. Such a story did not *cause* depravity, novelists argued; it actually prevented depravity by previewing its awful consequences in all their tragic inevitability. This is what happens to females who do not take sufficient care of their virtue, novels warned ponderously. *This could happen to you.*

Many novelists took an even further step to overcome their reputations as dangerous fantasists. They justified their fiction by employing another fiction: they presented their work as true. Defensive subtitles — "A Tale of Truth," "A Novel Founded on Fact," "The Fatal Effects of Seduction" — became an almost obligatory part of any novel's title page. They offered both a guarantee of the writer's good intentions and a license for the reader's guiltless indulgence.[8]

The fallen woman soon became not just popular but also indispensable for the novelist. Peter Brooks perceptively argues that prostitution had a special role in the nineteenth-century urban novel. Eminent writers like Eugène Sue and Honoré de Balzac found deviance in general to be "the last refuge of the narratable," the only interesting story left in a world otherwise orderly, happy, and boring. The prostitute, as an "essentially theatric being, capable of making mask into meaning," was perhaps the most versatile and manipulable of all possible characters, a novelistic wildcard.

Still, as Sue made clear in his massive 1843 blood-and-thunderer *Les Mystères de Paris*, even a novelist honors certain limits to realism. His heroine, Fleur-de-Marie, was a grand duchess lost in infancy and thrown, through no fault of her own, into a life of the vilest degradation. Rescued and restored to her family, the poor creature realized nonetheless that nothing could efface the stain of her early dishonor. She refused the hand of her princely suitor and died decorously in a convent.[9]

America's queen of the genre of seduction was Susanna Rowson, and the paradigm of female misery was her poor ruined Charlotte. Rowson's *Charlotte Temple: A Tale of Truth*, first published in the United States in 1794, was the best-selling novel of the eighteenth century and went through more than two hundred editions in the ensuing decades. It told the tale of a beautiful and accomplished young innocent who was inveigled away from her rural boarding school by a plausible rogue and a depraved older woman masquerading as a well-meaning friend. The consequences were inevitable: ruined and abandoned, the "fair bud of innocence . . . blasted ere it was half blown," fled to the anonymity and debasement of the big city, where she gave birth to a daughter and died of her shame.

Many readers preferred to believe that Rowson's was indeed a "tale of truth," perhaps even based on the experience of one of the author's own relatives. For years, votaries made the pilgrimage to Trinity Churchyard in Manhattan to weep at the tomb that actually bore Charlotte's name.[10] But it scarcely mattered that the dozens of Charlotte look-alikes who sprang up in her wake were free of even that tenuous anchor to fact.

Burnished by tradition, sanctified by a soulful public's calculated acquiescence, "true" tales of pure young schoolgirls and defenseless orphans preyed upon by wolfish men flourished in pamphlets, poems, songs, stage plays, almanacs, and magazines.

The topic was inexhaustible and endlessly versatile. "So obsessed were American writers with the importance of rape and seduction that by 1823 these were discovered to have been the real causes of the American Revolution." In the 1823 novel *Seventy-Six*, by the ardent nationalist writer John Neal, "it was only when rape became an issue that the Revolution really got under way: 'Men of America! — will ye ever forget it? . . . These things, at last, drove us mad. We arose, as one people — a nation, about to offer up its enemies in sacrifice.'"[11]

The Poor Unfortunate was a sinner, to be sure, one whose misdeeds threatened the most basic canons of bourgeois morality. Yet her fall was not entirely unforgivable. It was due to frailty and the arts of men, not to evil; it was only human; *she did not like what had happened to her.* Better yet, she was suitably punished. Death entitled her to both pity and gratitude. By dying in a decent and timely fashion, considerately removing from the community the embarrassment of her indelible smirch, she demonstrated to her fellow citizens that cosmic justice and social order could prevail.

The Siren, on the other hand, was evil incarnate. All the accumulated weight of tradition, religion, and morality required the annihilation of any woman who betrayed both sexes by indulging herself in illicit sex of her own free will. Many of the archetypal Sirens had died in peculiarly horrible ways: Clytemnestra was murdered by her son; Messalina was executed by her husband. Others, like Guenevere and Helen, were damned to survive long enough to witness the cataclysmic destruction of entire civilizations on their account.

The Siren *had* to pay a penalty. She did not merely threaten morality and order; she kicked them in the teeth. The proposition that a woman, an angel of purity, could not only feel lust but actually enjoy it was ghastly. The idea that a female, who should have been mild and pliant, could viciously set out to grapple a man down to her vile level was abhorrent. And there was no redemption, no pity, no softening possible even in her death. The only conceivable emotions could be joy and relief if the community lived through the excision of so fearsome a cancer.

The conflict between the two different versions of Jewett's life in the penny papers was, at bottom, a disagreement over which mythic heroine more truly reflected the state of society — an argument in which the prostitute turned out to be fully as indispensable and fully as manipulable in real life as she was to the novelist. Both the *Sun* and the *Transcript* (as well as, perhaps, Jewett herself, if she had indeed given the seduced-while-away-at-school version of her life to the *Transcript*) championed the Poor Unfortunate. In giving the young woman a respectable childhood at a boarding school, attributing her ruin to the devious arts of an unprincipled libertine, and celebrating her attempts to cling to the tattered remnants of decency and honor despite all, they were reviving poor victimized Charlotte Temple under a new name. The *Herald*, on the other hand, embraced the Siren. Luxuriating in lurid details about the madam's devil eyes and the prostitute's marble bust, Bennett titillated readers with his portrayal of life among the lascivious.

At first glance, this choice seems odd. If indeed the editors of the *Transcript* and the *Sun* were trying to publish "alternative" newspapers, one might expect their editors to choose the "alternative" myth, the subversive story of corruption and profligacy. If indeed Bennett of the *Herald* was trying to appeal to a broader and more respectable readership, one might expect him to prefer the milder version already sanitized and sanctified for middle-class consumption.

Yet like any good myth, the tales of the Poor Unfortunate and the Siren were stratified with meaning; both conveyed messages much deeper and subtler than were at first apparent. To readers of the Jewett tale, seeking hard explanations for how and why sin could happen, the most important character in each version was not the victim. It was the victimizer. The significant question in each case was: who was to blame for evil? Bennett's choice was indeed calculated to endear him to the sort of readers most concerned with protecting the social order. By their choice, Day and Lynde did indeed loose a tiny flurry of social subversion.

The Poor Unfortunate character chosen by Day and Lynde — the deluded sinner who dies rather than confound the moral universe — was in fact a subversive heroine. She mounted a much stronger challenge to the bourgeois social order than the Siren did and appealed much more strongly to the many mechanics, laborers, and artisans who had themselves struggled to confound the status quo. For Jewett was one of them.

If she was indeed a betrayed and exploited innocent, then her betrayers and exploiters were scoundrels, brutes, perhaps even criminals. And since those scoundrels were rich, powerful, middle- or upper-class men, then

Jewett was — like the Working Men before her, like the mechanics and laborers left powerless by their co-opted revolution, like the drunken rampagers who chose brothels as their target — an oppressed victim of privilege. Those brothel rioters, in fact, may even have mustered some sympathy for Jewett herself, Jewett as a woman, now that she would never again trouble them with her superiority — now that she had died of her superiority, which had proved too frail to withstand the power of the society's *real* oppressors. The myth of the Poor Unfortunate thus found the root of sin in the very structure of the community itself.

The *Sun* and the *Transcript* may actually have gotten their version of the story directly from either Jewett or someone who had known her; they may have embroidered the facts they knew. In the end, however, the source of their story is less important than the fact that, by choosing that particular version, they were also choosing to launch an indictment against society, power, and influence.[12]

Day and Lynde showed no hesitation in expressing their solidarity with the wronged women and their bitterness toward the victimizing men. On 18 April, in the *Sun's* long and caustic critique of the *Herald's* support for Robinson, scarcely a reference to either Townsend or her boarders escaped free of the prefix "unhappy," "persecuted," or "unfortunate." The men involved, on the other hand, were "unprincipled scoundrels, whose constant association with the depraved and unfortunate beings whom they seek to involve in the ruin which overwhelms their companion, has sunk them to a level (if not to a greater depth of infamy) with those they would sacrifice to revenge and the guilt of their companion."

The following day, under the heading "Shocking Perversion of Mind," the *Sun* printed a "dreadful" letter from a young man, himself a confessed roué, who roundly declared his disgust at "see[ing] so young a person [as Robinson] sacrificed for ridding the city of so great a disgrace to her sex." "So then this cold blooded, treacherous murder," the *Sun* fumed, "has merit in it!... It is a merit to murder, by the most detestable treachery and savage violence, a woman who is a disgrace to her sex; and this is said by a person who unblushingly admits his own disgraceful participation in the very crime which he deems sufficient to render her murder meritorious! We will not say that the writer of this atrocious sentiment has convinced us that it would be an act of merit to murder him; but we hesitate not to say that we think him qualified to commit a murder himself."

The artisan-editors' sympathy for their fellow victim was profound but unavailing. It was a viewpoint from the fringe, from the disaffected and disenfranchised of society, and in the end, as even its supporters must have suspected, it made virtually no headway in bringing a murderer to justice. Yet in propagating their version of the Jewett story, the editors did post one triumph that was in its own way just as important. They participated in the public debate. They voiced their own opinions. They disagreed with the established point of view and they said so. The rhetoric of egalitarianism complemented and upheld the classic myth of the poor oppressed victim, producing for working-class readers a clear and comprehensible explanation of who was to blame for evil.

While the *Sun* and the *Transcript* were cajoling laborers and artisans with classic subversion, the *Herald* was teasing a different class of readers with something just as dear to their own hearts: a fervent defense of the standing order. And in the process, Bennett rejected the single most cherished principle in the short history of the cheap alternative press.

When he reported in his *Herald* that Townsend, Jewett, and the other boarders were abandoned wantons, he did more than thrill readers. He also exonerated them. If Townsend was indeed a "woman lost to virtue and to principle," an "old miserable hag, who has spent her whole life in seducing and inveigling the young and old to their destruction" and who was possessed of a soul of "passion and malevolence" — if indeed all this were true, then who could blame her customers for falling prey to her evil designs? Throughout history other men, perfectly respectable ones, had done as much.

Even the wretched Robinson, argued Bennett, deserved compassion. "Robinson, it is too true, and 'pity tis, tis true' has to answer for 'debaucheries and iniquities' quite enough, besides the murder he is accused of. He like many others, has fallen a victim to the seduction and blandishments — the splendid air and gay revelry — the sparkling champaigne and polite attentions of such persons as the amiable and accomplished Rosina Townsend."

Bennett could have devised no better strategy for upholding middle-class morality than to blame immorality on anyone *but* the middle class. By selecting the members of society most deviant, most on the fringe, to bear the guilt for Jewett's death, the solid citizens of New York could enjoy both righteous indignation and relieved absolution.[13]

Bennett clearly recognized the appeal of this ploy to the more respectable class of readers he hoped to win, and he worked hard to distinguish himself and his press from the other, humbler penny papers aimed chiefly at the laborers and artisans. His effort required, first of all, that he abandon one of the proudest and most distinctive traditions of the artisan press. While the editors who had been Working Men continued to support natural rights, Bennett carefully avoided a topic so controversial, even painful, for masters and capitalists. Rare in his columns were any glimmerings of intellectual egalitarianism, any principled embrace of all people's right to know. Although he did issue declarations as ringing as any to be found in the penny press, *his* rang in support of an entirely different polestar. Bennett's coverage was based firmly on all people's responsibility to behave.

To hear Bennett tell it, society was in desperate danger, tottering on the brink of surrender; schemers and evildoers threatened everyone, everywhere, and even the righteous needed support. "The world is surely coming to an end," he preached on 14 April 1836, and "the vengeance of Heaven can be staid no longer." In such a benighted world a newspaper's main duty was not to inform so much as to regulate, to function as a sort of social chastity belt. As he put it five days later, "The aim of a lofty, intelligent, independent, educated and philosophical press . . . is to investigate the state of society which produced so horrid a catastrophe — to develope [*sic*] the current of moral feeling which that sad affair has developed — to lay open the principles and springs of that society in which so great a crime could have originated." His lively and plentiful coverage of the Jewett affair was, he argued, both justifiable and beneficial.

"Instead of relating the recent awful tragedy of Ellen Jewett as a dull police report," he argued on 30 April, "we made it the starting point to open a full view upon the morals of society — the hinge of a course of mental action calculated to benefit the age — the opening scene of a great domestic drama, that is yet to be completed by the trial of Robinson — a drama that will if properly conducted, bring about a reformation — a revolution — a total revolution in the present diseased state of society and morals."

Thus Bennett clearly distinguished his vision of the public duty of the press — and clearly marked out which public *his* press was intended for. Where the *Sun* and the *Transcript* endorsed the right of the excluded to challenge the social order, Bennett endorsed the right of the powerful and respectable to uphold it. Where the former Working Men demanded information, Bennett cried out for reformation. Where the other two papers defied authority, Bennett embraced authority.

The upstart Bennett was not always convincing in his wrath. Although some readers may have believed him sincere, many others maintained that the loftiness, intelligence, independence, education, and philosophy of Bennett's particular press were themselves a descent into dark ages of barbarism. "We would rather see," lamented the stalwart sixpenny *Commercial Advertiser* on 28 April, "[the penny press] columns filled with the dullest common-places or the most trivial records of overgrown beets and turnips; with wearisome disquisitions on any thing and nothing; aye, or even with dull speeches on the floor of congress, than with such matters, however entertaining or exciting they may be, as tend to vitiate the moral feeling or blunt the moral perception of the reader."

Yet even the veiled barbarism of Bennett's prose was itself another classic ploy to win his preferred readership. To anyone actually looking for results, his breast-beating about moral reform, his bloodcurdling prophecies about the wrath to come, and his pious laments about unprincipled men betrayed themselves as pure bluster. But even readers who recognized the editor as a moralistic poseur had some cause for gratitude that he posed at all. They knew that Bennett was the best source for a cornucopia of fascinating and fanciful detail about the world in need of reform — that distant and glamorous demimonde of false names, champagne, and beautiful courtesans who read Byron.

To say that orderly and respectable people harbor a secret curiosity about the underworld of disorder, vice, and sin is a gross and unfair generalization. It is also often true. And for those so inclined, donning the fig leaf of moralism made visiting this underworld permissible. In that age of mounting concern and activism about social evil, in fact, many writers, including novelists, were making an industry out of describing the evil and leaving out the activism.

One scholar has named this the subversive school of reform literature. "With increasing frequency and purposefulness," he writes, "popular American lecturers and writers learned to manipulate the rhetoric of reform instead of using it with high seriousness.... [They] deemphasized the remedies for vice while probing the grisly, sometimes perverse results of vice, such as shattered homes, sadomasochistic violence, eroticism, nightmare visions, and the disillusioning collapse of romantic ideals. Ironically, even the most grossly immoral reformers ... righteously proclaimed pure moral intentions."[14]

Thus Bennett's clever manipulation of the myth most antithetical to established social values pandered to those who upheld them. In the process, Bennett did little to clarify the ambiguity of the culture of morality. What he did instead was to claim the moral sphere as his own particular bailiwick. There he could allow bourgeois readers the indulgence of feeling morally superior, thus clarifying their own ambiguous standing in the social hierarchy.

That was what the public duty of the penny press was all about. Despite the apparent contradictions and falsehoods in the various reports on Jewett's life and death, Bennett and the other editors *were* fulfilling their public duty as journalists. They were giving their readers what they expected, in language they knew and understood. They were confirming their audience's general assumptions of how the world worked, reinforcing the facts they already knew, and upholding the beliefs and ethics they already cherished. They were allowing readers to cement their own sense of self and communal identity and to distinguish themselves from other communities. They were making sense of a society growing ever more confusing by assuring their readers that things happened in understandable, even predictable ways.

In the penny press, at this point, a true incident was one that harmonized with generally accepted and generally understood patterns, not one that forced the assimilation of extraneous and difficult variations. Even the editors' vigorous yet conflicting protestations of truth were part of the plan. Readers expected that a world conforming to their expectations would be defended as true.

The penny papers' mythic interpretations of Jewett's life attempted to explain a cosmic imbalance: why did evil happen? But they had still another puzzle to address, one much more mundane and much less intractable — one that could actually be solved by human reason. Who did it? Who was to blame for this particular evil? As they reported their solutions to the puzzle, the penny editors again sought to protect their readers' beliefs and their ethics, to harmonize with the patterns they knew and the assumptions they cherished. One editor was lucky enough to harmonize with reality as well.

GETTING AWAY WITH MURDER

The journalistic debate over Helen Jewett's life was at bottom a search for the most felicitous myth, a mighty truth that could explain the inexplicable. In the debate over Richard Robinson's guilt, on the other hand, New Yorkers already had their truths, and those were not mighty. They inhabited not the universal precincts of myth but the sordid under-belly of New York City politics. Corruption, ambition, power, influence, privilege, resentment — these are underground, shabby, and ubiquitous realities of everyday life. Yet more truly than any confusion over the validity of an alibi, they explain the brouhaha over whether the clerk killed the prostitute. More directly than any abstract journalistic principle, they inspired, at last, the only analysis of the crime that was just as accurate as it was truthful.

The exposé was long in coming. Not until after the rivalry and chaos of the spring's reporting, after the circus of the trial, after the jury deliberated for eight minutes and declared Richard Robinson innocent — only then, on 9 June 1836, did Benjamin Day of the *Sun* make his charges explicit, angry, and clear.

"By the verdict of a jury," Day reported,

> Richard P. Robinson stands acquitted of the awful crime of murder with which he was charged. Whether he be also acquitted by the jury of the public, is not so certain a result. . . . That the public have now as good an opportunity of forming as correct an opinion of his guilt or innocence as the jury who tried him, the fidelity with which the evidence adduced before them is reported in all the public prints, renders obvious; and that the public have a right to express that opinion, whatever it may be, is undeniable. . . . We hesitate not to say, that our opinion, calmly and dispassionately formed from that evidence, is that Richard P. Robinson is guilty of the wilfull and peculiarly atrocious murder of Helen Jewett.

Having finally begun, Day went at the task in good earnest, launching the most reasoned and realistic analysis of the entire affair to appear in any city paper. It was also devastating. "Any good-looking young man," he summed up, "possessing or being able to raise among his friends, the sum of fifteen hundred dollars to retain Messrs. Maxwell, Price and Hoffman for his counsel, might murder any person he chose, with perfect impunity. And hence it was that from the time it became known that these eminent advocates were retained for Robinson, there was but one opinion as to the result of his trial."

The *Transcript*, too, published a number of columns criticizing the corrupt handling of the affair, and several of the sixpenny papers joined in with a few mild complaints about irregularities in the trial. But Day remained the leader of the investigation. For days on end he published a series of long, detailed, and analytical articles under the heading "The Solemn Farce" — a title "at once accurately descriptive of its object," as he explained on 14 June, "and expressive of public opinion concerning it. It is one to which nine tenths of our intelligent population have stood sponsors."

Day commented on virtually every piece of evidence and every witness with a sturdy precision that suggests an extensive personal investigation. The jury had been packed with Hoxie's friends, he said. The rowdy audience jamming the courtroom had been permitted to whoop and cheer any testimony favorable to the prisoner and to boo anything critical. Hoxie had first tried to induce a theater manager to swear an alibi for Robinson weeks before finally settling on Furlong, the grocer. Day even managed to ferret out grand jury testimony that clarified Robinson's motive. Robinson, newly engaged to a respectable young woman, had previously been suspected of seducing and murdering one Emma Chancellor, and the jealous Jewett knew it and threatened to tell. Rumors of that first murder, said Day, had been afloat throughout the city during the trial and should have been examined and tracked down.

Day also minutely analyzed the various disputes that had erupted between the legal teams. One column contemptuously dismissed the claim that because Townsend had been the one to suggest searching her backyard for clues to the murder, she must have planted the cloak and the ax there. As the owner of the house, Day said, she could have planted a cloak anywhere she pleased, and how could she have gotten hold of Hoxie's ax from Maiden Lane, anyway? He pointed out inequities in the treatment of witnesses. The district attorney knew the names of the six men caught visiting at Townsend's when the cry of fire was raised, Day said, but he never required their appearance in court. Furlong's testimony had been accepted even though riddled with inconsistencies, while Townsend's was excluded even though credible and judicious. The automatic exclusion of any testimony from a fallen woman was, Day argued, foolish and dangerous: it meant that no crime a prostitute happened to witness could ever be punished.

All told, it was an astute, vivid, and convincing analysis, consistent with everything else we know about the trial, and it was contradicted by no known contemporary commentator except James Gordon Bennett. It was also, given its allegations of corruption in high places, a daring and perhaps dangerous analysis. Yet Day did not waver. Throughout his weeks of investigation, he declared again and again that challenging the official version of the case was nothing less than the right and the duty of every citizen. With a fearless press as their guide, all people could make up their own minds and express their own opinions on public matters.

"We mean not to say," he wrote on 20 June, "that the opinion of a majority of the press is necessarily an acurate [*sic*] expression of public opinion; but we do say that a popular opinion formed upon a fair report of a trial in the public papers, is a solemn authority which every judicial functionary, whether judge, public prosecutor, or jury, is bound to respect. It is the very authority which founds and sanctions the laws by which every free community is governed." Here, at last, the rhetoric of the right-to-know so cherished by the artisan editors was actually being put to use. Day was invoking the principles of egalitarianism to challenge, not a myth, but a real-life miscarriage of justice.

All through the last half of June, while the *Sun* was carrying out its mission of analysis and exposure, the great investigative journalist Bennett was not silent either. On the day after the *Sun* explicated its choice of the title "Solemn Farce," Bennett explored Robinson's first meeting with poor Emma Chancellor, who, he said, was *not* dead. "He danced," the *Herald* gushed, "he talked — he sentimentalized — he took her in his arms — he kissed her — he fondled on her ripe, rich, ruby lips."

As days passed, Bennett went on to promise to spill the lurid secrets of murder, bloodshed, kidnaping, and poisoning at other houses of prostitution. He chivied Day as an infidel, a sealbreaker, a consorter with prostitutes. On 20 June, he recalled the great days of the trial with a swooning nostalgia but managed to pull himself together at the last minute: "Who can forget the spirit displayed in the testimony of the lovely but bitter Emma French — the cool but enchanting Eliza Salters — the calm but persuasive Elizabeth Stewart — the affectionate but *passé* Mary Gallagher — the vindictive but black bright eyed Rosina Townsend? . . . When will the lightning of High Heaven purify the immoral atmosphere of this Sodom and Gomorrah?"

If credit is due anywhere for a rigorous and factual analysis of the Helen Jewett murder case, it must go to the *Sun*. Anyone who absolutely requires a heroic journalist for the infant mass press might, in the end, find that hero in Day. Yet the *Sun*'s editor accomplished one more feat with his stinging critique of the trial. He also gave his particular community of readers a compelling, familiar, and comprehensible story that conformed to their expectations and made sense of their world. As pioneering and progressive as his investigation appears, it was, at bottom, a humbug too, sharing distinct similarities with the Moon Hoax, the fantasy of Jewett's life, and Bennett's own edition of the killer's identity. Day's analysis was a crystallization of sentiments, wishes, and theories that had been roiling New Yorkers even before Jewett was found slashed to death in her flaming bed.

The giveaway was the cast of characters. Every single person involved in the prisoner's defense belonged heart and soul to the more conservative and privileged echelons of society. The young man's father, who reportedly sat next to him at every session of the trial, was a pillar of his Connecticut community and had served seven terms in the state general assembly. Nor did the defendant's family sink under its disgrace: the elder Robinson entered on his eighth and last assembly term in 1837, *after* the murder.[1]

The attorneys who argued Robinson's case were prominent and influential, the cream of the city's legal profession and the pride of its social elite. William Price was something of an anomaly, a "violent, brawling Federalist" until "he found he could get nothing by that [and] became a Democrat and Tammany man, more violent and brawling." He nonetheless enjoyed a reputation as a genius in dandy's clothing. Not only was he considered "the foremost criminal lawyer in New York City"; he also was admired for the "surpassing urbanity of his manners" and was widely sought as the "chief adornment of the social board." Hugh Maxwell, a former district attorney, had earned his greatest fame as the prosecutor of a bitter fraud case involving the failure of an insurance company in the business depression of 1826. For decades afterward, the defendants continued to denounce the trial as a conspiracy of the "moneyed aristocracy."[2]

Robinson's third attorney, the talented Ogden Hoffman, widely considered the "American Erskine," was also seen at the time as either a political turncoat or a prodigal son returned, depending on one's point of view. His Whig lineage was impeccable: he was the great-grandson of a Loyalist lieutenant governor, the son of a wealthy landholder and superior court judge, the brother of Washington Irving's ever-lamented Matilda, and the half-brother of Charles Fenno Hoffman, who spent his life trying to become Washington Irving. As a young man, Hoffman had broken with his august family's traditional Whig politics to join Tammany, but he had recently and publicly returned to the fold, renouncing the Democrats in disgust over Jackson's enmity toward the Bank. His performance in Robinson's trial doubtless went far to confirm the genuineness of his new political identity. In the fall elections later that year, the overwhelming support of the city's richest men helped send the lawyer to Congress as a Whig.

Ogden Edwards, the presiding judge at the trial, was also a Whig and also came from an important and influential family: his cousin was Aaron Burr, his grandfather the hellfire theologian Jonathan Edwards. Throughout that spring of 1836, furthermore, he had been busy earning himself a reputation among the city's working class as a union buster and enemy of republican rights. For weeks, the city had been torn by strikes, mass meetings, and protests as laborers and journeymen from a dozen or more trades resisted their masters' attempts to cut their wages. Edwards had recently presided over the trial in which twenty journeyman tailors active in the resistance were convicted of conspiracy to combine in restraint of trade, and the very week of Robinson's trial he sentenced them to an onerous fine. Thus even as Edwards was hearing the case presented by Robinson's wealthy, well-connected supporters and protectors, mechanics were plastering the city with handbills denouncing the judge as "the tool of Aristocracy" and preparing to hang him in effigy from the gates of City Hall Park.[3]

Joseph Hoxie, too, was a highly provocative player in the drama. Everyone knew he was Robinson's employer and patron; many also believed he was the young man's savior. As we have seen, he probably bribed Bennett into supporting Robinson. It was he who paid the eminent attorneys' large bill. And after the verdict, unsubstantiated hints continued to circulate that he had bribed the jury and some of the witnesses as well.

Yet though Hoxie's activity on Robinson's behalf was distinctly shady, his reputation until then had been that of a model citizen and benevolent employer. He was apparently a successful businessman: the dry-goods store he and his partner kept in Maiden Lane employed a bookkeeper and two other clerks besides Robinson. It must have been a profitable business indeed if Hoxie could afford all the payoffs as well as the lawyers' fee of fifteen hundred dollars.

For Hoxie, however, living properly required more than just making a good living. He was a perfect example of a new and increasingly prominent kind of New York businessman, the evangelical who carried his religious and moralistic zeal deep into the city's social and political life. Robinson's employer was a guiding member of several important philanthropic and fraternal organizations, among them the American Institute, which encouraged the development of native resources and manufacturing, and the General Society of Mechanics and Tradesmen, which sponsored schools and wholesome libraries for working people and campaigned for favorable trade conditions. He wholeheartedly embraced the work of the recently established New-York City Temperance Society — along with fellow members Hugh Maxwell, one of the men he hired to defend Robinson, and Judge Edwards himself.[4]

The stated purpose of these organizations was to improve the minds and morals of mechanics and artisans. Yet they had a second, less obvious purpose: to advance the interests of America's first generation of "capitalists," the *master* craftsmen and merchants who led the mechanics. It was not necessarily an insidious intent. These masters, fired by evangelical conviction as well as entrepreneurial sense, genuinely believed that what was good for them and their businesses was good for their workers and their city, too. An employer who brought the souls under his care to diligence, sobriety, and Jesus was both bestowing and earning blessings. By behaving with responsibility and humanity toward his inferiors, as any good citizen should, he was surely earning stars in his own heavenly crown — *and* increasing his earthly profits up to 25 percent as well.[5]

Not surprisingly, however, the aggressive benevolence of the evangelical leaders did not always please the people they hoped to improve. Many workers had not the slightest interest in embracing either temperance or Christ; many resented their employers' meddling in their lives. In the decade before the Jewett murder, as we have seen, the Working Men's efforts to declare social independence from the masters had led to a brief radical movement that embraced the ideals of Thomas Paine and Fanny Wright. Benjamin Day of the *Sun*, along with Willoughby Lynde and William J. Stanley of the *Transcript*, had been on the side of the freethinkers. And the relentlessly benevolent Joseph Hoxie had been a member of the more aristocratic Cookite faction that had managed to seize control of the Working Men's party and to kill off radical artisan insurgency.[6]

Six years after the failure of the Working Men, a young woman was found dead in a high-class brothel. The victim was a social outsider without acknowledged friends; the accused killer was a prepossessing youth of good family, defended by prestigious attorneys, heard by a judge widely considered hostile to the interests of the working class, and employed by a merchant with a history of social and economic manipulativeness. Rumors abounded that this merchant had used money and influence to ensure the prisoner's acquittal. The penny editors had long since set the guidelines that truth was whatever their own particular community of readers needed it to be. Now several different communities of New Yorkers were again confronting the old story: the capitalist's belief that he was entitled to mold people and society into the forms most convenient to himself.

Whether he did it for pay, for notice, or both, Bennett, by painting Robinson as the innocent victim of a foul conspiracy engineered by the conveniently depraved Rosina Townsend, was doing his best to ratify the social scenario preferred by Hoxie and his powerful friends. The editor's vicious attacks on critics, his invention and manipulation of evidence, and his purple passages of weal, woe, and wantonness were all carefully crafted to support a fantasy dearly beloved by a large and influential group of New Yorkers.

The occasional puffs of egalitarian rhetoric Bennett also sent up were sops to the humble reader, hollow indulgences in the rodomontade of victimhood, and they could have bamboozled no moderately observant New Yorker for long. Bennett's pious assertions that the poor "young and pennyless" Robinson had been scapegoated because of his "obscurity of situation" were clearly absurd. No one *truly* obscure could have enjoyed the support that Robinson had from an influential patron well known as an opponent of artisanal aspirations. No one *really* "pennyless" could have benefited from the legal counsel of the best and most prestigious defense team in the city, whose services commanded a larger fee than many skilled laborers could earn in four, five, even six years of steady work.[7]

No one who daily endured the zealous evangelical meddling of powerful employers and masters could have taken kindly to Bennett's frenzied calls for yet another general moral makeover. No one from the sadly experienced ranks of the mechanics and working men could possibly have believed that the "conspiracy" Bennett described would end up oppressing anyone other than themselves. None of society's authentic scapegoats, in short, could have believed for a minute that either the prisoner Robinson or his defender Bennett was at heart a brother in affliction. Bennett was clearly identifying himself with the aspiring and the respectable, and so were the readers who chose him.

The story of the murder offered by the *Sun* and the *Transcript*, on the other hand, was a calculated rebuttal of everything Bennett stood for and a purposeful protest against manipulation and oppression. Their version of Jewett's biography had cast her as an oppressed victim, and their depiction of the killer was a perfect complement: in their pages, Robinson was no "innocent boy" but rather a villainous man-about-town who found aid and comfort in the solidarity of wealthy and powerful friends.

Throughout most of the spring, the message was muted. Day, Stanley, and Lynde, chastened perhaps by the memory of the Working Men's failure, at first launched little overt criticism of their social superiors. Nor did they scruple any more than Bennett had to support the story they preferred in any way they could. They concocted convenient fantasies and indulged in blithe inconsistencies. They gleefully slung mud — at Bennett, at each other, and at anyone involved in Robinson's defense; they may have accepted bribes from Townsend; they may have colluded with the police.

The delivery of the verdict in Robinson's favor, however, finally goaded Day into venting his fury. To many New Yorkers, but particularly to the city's authentic scapegoats, the verdict must have been as predictable as it was infuriating. Day's investigation simply confirmed and publicized what readers had known all along. No one was surprised that this "good-looking young man, possessing . . . the sum of fifteen hundred dollars . . . might murder any person he chose, with perfect impunity." Privilege could and did sculpt society's progress. Money and influence could and did triumph over justice.

Privilege, money, and influence also, it turned out, changed history — in retrospect, that is. Not only did the manufactured Bennett/Hoxie/Hoffman version of the murder win the day in court; it also won the decades in the history books. Virtually every scholar who has ever written about the *Herald* has heaped praise on Bennett's brilliant coup of investigative journalism that saved a poor youth from a terrible miscarriage of justice.[8] For all the heat and excitement of the public debate — for all the egalitarian thrill that Day and his readers found in expressing their opinion just like anybody else — that much more credible opinion died a speedy and quiet death. The truth that ultimately prevailed in the marketplace of ideas was a truth that only the richest and most powerful New Yorkers could afford.

THE END OF THE AFFAIR

For years after her violent death, Helen Jewett lived on in legend. Her archetypal story was a natural for the novelist. Joseph Holt Ingraham used it in 1843 as the basis for *Frank Rivers; Or, the Dangers of the Town*, one of the dozens of racy paper-covered thrillers he wrote before embracing religion, and nearly a century later it inspired the former journalist Manuel Komroff's popular 1932 novel *New York Tempest*. Even more recently, in 1982, Raymond Paul turned the case into a detective story, *The Thomas Street Horror: An Historical Novel of Murder*. None of these authors scrupled to apply his own imagination to the tale. In Ingraham's version the young clerk was innocent and truehearted, a near victim of a hideous concatenation of coincidences. Paul fingered the prostitute Maria Stevens as the killer, discarding the inconvenient reality that she had died of a burst blood vessel just before the trial. After all, they were writing fiction.

Yet Jewett also lived on for decades as the protagonist of "real-life" cautionary tales that were presented as true even though they were no more authentic than the novelists' fantasies. As late as 1866, thirty years after her death, newspapers were still referring to a prostitute's murder as "a Helen Jewett affair."[1] When the spicy *National Police Gazette* was new, it declared itself dedicated to "merely stating facts," avowed itself "only bound to make true statements," and promised to furnish only "the most full and particular history." Over several months in 1848 and 1849 it spun out an endless "true" version of the Jewett tale and then reprinted the whole turgid thing in pamphlet form. Only after 115 double-column pages of tiny print detailing the tragic ruin of yet another girl who ended up a prostitute at Rosina Townsend's, or the wicked history of yet another vicious debauchery by the black-hearted Robinson, did the villain finally sink his ax into his helpless victim's skull.[2]

By the waning of the century, Jewett's tale even managed to melt America's most hard-bitten cop. Thomas Byrnes, the redoubtable inspector of the New York Police Detectives (a "Czar, with all an autocrat's irresponsible powers," as Jacob Riis called him), was famous for his ruthless and unscrupulous but thoroughly pragmatic dealings with the city's criminals. In 1886 Byrnes compiled an encyclopedia of the lives of famous crooks. There, amidst a bloodcurdling array of blackguards like Funeral Wells, Broken-Nose Tully, and Kid Glove Rosey, he paused to muse tenderly over the "brutal and unavenged" murder of "the fair cyprian," who had been found "clad in a dainty night-dress," her "fair forehead . . . almost divided by a ghastly axe-stroke," in a room that was a "marvel of luxury." The young woman's fate had been sealed, said the terrible inspector, when, gripped by "the maddest infatuation" for the handsome Robinson with the golden-brown curls, she had demanded marriage.[3]

As late as 1919, another source went on record with the "checkered and extraordinary" life story of the "graceful and voluptuous" courtesan whose "eyes flash[ed] with ardent fire." By now her first descent into vice was laid to her having fallen unwisely in love with a winning young sailorboy home from the China seas. After the collapse of that romance, she fled to the big city, where she enjoyed a lustrous career as the "Queen of the Pave" and entangled herself in "numerous intrigues"; once she nearly inveigled an unsuspecting broker into marriage, but an anonymous letter enlightened the "astonished gentleman" on the eve of the wedding. All ended, however, when she found herself "lov[ing] with a fiery passion the handsome Robinson."

This version appeared in John Lawson's *American State Trials*, a sober, respectable, seventeen-volume compilation of important cases that is still consulted by lawyers and historians today.[4]

Thus the years played havoc with Jewett's story, and those of us who can trace its permutations from our safe perch decades down the road will appreciate the joke of it. Space, however, can be as mischievous as time. In Jewett's own day, the miles also played havoc with the story, and many Americans who lived far beyond New York received versions of the tale as travel-stained as anything that finally reached the scholarly John Lawson. They, however, were not amused. And therein lie the gravest consequences of the penny papers' blithe rearrangement of fact for commercial and communitarian advantage.

Americans loved newspapers. The country boasted hundreds of them, and they were read with passionate dedication. Alexis de Tocqueville noticed during his travels of 1831-32 that "hardly a hamlet in America [is] without its newspaper" — or more often *both* its newspapers, one supporting each political party; around the same time, the assiduously discontented Mrs. Trollope ridiculed the Americans' "universal" habit of reading newspapers to the exclusion of any worthier fare. "If you buy a yard of ribbon, the shop-keeper lays down his newspaper, perhaps two or three, to measure it," she sniffed. "I have seen a brewer's dray-man perched on the shaft of his dray and reading one newspaper, while another was tucked under his arm."[5]

The newspaper of the hamlet was something very different from the urban press, both penny and sixpenny. Printed every week or two in minute quantities on presses that had been arduously shipped overland or hauled in pieces in saddlebags, held hostage to the timely arrival of the paper supply, set in type too battered to read without effort and too expensive to replace without pain, the rural weekly looked precisely like the country cousin it was.

Country editors could never have survived on the proceeds of their fragile little newspapers alone. They also cranked out almanacs, broadside announcements of stolen horses or runaway slaves, blank forms and business cards, and — if they were lucky enough to have supported the party in power — the official laws and other town business whose publication was mandated by statute. Payment for goods and services was rarely on time and rarely in cash. In a tiny community not far from Harpers Ferry in what is now West Virginia, one Nathan Haines paid for part of his 1837 subscription to Charles Town's *Virginia Free Press* with thirteen pounds of mutton worth eighty-one cents. Humphrey Keyes exchanged shoes, red flannel, nails, and horse brushes for the advertisements he placed between 1837 and 1842. And George Zeaman, when pressed in 1853 to pay $47.50 for the last nineteen years of the subscription he sent his brother, replied that the editor was supposed to have been taking hats from his shop all that time instead.[6]

Getting the news was a particular trial for the country press. The nation possessed just a few hundred miles of railroad tracks, and the big highways and canal systems were just beginning to creep into the interior. Much of the nation still slumbered in isolation every winter when rivers froze and raw roads filled with snow. There was no telegraph. By courtesy of the post office, editors across the country were permitted to exchange their papers with one another postage free, and most country newspaper proprietors gathered their news mainly by reading and copying from other papers, printed closer to the source, that had made the laborious journey through the mail.

On 16 April 1836, Elihu Stout, the editor of the *Vincennes Western Sun* in Indiana, shared the shocking news about the siege of the Alamo with his fellow citizens in the little cluster of communities along the banks of the Wabash. He had, said Stout, copied his report from the *Louisville Advertiser*, which in turn had copied it from an *Arkansas Gazette* extra, which had gotten it from Louisiana's *Natchitoches Herald*, which was indebted to the "politeness of a gentleman at San Augustine" in Texas, who had just received an "express" from San Antonio. By the time the good citizens of Vincennes, Owl Prairie, Slinkard's Mills, and Turman's Creek got the news of the massacre, Davy Crockett and Jim Bowie had been six weeks in their graves, and troops were massing for the revenge strike at San Jacinto.

Yet this chain-letter version of national and international news, however stale, was the fare of choice for the country weekly. In the odd spaces left between the plentiful advertisements and the weighty news items, many small-town papers did include brief tidbits, copied from larger journals, of poignant, peculiar, or gruesome happenings around the nation: the Indian murders in Tallahassee, the fire that consumed Wall Street, the woman who had borne two sets of triplets and three of twins.

News of purely hometown affairs, however, rarely surfaced in purely hometown papers.[7] The paper that enjoyed the support of the local party in power, to be sure, did devote some attention to the official business of the statehouse or the town council. But news of everyday life was virtually invisible. It would have been both unnecessary and profligate to waste one precious column-inch of that eagerly awaited stock of paper, and to subject that poor battered type to one more punishing press run, simply to describe at length the hailstorm that flattened the crops, the wedding party of the minister's daughter, or the arrival of the traveling circus. It would also have been pointlessly painful to dwell any further on the case of the mischievous boy who set fire to the barn or the hapless clerk caught with his hand in the cash drawer. Long before the waddling and costly apparatus of a weekly paper could embalm these events in print, they would have been thoroughly plumbed and discussed by the same people who lost the crops, attended the wedding, or knew that the firebug was a good boy at heart, really — just a little wild.

Country editors in the 1830s had one further incentive to use the utmost gravity and care in filling their columns: they knew that their papers were the only source of news many of their neighbors encountered with any regularity. Certainly the wealthier or more educated townspeople did read a big-city paper or two in addition to their local journal. The young Henry Bedinger, scion of a prominent Virginia family that owned a large house not far from Charles Town, kept a journal while reading law with a local attorney in 1833. He often mentioned reading the newspapers, usually his way of complaining of the dullness of his social life ("Newspapers and children," he sighed on 28 October; "wonder people have no more brains and decency"), and once he specified the *Cincinnati Mirror* as his fare.[8] But small farmers and petty merchants like Nathan Haines would doubtless have been hard pressed to spare enough mutton to pay for *two* annual subscriptions.

Thus even though the *Virginia Free Press* opposed Andrew Jackson and tried to ignore national politics as much as possible during his tenure, on 10 March 1831 the editor reported that he "deem[ed] it proper" to publish a full sketch of the split between Jackson and his vice president, John C. Calhoun. "Many of our subscribers," he explained, "read no other paper, and . . . the divisions of a ruling party must be interesting to every one, whatever may be his political creed."

In a country paper, in other words, news was no humbug; it was serious business. For the simple outlay of eighty-one cents' worth of mutton and a horse brush, one could connect oneself with great things, distant things, alien things. And the editor who reigned over these things, who provided the link with that wider and wilder world, spoke with a voice not of teasing complicity but of weighty authority. The editor's public duty was to give readers not the news they preferred, but the news they did not know.

This authority, this larger connection, may have been what made the local paper into something almost talismanic to many Americans. It is otherwise difficult to explain the eager devotion, almost reverence, accorded by expatriates and exiles to hometown papers that contained so little hometown news. The daughter married to the out-of-towner, the son gone west to seek his fortune, or the sweetheart away at college could actually have learned very little from the paper itself about the folks they left behind, yet informal family exchange networks seem to have been nearly as common and vigorous as the official ones among editors.

Elihu Stout, for one, was proudly conscious of his heavy responsibilities and arrayed his news for his readers with the dignity and care of a shop owner with a new stock of bombazine. "Of foreign news, I have none of importance, or of general interest," he informed Vincennes three weeks after the news of the Alamo broke. "France appears to be in a state of quietude, and the new Ministry popular. — The intelligence from Spain is rather unfavorable to the cause of the Queen. — At home I have nothing of consequence to detail. Congress appears closely and laboriously engaged in doing nothing — a subject that will require a great deal of patience and perseverance to get through the present Session."

When an adventurous young Bostonian named Hiram Abiff Whittington went off to Little Rock to make his fortune, he religiously sent the *Arkansas Gazette* to his family and pleaded with them to return the favor with papers from home. In July 1828, having just received a letter dated 13 April — eleven weeks earlier — he wrote his family a plaintive request for more mail. "I consider the sending of a newspaper the same thing as if I wrote a letter," he said. "Recollect that I am a stranger in a strange land."[9]

Yet in one area the omniscience of the country editor stumbled and the credulity of the country reader played traitor. Despite the harsh difficulties of transportation, sometimes the *Herald* or the *Sun* or the *Transcript* did make their way into the hands of Americans far from New York. When that happened, readers often made a terrible mistake. They accorded to the penny press the same trust and faith they gave their local *Sun* or *Press* or *Gazette*. They believed the city papers were telling a straight story.

For some country editors, getting news from New York was so difficult, and reading it was so disgusting, that they preferred to ignore the city almost entirely. Elihu Stout of Vincennes never even mentioned the Jewett affair in his paper; if he came across the story at all, he must have considered it beneath notice. Others, however, were willing both to notice and to disseminate it. Three typical country papers from three representative American towns — one on the fringe of New York's orbit, one in the South, and one on the great frontier — each accepted the story with wide-eyed wonder.

Residents of Princeton, New Jersey, were close enough to New York to know and fear its dangerous influence. Thus when murder happened there, the editor of the local *Whig* told his readers to get their information there, too. To some extent his decision was pragmatic. Complete transcripts of the trial were not only "entirely too voluminous for insertion in a weekly paper," as he noted on 10 June; they were also readily available in the New York and Philadelphia papers.

But the editor also had doubts about the appropriateness of the story for a family newspaper. "We have abstained," he told his readers, "for reasons that appear to us imperative, from publishing the report of this case — but we have not been inattentive to the proceedings." That attentiveness, he went on to say, had prepared him for the acquittal. "It was impossible, as it seems to us, with such evidence as was given, that the Jury could have arrived at any other conclusion — and so indeed they were distinctly told by the Judge." Yet whereas the entire affair obviously pointed to a "moral to be drawn from the perilous position in which — not certainly without fault on his side — so young a man has been placed," the editor was apparently *not* prepared to elaborate on that moral, promising vaguely to do so "at another time."

In Charles Town, readers of the *Virginia Free Press* followed with grave interest the sordid and exotic affairs of the faraway big city. For editor H. N. Gallaher, however, getting the news from so far away was arduous and time-consuming. He published his first account of the "Horrid Murder and Arson" nearly two weeks after the event, on 21 April. It was a long but sketchy notice, derived mainly from the columns of the *Baltimore Patriot*, which in turn had gotten its account from the *New York Daily Advertiser*; a stray excerpt from the *Journal of Commerce* was probably copied second-hand as well.

By the following week, however, Gallaher had apparently gotten hold of some aging New York papers for himself. He filled in details of the crime from the *Courier and Enquirer,* the *Times,* and a single issue of the *Sun.* Drawing on the penny paper for 15 April, the Charles Town editor earnestly informed his readers that Robinson's journal revealed his "cold and unfeeling heart," and his "striking emaciation" and sleeplessness were so fearful that he might not even live to stand trial. The prisoner's guilt, Gallaher concluded, looked certain.

But his coverage of the case began to wane soon after this as the full extent of the luridness of the affair became evident. Except for a short note on 2 June that Robinson had been arraigned "to-day" — that is, 24 May — Gallaher had no comment on the case until the opening of the trial. On 9 June, the day after the verdict had been rendered in New York, Gallaher reported on the first day of the proceedings. He took three paragraphs from the *Commercial Advertiser* on the empanelment of the jury, then added merely that the examination of the madam Townsend, the first witness, occupied some time but was "rather disgusting."

So disgusting did the case reveal itself to be that Gallaher shrank from it entirely thereafter, confining himself solely to the stray human-interest anecdote. From an unnamed "New York paper" (the *Transcript* of 26 April), he copied an affecting tidbit about the comfort Robinson was taking in the visits of his sister, who was "relieving his wounded spirit, and binding up his almost broken heart." The editor's last word on the affair, on 23 June, came from the *Sun*: it concerned the "marvellous" circumstance that during the trial a window in the courthouse had been accidentally broken into a "strong profile of Rosina Townsend."

Arkansas, in 1836, was a territory on the brink of statehood, a densely forested, sparsely populated outpost of semicivilization bordering on Indian lands and the turmoil of Texas. It required a rather different kind of newspaper than sedate places like Vincennes or Princeton — a paper for a frontier, not a town.

For years the *Arkansas Gazette* was the only paper produced in the territory, and for years after that, few of the tiny hamlets squatting in forest clearings could have supported a newspaper of their own. Even though readers in Fayetteville, in Arkansas's northwestern corner, would have had no journal more local than Little Rock's *Gazette,* they would been quite outside the informal, face-to-face communication networks Little Rockers enjoyed. The sort of grapevine that easily stretched from Slinkard's Mills to Vincennes in Indiana would have snapped and withered somewhere in the Ozarks of Arkansas.

Thus the *Gazette* published much more local news than a paper like the *Western Sun* did. Accounts of barbecue parties, stagecoach lines, and Independence Day celebrations helped to instill community pride and cement community ties. Reports of smallpox epidemics and Indian sightings helped to save lives. And news of local crime and murder brought forth a complicated variety of emotions.

A few cocky citizens professed themselves proud of their wild reputation. Upon his arrival in late 1826, Whittington, the young Boston transplant, had been horrified by Little Rock's viciousness; the town and perhaps the entire territory, he wrote his brother, were "inhabited by the dregs of Kentucky, Georgia and Louisiana, but principally from the former, and a more drunken, good for nothing set of fellows never got together. . . . There have been more than a dozen murders committed here, but the murderer was always acquitted."

Within four years, however, Whittington had become either resigned to or seduced by the swagger and bravado of the place. In 1830, when the murder of a wealthy Salem sea captain seized the attention of newspapers across the country (notably the *Courier and Enquirer* and its young correspondent, James Gordon Bennett), Whittington dismissed the "great fuss" as puerile. "Why, we might have a dozen murders here," he wrote his brother, "and not half so much noise made; it is nothing for a man to kill two or three before breakfast. There have been 20 or 30 killed in Arkansas since I have been here, and only three hung — this is what I call a free country. . . . Murders here are committed in the heat of passion, and on that account are more excusable. If a man insults another here, it is only to draw a pistol and shoot him; an insult is generally followed by the death of one or the other."[10]

Others, though, remained deeply troubled by the frontier tendency to violence. On 4 June 1828, the *Arkansas Gazette* mourned its "mortifying and painful duty" to report yet another homicide in "our unlucky and ill-fated little town (already too notorious at home and abroad for such occurrences)." Yet it continued to perform that painful duty, doubtless hoping that publicizing such sad events might eventually help celebrate the citizenry's virtue and sagacity in catching the perpetrator, while serving as a warning to any other reprobate who might be considering Arkansas a haven for the lawless.[11]

Sadly, "eventually" often meant "never." John Hill, alias Nixon Curry, had twice been elected to the Arkansas legislature before he was discovered to be a fugitive from North Carolina on a fourteen-year-old charge of Negro-stealing and murder. When he was caught in Conway County, the *Gazette* crowed on 6 September 1836 that "Arkansas, we are pleased to see, is getting to be one of the worst retreats for these cut-throats and robbers!" The *Gazette's* report, just a week later, that Hill had escaped and was making for the Indian Territory was considerably more brusque.

Luckily for the battered self-respect of Little Rock's citizens, however, their town was not the only place in America troubled by crime. The *Gazette's* commentary on the Jewett murder was uniquely detailed and notably caustic for a country paper. The first notice came on 24 May, some six weeks after the crime:

> The lackadaisical sighs and tears of some of the contemptible penny papers in New-York for the fate of *Ellen Jewett,* (an abandoned profligate who was recently murdered in that city,) were ridiculous, and harmless — but that those romantic fabrications about her youth, innocence, beauty and seduction, &c., should have been copied into so many newspapers pretending to character, is marvellous enough. . . .
>
> The attempt of individuals as well as newspapers, to create an interest about her life, and to convert her into a heroine, betrays a vicious and culpable taste. And some wretch in New-York as if to signalize his want of decency, proposes to publish the *"Life of Ellen Jewett."* What in the name of common sense was there in the example or acts of such a being, that ought to perpetuated!! The facetious scribblers in Gotham, and sometimes those of the city of "brotherly love," are given to the fun of showing up the inhabitants of Arkansas and the "settlements" in no enviable light — but if one of their "down easters" were to come here and propose to publish the "Life of Ellen Jewett" he would be *Lynched.*

All things considered, the horror and outrage expressed in the *Arkansas Gazette* over the forthcoming "Life of Ellen Jewett" were hardly surprising. Without having seen the long debate over the "true" origins of the murdered woman, however, readers could not know that the appropriate question to ask was not, "What in the name of common sense was there in the example or acts of such a being, that ought to perpetuated!!" The real question at issue for New York readers was, "Which life?"

The *Virginia Free Press* earnestly reprinted remarks from a solitary issue of the *Sun* about Robinson's "striking emaciation" and sleeplessness. Readers in Charles Town, however, could not realize that those remarks were intended to refute another newspaper's claim that the accused was whistling and smoking, confident of his acquittal. Not even the nearby *Princeton Whig* quite got the idea. All it told Princeton readers about the story was that they should not sully themselves with it.

Country editors and their readers thus missed *all* the truths of the story. None had any idea that the prisoner's patron was regarded in some quarters as a snake in the grass, or that the victim was neither a poor unfortunate nor a siren. None realized that the penny papers' account of Jewett's murder was just the latest installment in a long history of class tension and economic anxiety. None recognized that the whole thing was a humbug specifically intended to force a choice between truths. Humbugs, in other words, were like spinach soufflés: they never kept long, they did not travel well, and they pleased only connoisseurs.

Yet even though country readers failed to interpret the episode from the New Yorker's point of view, they found important truths of their own in it. In fact the destiny of the Jewett story seems to have been to fulfill the personal myth and clarify the personal identity of every last reader who came across it. The murdered prostitute of Thomas Street performed an important service for readers of the country press — for the citizens of Charles Town, Princeton, and Little Rock, for the people of Augusta, Maine, and for thousands of other Americans in hundreds of other communities. She assured them that they were right — in every sense of the word.

Many rural Americans cherished a deep suspicion that New York was a weird and terrible place. These suspicions were inspired by America's most cherished mythic vision of itself as the peaceful republic of virtuous yeomen — they were fed by rumor, protected by clergymen and other moral leaders, and nurtured by fiction. Scores of novels, from *Charlotte Temple* onward, earned their popularity by portraying the city as a pandemonium of iniquity, perversion, and despair, in contrast to the calm natural peace of rural life.

Still, few rural Americans ever actually traveled to the city; the rumors were only rumors, the suspicions unconfirmed. With the Jewett story the penny press, while giving its own readers the news that best fit their requirements, was at the same time ratifying, in the incontrovertible authority of newsprint, an entirely different vision for an entirely different audience. The news may have come to the country reader only in snippets, but who needed more than a snippet when it concerned cold and unfeeling hearts, a jealous prostitute who read Byron, and a guilty teenaged lover wasting away in prison? Hadn't country readers always known that New York was the sort of place where a broken window could trace a profile of the devil-eyed keeper of an elegant brothel?

In contrast to that brazen city, any community could consider itself safe, secure, and law-abiding. Even beleaguered Arkansas could savor its superiority to a place where such "vile and filthy" practices could occur, and indeed beleaguered Arkansas's *Gazette* devoted more space than any other paper to covering the story — as well as denouncing it bitterly, lest anyone miss the message. Thus rural Americans neither wanted nor needed to understand what the New York papers told New York readers, as long as those papers confirmed for them their own congenial myth: the big city was evil and sordid. The urban penny press in its infancy, before anyone knew it would grow into a giant, served more to reinforce the misapprehensions, prejudices, and boundaries that divided Americans from one another than to bond them together into any great community of readership.

Five years after the Jewett case, the penny-press coverage of another notorious murder would point out how drastically all that had changed.

FROM HUMBUG TO AUTHORITY

10

DEATH OF A PRINTER

One damp autumn afternoon in 1841, Samuel Adams left the office of the *Missionary Herald* and was never seen alive again. Soon after the young printer's worried wife advertised in the newspapers for information on his whereabouts, a teacher of bookkeeping and penmanship in a large office building across from City Hall came forward to relate a suspicious incident he had overheard that critical Friday afternoon, the seventeenth of September, in the room next door to his.

He had heard strange noises there, the teacher said, like the clash of fencing foils followed by a heavy thud. His curiosity aroused, he had gone into the hallway, peered through the keyhole of the other office (after first poking the inside keyhole drop aside with a pen), and glimpsed a man apparently bending over something on the floor. Later he borrowed a key from the custodians, a couple named Law and Mercy Octon, and entered the office. No one was inside, but he noticed that the floor had been scrubbed and that a large crate was missing from its customary spot.

Further official inquiry revealed that the tenant of the mysterious office, another teacher of bookkeeping named John C. Colt, had been seen on Saturday morning grappling a large crate down the stairs, and further advertisements in the papers brought forward a carman whom Colt had hired to carry the crate to a New Orleans–bound ship called the *Kalamazoo*. The ship's sailing had been delayed and she was still at her berth at the foot of Maiden Lane. A crew of stevedores ventured into the putrid hold and found the crate Colt had sent aboard more than a week earlier. Jammed inside was a body. Its head was badly battered, most of its clothing had been removed, and it had begun to decompose, but a gold ring on the little finger and an unusual scar on the leg proved that it was the missing printer's. Mayor Robert Hunter Morris himself headed the delegation of officials sent out to arrest Colt.

Like the accused killer Richard Robinson, Colt, then thirty, had a unsavory past. He had committed a perjury to join the Marines and a forgery to escape and had then progressed to professional riverboat gambling and a torrid public affair with the octoroon mistress of a rich planter. Later, in New York, he had been arrested for burglarizing his employer's crockery shop, and at the time of the murder he was living with a woman not his wife who was about to have a child.

But again like Robinson, Colt was a forgivable rake, lucky in his relatives and possessed of friends in high places. His brother Samuel was the celebrated inventor of the revolving pistol, his brother James a prominent lawyer in St. Louis. John Howard Payne, the dramatist whose signal achievement was the composition of the lyrics to "Home, Sweet Home," and man-about-town Lewis Gaylord Clark joined other family friends to maintain staunchly and publicly that the prisoner's crime had simply been an unhappy accident, the result of a quarrel that had gotten out of hand.

More than a decade after the incident, Herman Melville published his story of a sleek Wall Street lawyer who, enraged and baffled by the stolid presence of the inscrutable scrivener Bartleby in his office, was reminded of the tragedy of "the unfortunate Adams and the still more unfortunate Colt." "Often it had occurred to me in my ponderings upon the subject," Melville's lawyer mused, "that had that altercation taken place in the public street, or at a private residence, it would not have terminated as it did. It was the circumstance of being alone in a solitary office, up stairs, of a building entirely unhallowed by humanizing domestic associations — an uncarpeted office, doubtless, of a dusty, haggard sort of appearance; — this it must have been, which greatly helped to enhance the irritable desperation of the hapless Colt."[1]

Colt's brothers assembled a team of capable defense attorneys for John. One, Dudley Selden, was a cousin of the Colts' and a former one-term Democratic Congressman who had made the defiant switch to the Whigs along with Ogden Hoffman, Richard Robinson's savior. Later, in the spring of 1845, Selden would finally cap a harrowing election season for New York's Whigs by losing decisively in a three-way race for mayor. Another member of the team, John A. Morrill, had earlier that year earned dubious fame with his defense of the notorious abortionist Madame Restell, who had finally been brought to trial after a patient of hers died. The third attorney, the smooth-tongued Irishman Robert Emmet, sprang from a family tree studded with both lawyers and martyred patriots. As part of their fee, the attorneys were given eight thousand dollars' worth of stock in the new company formed to manufacture Samuel's latest invention, the submarine battery.[2]

Shortly after Colt's arrest, some of the New York newspapers published extracts from a confession the prisoner had made to a friend. In his statement, Colt admitted killing the printer but claimed that he had been acting in self-defense. Adams, who had printed several of Colt's works on bookkeeping, visited him to collect a small debt, the prisoner said. A disagreement arose over its exact amount, the two came to blows, and when Adams began twisting Colt's cravat so tightly as to cut off his wind, the desperate bookkeeper seized an object lying on the table and struck blindly at his adversary's head. To his horror the object turned out to be a lethal weapon, a double-sided tool topped with an ax blade and a hammerhead.

Later, Colt revealed more details of the terrible aftermath. He sat in the office for a time, dazed and sick, until his fear that the huge spreading pool of blood might seep through the floor roused him to mop up the mess with a towel. The blood filled one-third of a bucket. The bookkeeper then quietly left the building and walked up and down City Hall Park for over an hour, pondering his situation. His fear that he would bring disgrace to his family, his conviction that his past misdeeds would further blacken the case against him, and his certainty that the newspapers would spread "original, false, foul, calumniating lies" about the incident led him to decide against going straight to the police.

Although Colt briefly contemplated burning down the entire building to destroy the evidence of the crime, he soon lit on the idea of hiding the corpse in the crate that stood in the office. It was a tight fit: even after he stripped the body and trussed it tightly with a rope and some pieces torn from an awning, the dead printer's knees still protruded over the top edge of the box, and Colt had to "stand upon them with all my weight" before he could nail on the lid. He then cleaned the room thoroughly, making several trips up and down the stairs with buckets of water. Into a nearby outdoor privy he tossed the dead man's clothes and the contents of his pockets, and before returning home he stopped at the Washington bathhouse on Pearl Street to wash out his shirtfront and the knees of his pantaloons. The next morning, Saturday, he paid a man two-and-sixpence to carry the box to the Maiden Lane wharf.

From the moment of Colt's arrest, most of the city papers declared themselves convinced that the prisoner was guilty of cold-blooded murder. So frustrated were Colt's lawyers by this loud and united condemnation that they petitioned Judge William Kent to forbid the press from covering the proceedings. The judge refused. "It would have been strange," he explained later from the bench, "if, in the city of New York, the public mind would not have been shocked by the murder, but I have no doubt that every justice has been done to the prisoner. The Court has kept everything uninfluenced by contamination from without."

As the January trial date approached, most public speculation centered not on whether Colt was innocent, but on whether murder or manslaughter would be the verdict. As for the defense, most onlookers were expecting a plea of insanity. It would have made a compelling case. The weekly *Tribune* for 30 October quoted James Colt as saying that "insanity is hereditary in the family": a sister had poisoned herself in a fit of madness years earlier, and John himself had "several times become insane."

The trial began slowly and calmly. The prosecution called a parade of witnesses, who gave their testimony stolidly: Colt's neighbor in the office building and his teenage students, whose suspicions had been aroused by the strange noises and odd behavior next door; the man who had carried the crate to the wharf; the mayor, who had accompanied the arresting officers and who found in Colt's room a pocketbook containing locks of hair from his dead mother and sisters. The condition of the body was described by the coroner and several medical men, including the Dr. Rogers who had operated on Rosina Townsend's eyes during her prelapsarian days in New York. A number of Adams's colleagues and employees described his character and business.

Soon, however, the contest developed into one of the rowdiest, most startling, and most bizarre the city had yet seen. The defense team, scorning the easy argument of insanity, attempted to prove self-defense: Colt had been forced to attack the hotheaded Adams to save his own life. Whereupon the prosecution countered with the peculiar argument that the doctors who had examined the body were wrong about the weapon that made the wounds in the skull. Those holes could, they said, have been made by balls from a pistol.

Not so, responded the defense, and they staged a performance to prove it. John did own a gun, one of his brother's six-shooters. So Samuel Colt himself was called to the witness stand to demonstrate, by shooting at a book propped up several paces distant, exactly what kind of holes the bullets from his invention could and could not make in a target. One ball cut through nine pages of the book and dimpled twenty-four more, while shots he fired from a patent pocket pistol "made very little impression" on the same book.

The relevance of this demonstration to John's defense is obscure, but there may have been a deeper, hidden purpose behind the courtroom circus. Samuel's six-shooter business was floundering in 1842, a worrisome prospect not only for Samuel but also for lawyers Selden and Emmet, both of whose families were deeply involved as investors; and since all three lawyers now owned stock in Samuel's new battery company, his business reputation was a vital concern of theirs. Not even this dramatic performance, however, would save Colt's revolver business from bankruptcy within the year.

The prosecutors' intent in raising the pistol question is also cloudy. It may have been an attempt to prove the crime a premeditated murder, rather than manslaughter in the heat of passion, by suggesting that Colt had planned the encounter in advance and armed himself accordingly. It may have been a clever — and ultimately successful — ploy to force the defense into correcting the record by releasing Colt's cold and repugnant confession statement to the jury. Or, if the attorneys had all along been plotting the scene that followed, it was a diabolical stroke of prosecutorial brilliance.

To allow the reexamination of the wounds in Adams's head, the dead man was ordered exhumed and decapitated. The coroner then carried the head into court and sat in front of the chamber, in full view of the spectators, cradling the thing in his lap until it was called for. Over the objections of the defense, Judge Kent ruled that "however painful it is, justice must be administered and the head produced, if the jury think it necessary." It did. Whereupon Dr. Rogers held the head high before the packed courtroom. As Colt shaded his eyes with his hand, the doctor demonstrated to the satisfaction of the jury that the axhead fitted perfectly into the cuts in the skull. The prosecutors' argument was soundly disproven. The prosecutors' case for the fiendishness of the murderer was even more soundly advanced.

Rather desperately, Selden tried to turn their opponents' tactic to Colt's advantage. After reading the confession statement aloud, the attorney argued that anyone who was coolly plotting murder to discharge a troublesome debt would never have chosen to do the evil deed with an ax, in broad daylight, in a large office building in the busiest neighborhood in town. Any reasonable man like Colt who already owned a pistol would have decoyed his victim to a remote spot and turned his efficient weapon on the defenseless man there. The arrant clumsiness of Colt's attack, Selden insisted, proved that the murder could not have been premeditated.

The question of premeditation was vexing, but the jury and the general public were even more disturbed by John Colt's behavior immediately *after* the murder. His graphic confession statement, including those precise descriptions of how he cleaned up the blood and manhandled the body into the crate, was entirely too callous for most tastes. His stoic and unremorseful demeanor throughout the trial only reinforced the public's conviction of his cold-bloodedness.

Colt's irregular domestic arrangement with Caroline Henshaw — a mundane transgression unenhanced by any of the exotic or erotic interest surrounding the Jewett affair — also aroused acute public distaste, which Selden struggled in vain to overcome. The lawyer attempted to introduce character witnesses on Henshaw's behalf, arguing that "[Colt's] relation with her was one of the acts for which he has been called upon by public sentiment to answer, but she was no prostitute except as regarded him. He did wrong and she did, but adverse circumstances alone caused them to live together in the illegitimate manner they did."

The judge, however, refused to admit their testimony. Slyly, prosecutor

James Whiting elaborated on the point in his summation. "God forbid I should say anything against [Henshaw]," he declaimed.

She was about to become a mother, and if there was any one who would pray for that man, that he might be blessed forever, and would come here to testify for him it would be her. She approached his bed, he threw her from him. She knew she was not his wife, and dared not press it. Had she been his wife, she would have persisted.

But do not blame her, do not blame that slight girl, blame the one whose heart was such that he could seduce her, and keep her in abjection. Had she been his wife, he could have poured his sorrows in her ear; she would have clung by him; she would have gone with him to his prison; she would have accompanied him even to the gallows. Let this be a warning to women, let them learn not to put their earthly and eternal happiness in the keeping of such a man as that.

Judge Kent instructed the jury that, since Colt had already admitted the killing, their task was to determine whether the crime had been murder or manslaughter. After remarking on Colt's "careless air" and "gay air" after the crime, which seemed to him signs of "intrepidity and coolness, such as rarely can be met with," Kent told the panel to decide whether "the firm manner in which he walked on a precipice, one false step on which would have been fatal, [and] the coolness of character he displayed" were "sufficient to believe him capable of premeditation." If they were, he told the jurors, then they must "bring him in guilty of murder."

At four o'clock on a Sunday morning, after nearly ten hours of deliberation, the jury returned a verdict of guilty of murder. The decision so agitated Lewis Gaylord Clark, for one, that he, the city's premier literary angel, found himself unable to attend an important meeting that night to plan the great dinner in honor of Charles Dickens.[3] Counsel immediately demanded a new trial. Months of agitation and pleading were finally brought to an end in September 1842, a year after the murder, when the state supreme court denied the final appeal, and Colt was sentenced to hang on 18 November.

Again the prisoner's friends worked strenuously on his behalf, but their pleas to the chancellor and to Governor William H. Seward for commutation were refused. Also unsuccessful were their alleged attempts to bribe the prison guards to allow Colt to escape disguised in Caroline Henshaw's clothes. Just hours before the scheduled time of the hanging, Henshaw was married to the prisoner in his cell by the Reverend Henry Anthon, rector of the prestigious Episcopalian church, St. Mark's in the Bowery. It was a private ceremony attended only by Samuel Colt, John Howard Payne, and a lawyer or two, and the guests took their final leave of the condemned man immediately afterward.

When the guard returned to conduct Colt to the scaffold, he found the prisoner dead in a welter of blood. The wretched man had managed to stab himself through the heart with a small claspknife apparently smuggled in by one of his last visitors. To his brother Samuel, at least, the suicide came as a great relief. After bidding John farewell, Samuel had spent the rest of the day weeping in his office at New York University. When a hackman rushed in with the news of the suicide, Samuel's expression changed to something nearly approaching joy. "Thank God! Thank God!" the inventor exclaimed.

The discovery of a fire in the cupola of the prison at the very moment Colt was supposed to be hanged inspired rumors throughout the waiting crowd that the commotion had been staged to cover an effort to smuggle him out of prison. Former mayor Philip Hone, in a touching but implausible assessment of the motley crowd's most immediate reaction to the cry of fire, noted that the conflagration was "from its coincidence very mysterious and alarming. . . . Many persons no doubt thought, as I did, of the description in Schiller's tragedy of 'The Robbers' of the burning of the village and the rescue from the gallows of their brother-robber, and apprehensions were excited without cause; for by this time all other means of escape but the dagger had been abandoned."

Although Colt's suicide was announced immediately and his body buried at St. Mark's, many who had followed the proceedings believed resolutely for years that an anonymous corpse from the morgue had been substituted for Colt's and that the murderer's friends had spirited him and his new wife away, alive and well, to California. Another persistent rumor held that in 1850 "Samuel Colt's friend, Edgar Allan Poe," received an unsigned manuscript from Texas in what Poe recognized and Lewis Gaylord Clark confirmed as Colt's handwriting. Poe and Clark, however, were actually such bitter enemies that they would have been unlikely to speak to each other at all, let alone confer about a mysterious manuscript. If Poe did indeed receive a parcel from Colt in 1850, moreover, it could only serve as proof positive that Colt never left the prison alive. Poe died in 1849.[4]

Compared to the Jewett affair of 1836, the Colt case — and the penny-press coverage of it — seemed much tidier, much less mysterious. A man was murdered. A killer confessed. A famous brother of the killer worked strenuously but fruitlessly to save his life. And a woman who had lived illicitly with the killer was made an honorable woman and a widow on the same day. Again unlike the Jewett affair, and despite the spatter of uncertainty over the prisoner's death, the Colt case featured a conviction won, a penalty paid, and a resolution achieved. Press and readers together shared the satisfying certainty that justice had been served.

The case also, however, bore at its very core a dark and shameful secret. If the penny press of 1841–42 had discovered that secret, it is conceivable — just conceivable — a different verdict might have been reached. As it was, John Colt died in unwarranted disgrace, and Samuel Colt died happy.

11

A NEW FACE

Horace Greeley wasted no time. He issued the first number of his *New York Daily Tribune* on 10 April 1841, and on the 19th he was already blasting James Gordon Bennett and the other penny editors for their eagerness to "poison the fountains of public intelligence, and fan into destroying flames the hellish passions which now slumber in the bosom of Society." Bennett, the very next day, likened Greeley to a large, galvanized New England squash. Five years after the Jewett murder, American journalism had left behind the Age of the Mythic Hero and entered the Age of the Heroic Editor.

In 1836 the murdered prostitute and her indicted lover, their characters suitably revised, enlarged, and edited according to need, had been the undeniable stars of the racy story that had so satisfied New York readers and so nonplused everyone else. But 1841 marked the exchange of the fabricated and fantastic brand of hero for two new flesh-and-blood ones whose renown increased with every issue of the *Herald* and *Tribune* they produced, even though neither had ever committed a sleazy murder or sported in an elegant brothel. Greeley's appearance on the journalistic scene — in itself both a token and a consequence of a growing dissatisfaction with the penny press among some of the reading community — signaled the emergence of a new brand of editor guiding a new breed of cheap press for a wholly new kind of world.

This new press was less prankish, less parochial, and infinitely less freewheeling, but also more intrusive, more unavoidable, more powerful, and more controversial. It was, in spots, developing a social conscience and a national outlook; it was certainly building a national subscription list. It was taking on broad new roles and creating new national heroes. It was revising its public duty, relinquishing the role of provocateur and readjusting its relationship with fact. It wasn't exactly sure, however, precisely what that new partnership ought to entail.

Its editors did know that this new role, whatever it was to be, required moving up in the world. The 1820s and 1830s had been an active time for the artisan and laborer, whose strikes and struggles had commanded the attention — and often the consternation — of citizens across the nation. The very first penny papers, as we saw, were directly inspired and shaped by the Working Men's movement.

By the 1840s, however, the urban worker was losing ground. The financial panic and depression of 1837 burdened the poorest people hardest and longest; over one-third of New York's laborers lost their jobs that summer, wages plunged for those who still had work, and organized union activism gave way to the brutally focused energy of scrounging for survival and rioting for flour. Ever more clear became the truth Bennett had glimpsed during the Jewett affair: interest and influence both were becoming ever more concentrated in the hands of the "middling sort" of citizen. As these citizens explored and solidified their own position in the social and economic life of the nation, the penny press began to reexamine its own relationship with them as well.[1]

In the 1840s, in fact, social changes were forcing Americans of all stripes to reexamine many of their traditional relationships. America was becoming an ever more unfamiliar place, a land teeming with exotic immigrants, bristling with huge and often hideous cities, throbbing and smoking with outlandish machines and ugly factories.

No place was stranger than New York, the nation's largest urban settlement — and the cradle of the penny press. Between 1835 and 1850 the city's population nearly doubled, most of that increase due to immigration from Ireland and Germany, and the chasm between rich and poor deepened almost as fast as the population grew.[2] In no other city clustered such an array of inhabitants and sights symbolizing both the triumphs and the ravages of immense social change: the fabulous Astors and the savage Dead Rabbit criminal gang; showy Broadway and crime-ridden Five Points; A. T. Stewart's vast emporium and throngs of desperate street peddlers; the amazing Croton reservoir and some of the foulest slums in the world.

Entrepreneurs, too, were spending the decade rethinking their traditional ways as countless livelihoods, from cobbling to mining, transformed themselves headlong from handicraft to industry. The mechanization and capitalization of business opened vast new opportunities for wealth and expansion. It also permitted spectacular failure on a scale hitherto unknown. Suddenly, the stakes for the experimenter were high, the potential rewards huge, and the risks immense.

The business of journalism followed a typical course. In September 1833, Benjamin Day's entire staff had consisted of a journeyman printer and a boy, and the three of them had printed the first issue of the *Sun* on a hand printing press that Benjamin Franklin — not to mention Gutenberg himself — would have recognized as an old friend. In an hour of strenuous and sweaty work, Day and his colleague could have printed at most two hundred sheets on one side only, and the entire press run of that first issue was at most a thousand copies. Two years later, when James Gordon Bennett squandered his last five hundred dollars on equipment and supplies for a new newspaper, he could at least rest secure in the knowledge that his extravagance had supplied him with everything he needed to start a publishing enterprise.

But as the demand for penny papers grew and the profits of the penny editors mounted, Day and the others began to haunt the shops and cheer on the efforts of a new and innovative generation of machinery builders, papermakers, and typefounders. The editors seized immediately on any device that might lead to cheaper, quicker, more efficient ways to reach an ever larger readership.

Even in the grimmest days of the economic depression, many of the penny papers continued to thrive. The hard times killed off some that had been wobbling in the first place — including the *Transcript* — and illuminated the weakest seams in some others, like the maladroit business intellect behind Horace Greeley's *New-Yorker*. But as the movies would prove to be a century later and in another depression, the penny papers were in general cheap but filling, an excusable but satisfying indulgence, the perfect entertainment for difficult times.

Within a decade after Day had produced his first issue, even the ingenious Franklin would have been overwhelmed by what he saw in any New York newspaper office. The dank, inexpensive basement holes favored by struggling editors in the 1830s had given way to grand offices occupying entire buildings. They bristled with scurrying staffs, and their floors trembled under the weight of the speedy new mechanized Napier presses that used steam-powered rolling cylinders instead of the traditional muscle-powered flat platen to press the paper against the type forme.

It all cost money. In 1841 Bennett placed an order with New York's most flourishing press builder, R. Hoe and Company, for two small double-cylinder presses at $3,000 each, two large double-cylinder presses at $3,500 each, and a steam engine for $1,000. Even after Hoe deducted $3,500 for a trade-in of Bennett's old press, the total cost came to $10,500 — a sum more than twenty times larger than his little puddle of startup capital — plus $175 more each year for maintenance.[3]

The *Sun* was booming, too. In a tenth-birthday salute to his paper in 1843, the *Sun*'s chief crowed that he was employing eight editors and reporters, twenty typesetters, sixteen pressmen, and twelve folders. The paper had already outgrown at least two generations of Napiers and had recently added two of Hoe's new "Pony" double-cylinder presses to meet the demands of its claimed circulation: thirty-eight thousand copies of the daily edition and twelve thousand of the weekly. As one longtime Hoe employee later recalled, the new machines, which featured improvements in the inking apparatus and the cylinder design, "could run 5,000 to 6,000 sheets per hour and the circulation of the *Sun* had increased to such an extent that they were required to run to their utmost capacity, and for a time in 1841 it was my especial business to keep them in order."[4]

Nor did the thousands of sheets spun off by these unceasing printing presses merely pile up in New York. Inspired perhaps by ambition, perhaps by vision, certainly by the expensive hum of their three-thousand-dollar presses and the costly pattering of their scores of employed feet, the editors of the 1840s were pursuing an audience much larger, more far-flung, and more heterogeneous than their predecessors could have hoped for — or even wanted — in 1836.

New York was the perfect base of operations for large-minded business entrepreneurs. The city's merchants had always made shrewd commercial use of the natural advantages of what was perhaps the choicest urban location on the East Coast. Throughout the second quarter of the century, their eager embrace and support of new transportation technologies turned a larger and larger chunk of the nation into one huge proprietary hinterland full of consumers for all sorts of city goods.

Bostonians snuggled ever deeper into their geographical isolation and cultural aloofness; Philadelphians fumed at the inevitable delays forced by the dozens of locks and the cumbersome trans-Allegheny portage railroad on their rugged Main Line Canal route to Pittsburgh. But New Yorkers reveled in the advantages of roundabout but easy inland-water connections with major midwestern cities, a thriving coastal steamship trade, and quick access by ferry to a network of railroad lines exploding through most northern states and some southern ones as well. Even if readers farther to the west and south were still too distant from New York to receive the daily newspapers with any timeliness, steamboat and railroad lines, supplemented by federal postal riders, could certainly manage delivery there at a slightly longer interval.

Its location, coupled with its economic and cultural strength, made New York "the London of the West," recalled a onetime *Herald* reporter after he emigrated to Britain in disgust over the Civil War; New York newspapers, he said, "penetrate everywhere . . . in St. Louis, New Orleans, Mobile, and Galveston, . . . in Boston, Baltimore, Chicago, San Francisco." But New York did not return the favor. "It is very rare," the former reporter continued, "that a daily paper, published East, South, or West, is sold in New York. . . . A curious law is observed . . . all papers go from east to west, with the sun, and scarcely ever in the opposite direction. The best magazine or weekly paper that could be published in Cincinnati, in the Ohio valley, would never cross the Alleghanies [*sic*]."[5]

Out there, with the sun, the middle-class reading audience was immense and ready to consume. The nation was nurturing a roaring appetite for education and self-improvement. Public schools, Sunday schools, academies, lyceums, lecture bureaus, and colleges were proliferating (although, like the railroad trackage, they were concentrated chiefly in the northern tier), and more and more middle-class Americans of both sexes were gaining both the facility and the leisure to read for pleasure. To reach out to those readers directly, the penny editors began publishing special "country" editions. These weekly papers distilled the most important recent news and brought the drama and color of New York even to those poor souls too far from the metropolis to succumb to the seductive song of the newsboys.

In 1841, at the very beginning of this great decade of change, a new and enduring journalistic rivalry was born, something completely novel in spirit. During the Jewett affair, the various editors had pursued two distinct audiences by telling them entirely different stories — by presenting an entirely different set of facts that they called "truth" — but they had all agreed implicitly on a more fundamental Truth: a newspaper's function was to discover and distribute whichever fundamental truths its particular audience most wanted and needed. For all their contentious hoopla, Bennett of the *Herald* and Day of the *Sun* had at bottom been teammates in a three-legged race. They were making for the same goal by the same route, in a manner wholly ludicrous to the uninvolved beholder, and the progress of each was helped as well as hindered by his partner.

The rivalry of Bennett and Greeley was different. Both editors wanted the same audience: the huge, influential, and important middle class. Greeley had come to realize that middle-class readers might welcome the novelty of a "decent" paper written specifically for them. For the canny Bennett, who had known all along that the respectable sort of folk had more money, power, and prestige than the penny press's traditional working-class audience, the consequences of falling behind in the circulation race grew with the same breathtaking swiftness that his business did.

Yet even though the editors wanted the same audience, they perceived their journalistic duties in precisely opposite ways. The two editors were perfectly and innately antipodal, separated by diametrically opposing philosophies, characters, aims, likes, dislikes, and styles; if they had been entered as a team in a three-legged race, they would have ended up with one leg apiece. The reader choosing between the *Herald* and the *Tribune* was choosing between sensationalism and moralism, amusement and education, voyeurism and verdict making, celebration of the city and fear of it, glorification of crime and condemnation of it. In essence, the reader was faced with the ancient dilemma that in the early days of the republic had come to seem specially American as well: Hercules' choice between Pleasure and Virtue.

In another specially American way, however, this dilemma was different. Hercules' choice — and, as good republicans always saw it, their own as well — had been rigged. If they decided on Virtue they got immortality, too, but if they picked Pleasure, the entire moral and philosophical tradition of the Western world demanded that they pay a price. For the American of 1841, however, who lived in a world growing ever more huge, disorganized, and threatening, all the rules were changing. Virtue's reward was not inevitable, Pleasure's price seemed small, and the partisans of each grew increasingly defensive in the face of the other side. Small wonder that anyone who could help make sense of this disarray would soon come to take on the status of a hero nearly as legendary and immortal as Hercules. How both the virtuous-minded Greeley and the pleasure-loving Bennett managed to achieve heroic status at the same time, in the same world, is the journalistic story of the decade.

This tidy two-way antagonism between the two editors required that even a moderate reader gravitate toward one or the other extreme, but for ten long years after the founding of the *Tribune*, no real middle option presented itself. One of the *Herald*'s earlier archrivals, the *Transcript*, had died in 1839, weakened by the economic depression and ravaged by the deaths or defections of its best editorial talent; one surviving partner suffered the indignity of ending up as a typesetter in Bennett's own composing rooms. By 1841 the *Herald*'s other great rival was investing its energies elsewhere. The *Sun* shone for New York workers alone in those days, and the *Sun*'s new editor, Moses Y. Beach, scarcely shone at all.

Beach's paper was still the circulation leader in the city, which ensured that it would remain a favorite target in any of the long-running feuds of Newspaper Row; and it still fought back with paper attacks on its rivals, both real and potential. But neither Beach nor his sons, who joined him as partners in 1845, were cast from a heroic mold. They never developed national personalities of any sort. Their interests and emphases were mostly local, they had no public characters to speak of, and they symbolized nothing in particular.

Caring little for political causes, conservative both financially and philosophically, they avoided the moral and social crusades of Day's era and preferred to invest their energies in technology. They invented devices to wet, fold, and cut paper and to print paper on both sides at the same time; they were active in the establishment of the New York Associated Press to pool newsgathering resources; they set up what may have been the first newspaper syndicate.

Alone among the major cheap papers of the 1840s, the *Sun* remained true to its original working-class roots. Artisans and laborers liked its offerings of romantic and potboiler fiction; its racy delight in news of crime, the theater, and sporting; its staunch refusal to follow the other papers in hiking its price to two cents; its Democratic slant — muted, careful, businesslike, but perceptible at least, and rare in this era; and that dazzling array of advertisements, including the best employment listings in town. Readers still approached it with a pleasurable wariness, on the alert for the lurking humbug, and sometimes they still caught a big, splashy, entertaining one — like Edgar Allan Poe's straight-faced 1844 story of a transatlantic crossing by balloon.

No longer, however, did they catch humbugs fraught with social and political meaning. The *Sun*'s quirky, mischievous, insurrectionary character was gone. In fact, it displayed scarcely any character at all. When a typical four-page, twenty-eight-column issue in 1840 devoted twenty-one-and-a-half columns to advertising, one to fiction, and one-and-a-half to the police court, distinguishing characteristics were simply squeezed out. So too was in-depth attention to the news, although particularly rich or exciting events sometimes earned their own special "extra" pamphlets.

Beach bought the paper in 1837 from his brother-in-law, Benjamin Day, who was in a panic over an impending libel suit as well as the recent bank collapses. Always more a manager than an editor, Beach made a great deal of money out of the paper while remaining as gray and opaque as his columns. Except for a brief interval around the beginning of the Civil War — when the *Sun* was bought, managed, nearly ruined, and finally resold to Beach by a group of evangelicals who held daily prayer meetings in the office and who urged the Union army to forbid attacks on Sunday — Moses Beach and his sons ran the paper for thirty-one straight years. Perhaps thirty-one people outside New York could have come up with their names.

Thus it was the great Bennett/Greeley rivalry for the trust and favor of the middle class that most definitively shaped the development of the penny press throughout the 1840s. The roots of that competition went back to the notorious episode that quickly and grandly came to be known as the Moral War. This battle — which took place in the spring of 1840, a year before Greeley even started his *Tribune* — is one of the most commonly cited events in the history of the penny press. It is also the most misinterpreted. The confusion is understandable. We do not often encounter a war named after its loser.

A WAR OF MORALS,
A CLASH OF CULTURES

The Moral War has come down through history as a conversion story: How James Gordon Bennett Saw the Light. For years, historians of journalism have told the tale of how the editor's sensational and heretical reporting finally goaded his opponents into fighting back. Cast in the role of the Crusaders who converted him were some of Bennett's most long-suffering enemies, the sixpenny editors Park Benjamin, M. M. Noah, and James Watson Webb — the "Holy Allies," as Bennett dubbed them. A cadre of prominent clergymen, bankers, teachers, merchants, and men of society also joined in the struggle. Hurling a bloodcurdling bounty of epic taunts against Bennett — taunts like "obscene vagabond," "turkey-buzzard," "moral pestilence," "profligate adventurer," and "prince of darkness" — they called for a public boycott of his paper and of any merchant who advertised in it.

Scorning the action as mere "piffle," Bennett retaliated with a galling campaign of self-congratulation disguised as self-defense. To the accusation that he had once been a mere street peddler he replied: "From my youth up I have been a pedler [*sic*], not of tapes and laces, but of thoughts, feelings, lofty principles, and intellectual truths. . . . I was educated and intended for a religious sect, but the Almighty, in his wisdom, meant me for truth and mankind."[1]

Despite his brave words, Bennett was demonstrably pricked by the "piffle." The *Herald*'s circulation figures drooped during the battle: purchases of the daily slid from 17,000 to 14,500 copies and of the weekly from 19,000 to 12,240.[2] And the charges of disreputableness may have helped shake Bennett into doing something he had avoided for decades. That June of 1840, at the age of nearly forty-five, the editor married. In a long *Herald* article on 1 June he hailed his step as a "new movement in civilization," and with placid resignation he bowed to the necessity of "giv[ing] the world a pattern of happy wedded life."

Bennett himself perpetuated the conversion tale. Upon his marriage he all but conceded that he had gone too far. In that "new and holy condition," he announced, "I anticipate some signal changes in my feelings, in my views, in my purposes, my pursuits." Not even Isaac Pray, his contemporary biographer and staunchest supporter, denied that the *Herald* had "indulged" in "latitude of expression" — although in Pray's analysis this indulgence had been intended solely for the readers' own good. Bennett was only trying, Pray argued, to cure their "affected prudery" and "mawkish refinement."[3] Many commentators have therefore viewed the episode as a turning point for Bennett — the moment when he began to moderate his tone in the realization that sensationalism had its limits as a marketing tool. It may not have been conversion by grace, but under the circumstances conversion by the sword would do.

There is only one problem with this story of redemption. It is a myth. Bennett may have seen some advantage in going through the motions of conversion, but the Crusaders' swords were obviously blunt. A closer look at the circulation figures shows that the boycott's damage to the *Herald* was only a flesh wound; the daily's losses never exceeded some 15 percent of its total, and it soon bounced back completely. Nor did Bennett entirely abandon his old gods. He may never again have quite replicated the full-blown torridness of his Jewett coverage, but other *Herald* features, like the regular smirky and smarmy society columns about the scandalous doings of various Miss B——s and Mr. ****'s, continued to come close. His marriage did not seem to help much, either; Henrietta Crean, an Irish-born piano teacher half the editor's age, soon found herself so harassed and vilified as Bennett's wife that she and her children spent most of their time in Europe.

During the Moral War, moreover, Bennett actually enjoyed a large measure of community support, some of it from quite reputable quarters. According to one widely circulated story, a committee of Moral Warriors visited the merchant and shipper Edward K. Collins to demand that he withdraw his advertising from the *Herald*. In their presence, Collins defiantly ordered his clerk to double the number of ads he ran in the disputed paper. Over at Gilpin's Exchange and Reading Room, where city merchants gathered to gossip and read the latest news, the manager obediently exiled the *Herald* — only to face such a vehement protest from his clients that he was forced to reinstate the paper immediately.

The war, in fact, was a stroke of luck for Bennett. His opponents' attacks brought him invaluable free publicity. And even though many respectable New Yorkers still refused on principle to go near the disgraceful sheet, others found the Moral War more intriguing than disgusting. Some were pleased that an upstart had mounted so ringing a challenge to moss-bound conventionality. For many others who had been both curious *and* uneasy about Bennett's reputation for excess, the editor's modest contrition satisfied all the right conventions and fostered the impression that he had undergone a change of heart — all the while saving him the trouble of actually going and reforming. A judicious public penance can be the best license to continue misbehaving.

The mythmakers of the Moral War have gotten the combatants as well as the consequences all wrong. It was not a battle between a courageous heretic (or even a deluded one) and "the establishment." It was not Bennett versus the bluenoses. Like all myths, the tale of Bennett's conversion was actually a metaphorical explanation for a cataclysmic clash. The adversaries were the traditional and the new establishments — the old elite, on the one hand, and the new middle class and the would-be plutocrats, on the other — and the stakes were nothing less than the social, political, and cultural leadership of antebellum America.

Indeed, the mere fact that Bennett was able to insinuate himself into the fight at all is irrefutable evidence that his heretic days were over. It was the older elite, the merchants, bankers, and social leaders, who started the Moral War in the first place. Yet they would never have noticed Bennett if the insurgent middle class had not *already* begun to accept him. Their ire was sparked by their recognition that so gamy a rag as the *Herald* was gaining favor among the part of the community that most threatened their leadership — and that was not the working class, the traditional target of the penny press.

Philip Hone is a perfect representative of the elite establishment that was most shaken by Bennett's growing success, and Bennettophiles have always enjoyed snickering at Hone's journal as the lay of the last fuddy-duddy. The former mayor was, to be sure, the classic Moral Warrior, a symbolic embodiment of all those clergymen, educators, editors, and civic-minded patricians who in the past would have been the unquestioned leaders of their communities. Then in his sixtieth year, Hone was through and through a Knickerbocker — Whiggish, wealthy, cultivated, conservative, and sure of his own good taste. He enjoyed friendships with a circle of gentlemen as urbane as himself, gentlemen who adored the polished literature of eighteenth-century England, collected books and art, entertained each other well, and lavished time and money on cultural and philanthropic causes.

To these gentleman, a taste for elegant literature was as necessary as a palate for good wine, a seat on the board of a cultural institution as inevitable as a pew in an Episcopalian church. Although Hone himself had been born poor, the son of a joiner, and never attended college, he was no less a Knickerbocker for that. At forty he had retired from his auction business to devote himself to travel, culture, and public service. He had, he decided, made quite enough money — the ultimate Knickerbocker statement. In the hustling commercial New York of the 1830s and 1840s, however, Hone and his elegant fellows were also the ultimate atavism.

During the Jewett affair, Hone had not even acknowledged the excesses of the vulgar new press, preferring a tactic of pointed but silent disdain. Although he had been fascinated as well as horrified by the prostitute's murder and described it at great length in his diary, he seemed to have found all the information he needed about the crime in the staid sixpenny papers. He spelled Townsend's first name as "Rosanna" and referred to the victim with the delicate phrase "girl of the town"; those variations were to be found only in two of the most respectable of the Wall Street papers, the morning *Courier and Enquirer* and the *Evening Post,* which copied and credited the *Courier's* report.

Soon, however, the ever-increasing reach of the penny press made it impossible to ignore. In 1840, just weeks before the Moral War began, Henry Brevoort held an extravagant fancy-dress ball for the highest of high society in his elegant new Fifth Avenue mansion. Some of his more sharp-eyed guests were surprised to recognize the knight clanking about in a suit of armor as "a Mr. Attree," who had sufficiently forgiven Bennett's old "Wandering Willie" barb to join him as "reporter and one of the editors of an infamous penny paper called the *Herald,*" as Hone put it.

But Hone (who went dressed as Cardinal Wolsey, in a new scarlet merino robe) reluctantly agreed with the host's decision to permit Bennett's minion to attend, in the hope that the capitulation would impose "a sort of obligation . . . upon him to refrain from abusing the house, the people of the house, and their guests, which would have been done in case of a denial. But this is a hard alternative to submit to. This kind of surveillance is getting to be intolerable, and nothing but the force of public opinion will correct the insolence." He was delighted when the Moral War broke out. "Write [Bennett] down," he chortled that June, "make respectable people withdraw their support from the vile sheet, so that it shall be considered disgraceful to read it, and the serpent will be rendered harmless."[4]

Bennett's partisans, however, were not entirely right in their characterization of Hone. He lacked the most distinctive hallmark of the true fuddy-duddy: he was *not* oblivious to his own antiquation. Even as he called down the wrath of public opinion on Bennett's head, he also knew quite well that his call would accomplish little. Hone betrayed himself in that call; it was the perfect summation of what had dammed him and his fellows into a backwater as the currents of change swept the nation. He was outraged not so much by the reporter's presence at the Brevoort ball as by the fact that some of the guests, notably the nouveau riche merchant prince Charles A. Davis, were making the ghastly Attree "hail fellow well met." Such attention could only countenance and encourage the "daily slanders and unblushing impudence of the paper" he represented.

Even if, as Hone speculated darkly, Davis was only trying to "purchase [Attree's] forbearance" toward himself and his friends, still the very fact that a respectable person should choose surrender to so repellent a character rather than a fight with all the classic weapons of social disapproval shows clearly that those classic weapons had lost their edge. Even if the better sort read the paper only to learn how high they had to hold their heads that day, still the altitude of those heads was a measure of how much power the press was exercising over their lives. In fact, it may have been more than the chance to shine in scarlet merino that drew Hone to impersonate Cardinal Wolsey. He must have known the speech in Shakespeare's *King Henry the Eighth* in which the stiff-necked Cardinal, discovering his own dispensability, bids "a long farewell" to all his greatness. The Brevoort ball and the Moral War together made painfully clear to the old elite that a "killing frost" was nipping their own greatness, too.

The Moral War was a turning point in the history of both the middle class and the penny press, a symbol of how powerful both had become in the public cultural life of the city. But the war told only half the story of the entente between bourgeois and Bennett — the top half, the challenge upward. Yet one's sense of identity is often shaped as much by what one rejects as by what one pursues. Just as Bennett continually worked to rise in the world, to solidify his position with the better class of citizen and loosen his association with the worse, so too did middle-class New Yorkers strive to distance themselves from the popular culture of the "common people" even as they sought to take over the cultural leadership of the elite. Their struggle to establish their position presented Bennett with a great opportunity — and a great complication.

More than an economic gap separated bourgeois and laborer in the 1840s. They were inhabiting ever more different worlds, embracing different cultural styles and heroes, pursuing different public lives. Ten or twenty years earlier, the theater, for instance, had been a meeting ground open and welcoming to virtually any New Yorker, to the merchants and professionals who occupied the pit and lower tiers as well as to the rowdy "gods" at the top of house. A typical program included something for everyone: a little tragedy, a little music and dance, a little farce to cap off the evening. Now, however, workers found their public entertainment at the taverns, the oyster cellars, the melodramas and minstrel shows clustering around the Bowery — and they read the *Sun*. Middle-class New Yorkers, on the other hand, preferred to amuse themselves in the uptown theaters, perhaps at the opera, with art and serious music, all of which required special knowledge, special codes of behavior, and special incomes to enjoy. They rarely touched the *Sun*.

This fragmentation of public life gave a new significance to intellectual and leisure pursuits. In this so-called age of democracy, culture was not so much democratized as differentiated. The books and periodicals one chose, the public amusements one attended, the taste in art one displayed, were becoming badges of identity and means of distinction. As "the haute bourgeoisie ... learn[ed] to employ a variety of means to keep the expansion of the class within the limits of recognition and taste; or rather, matters of taste, character and entrance had to be channeled, discussed and formalized," it became clear that in matters of culture no less than in food, one *was* what one consumed.[5]

The new significance of leisure helped to produce a new profession: that of the entrepreneurs of culture, who created and marketed the stuff that dreams — and social distinctions — are made on. Business success came to those marketers who best divined and supplied the psychic bread and intellectual meat that would help their consumers clarify how they fit into their increasingly complicated society.

Even so quiet a pursuit as reading conveyed complex messages. The wide availability of printed matter was turning reading from shared ritual — as it had been when scarce books or papers were cherished, passed from hand to hand, and read aloud as a social occasion — into a much more private, more isolated, more socially fragmented event. Although the lines were often murky, often crossed and recrossed, readers were striated according to geography, sex, income, and class. Urban readers had access to more variety than country readers, bourgeois women had more leisure to read than men, and not even the technological revolution in publishing had yet made books easily affordable for working-class people, who stuck mainly to their large selection of newspapers, periodicals, and pamphlets.[6]

Thus for New Yorkers of the middle class, reading served other purposes than mere entertainment. One, of course, was practical: it could be a direct way of gaining authoritative instruction in the rules, boundaries, and practices of their class. Yet the symbolism of their chosen reading matter — what they could *afford* to read, what they had *time* to read, what they had the *taste* to read — was equally important, still another way to separate themselves from the pursuits of the common folk.

A prime example of the complex intersections of literary culture, consumption, and class was the sentimental domestic novel, a wildly popular genre churned out in prodigal abundance from the 1840s through the 1870s and devoted to the adventures of pious young females beset, but not bowed, by the snares of the world. Novels like Martha Finlay's *Elsie Dinsmore*, Harriet Beecher Stowe's *My Wife and I*, and Susan Warner's *Wide, Wide World* became best-sellers among bourgeois women not for their great literary merit, not for the interest of their plots (which were virtually indistinguishable and mainly confined to the bourgeois woman's spheres of expertise: tears, moralism, saintly death, and buying, consuming, and wearing things), but because they were *meant* to be best-sellers. The authors of these novels were mainly women themselves or clergymen, two groups who were feeling increasingly marginalized in a society that defined itself more and more by competition and commerce. Writing gave them a place in the world of the producers, even as their books trained, validated, and reassured a limitless market of consumers.

Sentimental fiction thus functioned as both a symbolic and a practical textbook to the art of being middle class. The authors knew that "literature was functioning more and more as a form of leisure, a complicated mass dream-life in the busiest, most wide-awake society in the world. They could not be altogether ignorant that literature was revealing and supporting a special class, a class defined less by what its members produced than by what they consumed."[7]

Few other producers of literary consumer goods would ever match the popularity of the ladies' novelists, but the ripe possibilities of the 1840s beckoned many to try. Scores of publishers, editors, authors, scribblers, zealots, malcontents, and hacks sought to devise commodities whose purchase would somehow clarify, validate, or reinforce the identity of that special class of consumers.

This was the competition now faced by James Gordon Bennett in his single-minded pursuit of the middle-class reader. Half of his job was just about done; through such ploys as doubling the *Herald*'s price to two cents, favoring the Whig presidential candidate instead of Andrew Jackson's anointed Democratic heir in 1840, and cutting drastically back on employment advertising for active tidy girls and well-bred Protestant women, he was making clear that he no longer cared for the scrounged pennies of the nursemaid, the laundress, and the journeyman. The message of the Moral War was that he no longer had to. Yet even as he seemed poised for success on an undreamed-of scale, Bennett was suddenly discovering an enormous new mass of rivals for the attention of his favored class.

There were, for instance, cheap and popular monthly magazines that guaranteed complete gentility. *Graham's* offered essays and stories with the safe spiciness of a cinnamon stick, while *Godey's Lady's Book* never departed from the sweet. By 1842 each had a nationwide circulation of between thirty and forty thousand, and each had tied up some of America's most famous authors with exclusive publication contracts.

Another cutthroat pair, the weeklies *New World* and *Brother Jonathan*, had a virtual monopoly on foreign literature, a favorite of the "cosmopolitan" reader. These weeklies had one great business ploy and one great business goal: to focus on British works, which were cheaper to publish than American fiction because they were unprotected by copyright in this country, and to print them faster and in a less costly form than the great book-publishing firms like Harper and Brothers could. In frantic haste the editors of these weeklies hustled the latest novels by Charles Dickens, G. P. R. James, Edward Bulwer-Lytton, William Ainsworth, and Mrs. Gore off the transatlantic steamships and through their high-speed presses, often reprinting an entire work in one fat "extra" pamphlet or in a mammoth issue that measured up to four feet across the sheet, all for ten or twelve cents. The penny papers, which could afford to allot perhaps a column or two to fiction only on days with no more pressing news, could compete with these massive hustlers no better than the Harpers could.

Even worse, these British reprints were muscling in on a province the penny papers had made their own specialty during the Jewett affair: the world of melodrama and high romance. Dickens's Little Nell died a death even more fascinating than Helen Jewett's; James, Walter Scott's protégé, began no fewer than seventeen of his sixty-odd historical romances with a long view of a "solitary horseman" or a "party of cavaliers" tittuping through the countryside; Bulwer-Lytton sealed his immortality with one of the most indelible opening lines in English literature: "It was a dark and stormy night."[8]

Besides these heavy contenders, the range of choice in reading material also included other penny papers; although few survived very long, the four dozen or so dailies that were started up in the decade following the highly auspicious birth of Benjamin Day's *Sun* constituted a distraction, at least, from the front-runners. There was an ever increasing torrent of specialized periodicals — religious, agricultural, scientific, mechanical, sporting, theatrical, juvenile. Each devoted itself with myopic intensity to subjects that the penny papers only occasionally managed to mention in passing.

There were the religious books and tracts published by huge interdenominational firms like the American Tract Society, the American Bible Society, and the American Sunday School Union. Some tracts were intended to shape the conscience and conduct of middle-class children; many others were distributed to the urban working class by armies of zealous middle-class volunteers. The Philadelphia Bible Society had been the first firm in America to print from the new tough, reusable stereotype plates instead of fragile type. The Tract Society had grasped sooner than most commercial firms the vast potential of the steam printing press developed by Daniel Treadwell in the early 1820s. As early as 1826 it had at least two of the ponderous machines installed in its specially reinforced printing plant, and it was soon producing as many as six million tracts, almanacs, and books a year.[9]

Matching the religious firms in their evangelical perseverance as well as their marketing savvy were some single-interest political organizations that used the new mass printing techniques to produce huge but cheap editions of pamphlets, broadsides, and papers espousing their causes. The American Anti-Slavery Society, a small group with only thirteen agents in 1835, sent out such an unprecedented flood of literature that their terrified opponents, behindhand in their technological expertise, became convinced the society must be receiving foreign financial help in a worldwide abolitionist plot.[10]

Then there were the semicolon tales — inexpensive sensation novels in paper covers that inevitably sported racy bifurcated titles like *Fanny H——; Or, the Hunchback and the Roué.* Joseph Holt Ingraham, one of the masters of the genre, would soon tread very close to the penny editors' toes when in 1843 he published *Frank Rivers; Or, the Dangers of the Town,* his own version, even more embroidered than theirs, of the Jewett tragedy. He followed up that success a year later with *La Bonita Cigarera; Or, the Beautiful Cigar Vendor* and a sequel, both based on the Mary Rogers murder.

And another rival was rising on a flank that had always seemed under the penny papers' particular protection. The passage in 1842 of federal laws forbidding the importation of erotic literature roused many enterprising Americans to fill the breach with homegrown products. The aggressively "saucy" *Herald* came to seem positively demure compared to a paper like the *Rake,* which got itself fined for gross obscenity, or to the thriving underground pamphlet literature that ran the gamut from the merely salacious to the queasily perverse — from "rose-tipped hillocks" and "portals of paradise" to nymphomania, incest, sadomasochism, and necrophilia.[11]

In late 1841, when news broke of the sort of sensational murder that would once have seemed the exclusive possession of James Gordon Bennett, the challenge facing him was enormous: to elbow his way through this vast thicket of print and figure out what would reward the public for reading *his* words instead of someone else's. But that was not all he had to contend with. He also had Horace Greeley.

13

FOR THE VIRTUOUS AND REFINED

The Moral War of 1840 was in some sense the Trojan Horse that slid Horace Greeley through the gates of the city. The war must have been bruising indeed if its shell-shocked survivors could bring themselves to hail so singular a beast.

Greeley was already well known as more than a squash by the time he and his *Tribune* took on James Gordon Bennett and the rest of the poisoners of public intelligence. A pallid, skinny, downy-haired, cherub-faced semivegetarian, Greeley was equipped with one of the city's most profane mouths and a long-thwarted ambition to publish a high-class newspaper at a working-class price. In a decade of work in New York, the immigrant New Englander had already sampled a variety of journalistic experiences that had brought him a reputation for a nice literary taste, a strict adherence to Whig principles, an interest in the affairs of the working man, a high moral sensitivity, an aptitude for all manner of crotchets and eccentricities, and an abominable business sense.

Nearly a year before Benjamin Day succeeded in launching a cheap paper for the masses in 1833, Greeley had participated in the failure of the very first such effort. He printed, briefly, the *Morning Post* for one Dr. Horatio David Sheppard, a physician by training, who had a theory about newspapers. If they cost no more than the peanuts or gingerbread hawked in the street, he reasoned, they ought to sell just as well. It was the only theory about newspapers the artless doctor had.[1] In his next venture, Greeley tried his hand at editing as well as printing; his weekly *New-Yorker* featured carefully selected literary matter, including poetry signed "H.G."; editorial articles on topics ranging from foreign relations to slavery, labor, and capital punishment; and nonpartisan political news. It was well respected among the literary and at one point boasted a subscription list of over nine thousand.

But Greeley was constitutionally incapable of conducting an orderly and efficient business. He would leave bundles of letters in his overcoat pocket, forgotten and unanswered for months, and he often paid his paragraphists not only more than they dared ask, but also more than he could afford. Greeley's fuzzy business head, combined with the economic depression that began in 1837, kept the paper mired in debt throughout its seven years of life.

Another of Greeley's strategies for eking out a living involved him with Thurlow Weed, the kingpin of the New York State Whig party. While continuing to publish the *New-Yorker* from Ann Street in New York, Greeley also served first as editor of the *Jeffersonian*, a campaign newspaper for the 1838 state races issued from the state capital, and then as an inner-circle Whig and editor of the *Log Cabin*, which boomed William Henry Harrison, Old Tippecanoe, for president in 1840. For a while Greeley traveled weekly by riverboat — and, in winter when the river froze, by sleigh — between New York and Albany to produce his two papers at opposite ends of the week. Then, as the presidential campaign heated up, he stumped in other northeastern cities as well.

By the end of the grueling campaign season he was exhausted, his poor

New-Yorker was suffering from neglect as well as disarray, and even though he professed to have no interest in political office, still "it *is* somewhat surprising," his biographer later sniffed, "that the incoming administration had not the decency to *offer* him something."[2] On 10 April 1841, just after the nation's first Whig president ungraciously died of the effects of a month in office, Greeley issued the first number of a brand new, much more independent venture, the *New York Daily Tribune.*

The *Tribune* was to be something unprecedented: a cheap mass-circulation daily with a sixpenny's modesty, a Whig turn of mind, and a broadbased, respectable readership drawn primarily from the middle class. In his issue of 3 May, Greeley pictured his target audience as exactly that: "the active and substantial Middle Class of our citizens — those who live by their labor or their business, and are neither above the necessity nor devoid of the ability to buy and sell to the best advantage." It would, however, he conceded shortly thereafter, be a difficult battle to dispel what he would describe as "the common presumption that a Daily paper afforded at so low a price as *Four Dollars per annum* must necessarily cater for the tastes and minister to the prejudices of the ignorant and the trifling."

In after years Greeley's business partner, the former bookseller Thomas McElrath, would explain that when the *Tribune* was born, the penny papers "were not generally taken into the families of the better class of the citizens. . . . The [*Sun*] was extensively circulated among the class of people from whom it received the largest share of its advertising patronage, the [*Herald*] was read 'downtown' by business men and clerks; but neither of them very often penetrated into the parlors or sitting rooms of the uptown residents. . . . It struck me that, however important the patronage of a political party, a circulation in the cultivated and influential families of the city was quite as important."[3]

Although McElrath was clearly underreporting the strength of the enemy *Herald* in the parlor, nonetheless Greeley had reason to believe that New York offered plenty of room for a new and different kind of penny paper. The Moral War of the previous year had solidified Bennett's position among many respectable New Yorkers, but it had also focused the ire of those others who were disgusted with the prevailing choice among penny papers, and it highlighted a vacuum that an alert and more polite journalist might profitably fill. In his memoirs Greeley himself recalled his goal as quite simple: he only wanted to produce a cheap paper that would present an alternative to the Democratic leanings of much of the penny press. But the new paper would also be "removed alike from servile partisanship on the one hand and from gagged, mincing neutrality on the other.... My familiarity with [the Whig press's] history and management gave me confidence that the right sort of a cheap Whig journal would be enabled to live."[4]

According to the new paper's prospectus, published in the same issue of the *Log Cabin* in which he announced President Harrison's death, Greeley saw himself as transcending the tenets of Whiggism to undertake nothing less than an evangelical mission on behalf of virtue and decorum. In a direct and explicit challenge to the *Herald* and the other penny papers, Greeley announced that he was dedicating the *Tribune* to the "Moral, Social, and Political well-being" of the people, which meant that the "immoral and degrading Police Reports, Advertisements and other matter which have been allowed to disgrace the columns of many of our leading Penny Papers will be carefully excluded from this, and no exertion spared to render it worthy of the hearty approval of the virtuous and refined, and a welcome visitant at the family fireside."

Unlike the wily Bennett, moreover, Greeley soon proved that neither his claim to a superior morality nor his commitment to educating the public was a humbug, though the alacrity with which he embraced reforms both practical and wild-eyed did leave him vulnerable to accusations of eccentricity at least, if not radicalism. On a lecture trip to New York in the spring of 1842, Ralph Waldo Emerson made Greeley's acquaintance over a vegetarian dinner at the editor's Grahamite boarding house (no meat, bolted flour, coffee, alcohol, constricting clothing, unventilated rooms, or sexual excesses allowed), and in a bemused letter to Margaret Fuller he analyzed the enthusiastic soul.

"Greeley is a young man with white soft hair from New Hampshire, mother of men," wrote Emerson, "of sanguine temper & liberal mind, no scholar but such a one as journals & newspapers make, who listens after all new thoughts & things but with the indispensable New York condition that they can be made available.... What can I do with such an abettor? He declares himself a Transcendentalist, is a unitarian, a defender of miracles, &c I saw my fate in a moment & that I should never content him."[5]

Emerson's perplexity over this hearkener after worldly trends and otherworldly miracles was not at all unusual. Few people could have entirely contented so zealous and wide-ranging and often perverse a soul. The editor was genuinely and passionately interested in improving the lot of the farmer and the laborer and for many years extolled Fourierism, a sort of Utopian republican communalism, as Everyman's path to an idyllic rural self-sufficiency. At various times he advocated government responsibility for education, internal improvements, and full employment, and he demanded the free distribution of public lands to farmers, all of which seared him, in many eyes, with the brand of the socialist. He took firmly — even belligerently — moralistic stands on the great issues of the day and once summed up his paper as "Anti-Slavery, Anti-War, Anti-Rum, Anti-Tobacco, Anti-Seduction, Anti-Grogshops, Brothels, Gambling Houses."[6]

His radicalism did, however, know limits, some of them quite narrow. While lauding the laborer, he maintained a fondness more than sneaking for capitalists and employers as well. He strongly supported the very Whiggish bankruptcy act of 1841 that was generally seen as favoring people of property. Some other reforms were too ultra for even his stomach, like the impious free-lovism of the freewheeling Fanny Wright — or suffrage for women.

Still, his integrity and earnestness were unquestionable. He broke with tradition and refused to accept the patronage of so-called "female physicians" like Mesdames Costello and Restell, who ran regular and prominent advertisements in all the other penny dailies that promised discreet relief for distraught women suffering from "suppression, irregularity, obstruction, &c., by whatever cause produced." Instead of regaling his readers with potboiler fiction, he pursued good writers and good literature; within his first six months he published excerpts from two of the year's most exciting new works, Dickens's *Barnaby Rudge* and Emerson's first series of essays. Lest anyone miss his point, he regularly reminded his readers of his superior virtue in long articles critical of the viciousness of the other penny editors, who soon honored the *Tribune* with the recognition of refutation and its editor with the label of "squash."

And as perverse and perplexing as Greeley could sometimes be on matters of political reform, on one particular crusade the editor of the *Tribune* was absolutely firm and unyielding. It was a rather unusual stance for an editor of a cheap urban newspaper that was supposed to have a mass appeal, and it marked one of the sharpest differences between Greeley and Bennett. It also served to repel many of the readers he most sought to attract, to keep a tenuous hold on others who otherwise had little sympathy for his philosophies, and to captivate a vast and completely new readership for the first time in newspaper history.

Horace Greeley hated and feared the city.

Distaste for the city was a common enough emotion among many established New Yorkers seeking something to blame for the disorders and threats that more and more encroached on their lives. Greeley's attitude toward the urban poor, like that of many middle-class social reformers of the time, was a complicated stew of humanitarianism, defensiveness, fear, and an anxious reaffirmation of the traditional but increasingly disputed role of the professional class as the moral leaders of their communities. Greeley was fervently and genuinely devoted to improving education and opportunities for the disadvantaged individual. Yet he feared the disorderly tendencies of the disadvantaged individual *en masse*, the horde of unskilled laborers, struggling immigrants, transients, paupers, loners, street urchins, and petty criminals who crammed into New York's poorer wards and who seemed immune to any form of social direction or control.

These were the creatures, "generally ignorant [and] devoid of any fixed moral principle," who were most vulnerable to "the worst influences" — who might be unhealthily excited by voting for a Democrat, watching a public execution, or reading the *Herald*. Greeley was convinced that both they and the city would be better off if they left it, and he campaigned continually for a great exodus of the urban poor.

But again like many other urban reformers, most notably Robert Hartley, who was shortly to found the influential New York Association for Improving the Condition of the Poor, Greeley believed that at bottom poverty was caused by innate character flaws, by flightiness or dullness or sloth. "[A]n extensive, protracted experience has led me to the conclusion," he would later remark in his memoirs, "that nine tenths of those who solicit loans of strangers or casual acquaintances are thriftless vagabonds, who will never be better off than at present, or scoundrels, who would not pay if they were able. . . .

"That the poor often suffer from poverty, I know; but oftener from lack of capacity, skill, management, efficiency, than lack of money. . . . The widow, the orphan, the cripple, the invalid, often need alms, and should have them; but to the innumerable hosts of needy, would-be borrowers the best response is Nature's, — 'Root, hog, or die!' "[7] The editor could neither understand nor sympathize if people so downtrodden refused to listen to reason — to pull themselves together, move out, and join Fourierite phalanxes or simply to heal themselves with the all-purpose tonic of the bucolic.

Besides encouraging New Yorkers to leave the city, Greeley also tried to dissuade outsiders from coming in the first place, and he was especially anxious to stopper the surging influx of restless rural youth. They were not, perhaps, as frightening as the urban slum masses, but even the most talented young people risked drowning in the great cesspool that was the metropolis, and others might well discover their more evil propensities when released from family supervision. His westering advice to the "young man" lives on in folklore, but for years he had been giving similar advice, in the columns of the *Tribune* and also in his private correspondence, to anyone who would listen.[8]

The city may seem an exciting and noble place — but don't come here, he wrote again and again; it is unhealthy, overcrowded, vicious, and teeming with young men, all desperate for a professional position. A youth starting out in life, he argued, would do best by avoiding both the city and the intellectual professions and by taking up some kind of wholesome manual labor in the healthier atmosphere of the country.

Typical of his convictions is a reply he sent to one H. Hubbard, a young man from the New York outback who had struck up a correspondence with Greeley after getting a piece published in *Brother Jonathan*. In a series of letters, the editor gave Hubbard friendly advice about his talents. "Do not publish poetry in a volume," he admonished in one such letter. "You write fair verses, but not such as the public will [illegible] buy because they can't do without them." But when Hubbard floated an inquiry about coming to New York himself, the editor's response was crushing. "Alas! my friend," Greeley wrote back, "you know not what it is that it is [*sic*] wanted of men who live by literary labor here, nor at what a dreadful cost any distinction must be purchased! I have been fortunate here, as the world says, but how? I need money badly, and I am an assemblage of pains. . . . You do not realize," the editor went on, "how little the mere talent of writing well has to do with success or usefulness. There are a thousand at least in this city who can write very good prose or verse . . . while there are not fifty who can earn their bread by it."

To Greeley's dismay, however, few young men heeded his advice. A generation later, he was still warning young men away with the same fervor and the same futility. In 1870 he advised the twelve-year-old Worthington C. Ford that "the professions are overcrowded, and all our people seem intent on living without producing positive wealth. Step out from this mob, by becoming a producer." Ford did not listen either; rather than producing positive wealth, he became a historian.[9]

The columns of the *Tribune* ceaselessly hammered home the same message. For several weeks in 1841, both the weekly and the daily editions carried extracts from a *Blackwood's* article on "The World of London" that warned heavily against seeking fame and fortune in the vast, impersonal city. The excerpt published on 25 September included a description of the folly of one Sam Patch, namesake of the celebrated daredevil who had recently leaped over Niagara Falls with the laconic battle-cry "Some things can be done as well as others" — and earned a blazing fame for proving his own slogan wrong.

In the *Blackwood's* article, the second Patch sought a similar celebrity by coming to London and hanging himself, "by way of a lark," from Waterloo Bridge. His pains earned him a fame lasting "some seconds less than five minutes." The ignominy was Patch's own fault, reported *Blackwood's*; he should never have wasted his efforts on so blasé an audience. If he had been clever enough to do the deed in a smaller town, "songs would have been sung, and sermons made about him. . . . Patch would have become a household word. . . . We would have had the Sam Patch quadrilles, and the Sam Patch magic strop, and the Sam Patch cravats. . . . There is no town's talk in London . . . try how you will, it is as impossible to astonish us, as it would be if you were to exert your abilities in that line upon a fossil elephant."

Greeley saw in the British article some serious lessons for Americans, too. "We have preached ourselves hoarse in entreating the mass of young men of our day not to covet what is called 'an education,' not to crowd into the professions," he commented in the weekly for 20 November, "but, above all, to resist that insane craving for city life by which the happiness of so many is shipwrecked." He entreated his readers to heed the article as "pertinent and vividly just."

The columns of the *Tribune* trembled with sincerity and urgency, with genuine concern for the city's moral well-being, and with legitimate, if ineffective, suggestions as to how to improve it. No penny paper had ever demanded to be taken so seriously before. With that demand, the *Tribune's* editor staked out a loyal readership among new communities of readers who had been yearning to take a penny paper seriously — and amused, bemused, and baffled most others.

Something about Horace Greeley appealed mightily to one group of readers who were entirely new to the cheap press idea. The weekly *Tribune*, a digest of the same news stories and editorial pieces that had appeared in the most recent dailies, was intended for readers who lived too far from the city to receive a paper every day. Americans who did *not* live in New York flocked to the New York paper that denounced New York. Established five months after the daily *Tribune* and drawing on the ready-made and wide-ranging subscription lists of Greeley's two previous efforts, the *New-Yorker* and the *Log Cabin*, the weekly for the country readership soon outstripped the circulation of the city daily.

Some of Greeley's appeal was obviously visceral. Born on a farm in New Hampshire, reared on a farm in Vermont, the editor embodied for many the flinty independence and iron rectitude of the American yeoman. As one journalist who knew him recalled later, Greeley was "adored by the farmers in New England and in the Western Reserve, who believed he wrote every word of the *Tribune*, not excepting the advertisements." This journalist ascribed the editor's popularity to his willingness to sacrifice "everything, advertisers, subscribers, and all else, to what he considered principle."

Yet more than admiration for his good republican virtues drew country readers to Greeley's paper. A former *Tribune* reporter explained Greeley's attraction this way, in an enthusiastically received lecture given for the paper's golden anniversary: "He was felt to be a representative American: not, indeed, because he flattered the mob, nor because he was said sometimes to stuff his trousers into his boots, or to tie his cravat under his ear, or forget his collar or one shoe [laughter], nor because of any eccentricity of dress or contact. It was because, with all his fond faith in America and American institutions, he knew, as the German proverb says, that beyond the mountains there are men also. [Applause.]"[10]

That was not all Greeley knew — or seemed to know — and the unfortunate editor was not merely adored from afar; he was pestered, beseeched, and besieged by people who seemed to believe he could fix any problem, cure any ill, move any mountain. An employee once described how Greeley finally had to move his office deep into the remotest reaches of the *Tribune* building to hide from the importunate masses of visitors "with the greatest possible variety of bees in their bonnets," some of whom had traveled miles to see him.

There were people with machines of perpetual motion; with theories about Spiritualism . . . ; with notions about the next election . . . ; with anxiety to become writers upon his newspaper; with manuscripts which they wished to have recommended to some publisher of books; with new

religions; with schemes for the abolition of every religion whatever ...;
widows whose sole claim upon him or upon anybody was that they were
widows; orphans, sometimes suspiciously well grown, with nothing to
plead but their orphanage. ... [Greeley] would try sometimes to be
extremely stern and repellent, but it was always a lamentable failure.

And he got letters, hundreds of letters. Many of Greeley's correspondents were doubtless motivated to write by the sentiment actually voiced
by one E. W. Durham of Irvington-on-the-Hudson. Durham began a nine-
page excursus supporting the resumption of specie payments with a forth-
right and unapologetic assertion. "Dear Sir," he wrote, "You are the property of the nation; and, therefore, without further preface, I take the liberty
of addressing you on a subject of vital interest to all."

In the course of his editorial career, the property of the nation received
letters from across the country, asking for a myriad of blessings: from
Ohio, requesting the name of an industrious young Whig interested in
buying a struggling newspaper; from California, seeking words of wisdom
to insert in a college paper; from West Virginia, begging a loan; from
Pennsylvania, looking for a husband; from upstate New York, pleading for
the real truth about Dr. Ball's Patent Improved Eye Cups. Legions of
would-be poets, most of them possessing half the talent and twice the
nerve of the aspiring young author Hubbard, seemed to believe that Greeley's notice was the only measure of literary success worth striving for.
One E. G. Holland of Geneva, New York, sent a verse entitled "The Snow
Drops" that began:

> I view thee upward far in air!
>> Downward coming mild and fair.
> I have watched thy downward move,
>> With a free admiring love.
> Tell me snow drop, what's thine aim,
>> What thou art, and whence thou came ...

"If these spontaneous outbursts of the *poetique*, should please you," the
blushing poet told Greeley, "you are at liberty to publish them."[11]

The ubiquity of his renown eventually became the stuff of jokes. By the
1860s, Mark Twain, wandering in the West, would be driven to distraction
by hearing the same dreary anecdote about Greeley's breakneck adventure
in a stagecoach, told to him "four hundred and eighty-one or eighty-two
times."

I have the list somewhere. Drivers always told it, conductors told it, landlords told it, chance passengers told it, the very Chinamen and vagrant Indians recounted it. I have had the same driver tell it to me two or three times in the same afternoon. . . . I never have smelt any anecdote as often as I have smelt that one; never have smelt any anecdote that smelt so variegated as that one. . . . I have heard it is in the Talmud. I have seen it in print in nine different foreign languages; I have been told that it is employed in the inquisition in Rome; and I now learn with regret that it is going to be set to music. I do not think that such things are right.[12]

Although country readers honored Greeley's wisdom about everything from specie payments to husbands to eye cups, for one task in particular they found him absolutely indispensable. Unlike the *Herald* or the *Sun*, the *Tribune* laid out for them, in clear, specific terms, exactly how hideous the big city was. During the Jewett affair readers had reached this conclusion for themselves, piecing together a confirmation of their belief in urban horror from the snippets and driblets of news that managed to toil their way. Now Greeley was doing the job for them every week. He confirmed their suspicions. He assured them they were correct in this matter so close to their hearts — and he should know. Country readers adored Greeley not because he tied his cravat oddly but because he both personified and personally validated one of their most important truths for them.

New Yorkers themselves, however, were much less enamored of Horace Greeley's *Tribune* than provincial readers were. Specific evidence about popular readership of this — or any — cheap paper is sparse, and determining exactly which city dwellers read the idiosyncratic paper is difficult. Also impossible to gauge is the exclusivity of the average newspaper reader's taste. The assumption seems safe, however, that although some New Yorkers may well have enjoyed sampling from the cornucopia of the city press, most readers devoted their loyalty then — as most do now — to a favorite paper or two. We do know that the *Tribune*'s numbers were low; circulation figures show that the daily *Tribune* never overtook either the *Sun* or the *Herald*, let alone its own sister weekly. Despite Greeley's championship of their rights, few urban lower-class readers rushed to embrace the *Tribune*, and few members of the city's business community were any more eager to lavish their advertising patronage on a sheet with so limited an appeal.[13]

The real targets of both Greeley's fears and his reformism, moreover —

the desperate underclass and the degenerates "devoid of any fixed moral principle" — probably never read his newspaper at all. The worst-off workers, the hardscrabbling day laborer or the seamstress who earned a hundred dollars in a good year, would rarely have had either the spare penny to buy any paper or the spare minutes to read one, assuming that he or she could read in the first place. And the true degenerates, the villainous "roughs," thugs, and bruisers who seemed to epitomize everything disorderly and frightening about the slums, favored a more functional literary fare. One eminent journalist remarked that these rowdies nerved themselves to the task of learning to read only so that they could follow the prizefights in the sporting papers. They would have avoided an uplifting and moralistic paper like the *Tribune* as sedulously as Huck Finn would come to avoid Sunday School.[14]

The more stable portion of the working class was a likelier pool for readers of newspapers of any type, and some may indeed have chosen Greeley's paper to acclimate themselves to the habits of the class they aspired to join. But many more would undoubtedly have been offended or dismayed by the *Tribune*'s rabidly anti-Democratic politics and its explicit disapproval of their own way of life. They remained unmoved by Greeley's fears concerning their susceptibility to evil influences and their propensity for grogshops; they rejected his simpleminded insistence that their lives would improve if only they lit out west and became farmers. They preferred the comfortable pleasures of the *Sun*.

Members of the middle and upper classes — the sorts of people who would actually have had the "family fireside" to which Greeley hoped his paper would be a regular visitant — were in general rather more sympathetic to the daily *Tribune*, but even they had mixed feelings about the paper. It did have a devoted following among New York's intelligentsia because of its superior writers and progressive thinkers. During its first decade such illuminati as Margaret Fuller, Karl Marx, George Ripley, Bayard Taylor, William Henry Fry, and Charles Dana labored on its staff, and the admittance of a new young writer to the paper's august columns would soon come to confer on the tyro, in the editor E. L. Godkin's words, "a patent of literary nobility."[15]

Many New Yorkers, however, who normally would have passionately embraced so warm a Whig paper, or who would have delighted in its empathetic understanding of their fear of disorder, were daunted by the editor's crotchets, his bizarre beliefs, and his most unpatrician descent into rank enthusiasm. Fourteen years after the founding of the *Tribune*, Greeley's own biographer James Parton, sympathetic though he was to his principal, conceded that the editor "is not a born journalist. He is too much in earnest to be a perfect editor. He has too many opinions and preferences."

The editor's reputation for the strength of his own opinions, in fact, combined with his practice of "giving every new thought and every new man a hearing in the columns of his paper," led "unthinking persons" to believe that he actively advocated every one of the myriad ideas and causes that made an appearance in his pages. "They thought the Tribune was an unsafe, disorganizing paper," Parton continued. " 'An excellent paper,' said they, 'and honest, but then it's so full of *isms!* ' "[16]

Just in time to make the third issue of the new weekly *Tribune*, a missing printer's battered and malodorous body was found crammed in a box in the hold of a cargo ship. Like the Jewett case, Samuel Adams's murder was the perfect story at the perfect time, an ideal showcase for a new pair of rival journalists to stake out their claims for the readerships they preferred by strutting their differences and, presumably, their strengths. James Gordon Bennett, predictably, welcomed the story with the fervor of a ringmaster confronting a midget tattooed woman with a beard. While Horace Greeley's reaction to the crime was somewhat different, his coverage of the affair was laden with enough *isms* to convince a substantial community of New Yorkers of exactly how excellent and honest a penny paper could be.

14

GREELEY EXPOUNDS ON A MURDER

When the missing printer's battered body turned up in a box aboard a cargo ship, Greeley welcomed the story with all the fervor of a diner confronting a fingernail in his sausage.

The *Tribune* editor was uneasy, apologetic, and resentful about devoting his columns to so lurid a story. It was, first of all, both enervating and boring to report. After it was finally over he confided to a friend that he had felt "hurried to death in 'York, worked all to pieces . . . while that everlasting Colt's Trial was in progress."[1]

Even more important, though, was Greeley's concern about the effect of the story on the moral well-being of the people. On 29 January 1842 he apologized to readers of the weekly edition, assuring them that "we shall very seldom publish reports of this kind." He had already asserted, in the same early article in which he accused Bennett of poisoning the fountains of public intelligence, that intense press attention to violence and crime was harmful to society. At that point Greeley was objecting to the other cheap papers' excited coverage of the brutal murder of a New Jersey banker by a dimwitted, shovel-wielding thug. That kind of journalism, he believed, bred a familiarity with crime that could harden the heart, blunt the humanity, and even encourage the practice of similar depredations "among a class of our population, generally ignorant, devoid of any fixed moral principle, and open on every side to the worst influences."

Even the unworldly Greeley could recognize, however, that some careful forays in the direction of the "immoral and degrading" might bring their more reputable rewards. As any evangelist knows, nobody can reform the people who do not stop to listen; they must be securely captivated first with an alluring bait. So Greeley supplemented his servings of political news, fiction by Dickens, essays by Emerson, and poems by Poe with his own version of the street-corner brass band. He followed the developments in the murder of the Beautiful Cigar Girl and even issued an extra on 17 August 1841 when a suspect was arrested. He regularly included a proven journalistic staple, a column recounting horrors from around the country: suicides, rapes, murders, fires, heartbreaking accidents to tiny children, gruesome encounters between careless people and ravening machines. He chronicled the careers of Wellington the Bigamist, who had four or five wives, and of Mrs. Jones the Female Impostor, whose spurious tales of important connections in England dazzled at least two young men into marrying him.[2]

He could even be prevailed upon to include the occasional item of sporting news. Greeley's associate Charles A. Dana would recall years later the dismay in the *Tribune* office around 1842 when the chief seemed to be resolutely ignoring an important horse race between Boston, the northern favorite, and Fashion, the darling of the South. A reporter finally confronted Greeley directly, insisting that "it will not do for The Tribune to appear day after tomorrow without any account of that event in which the whole public mind is absorbed." Dana quoted Greeley's reluctant decision: " 'Well,' said Horace, 'I don't know.' Finally said he, 'We have to report hangings, anyway.' "[3]

All of these descents into the immoral, however, were carefully balanced and justified. They all, in Greeley's hands, became object lessons on behalf of their antitheses: the good, the moral, the virtuous. Because the Colt affair, which stretched out for over a year, provided a whole parade of such lessons, Greeley managed to put aside his disgust enough to cover the case at length. He did not even balk at including the inevitable and endless verbatim transcription of the entire trial. The *Tribune's* transcription was widely admired for its accuracy and completeness — due mostly to the lightning pen of Greeley's overworked young assistant, Henry J. Raymond, who a decade later would establish the *Times* and overwork himself into being his old boss's great rival.[4]

But the transcript was the only part of Greeley's coverage that would have been familiar to connoisseurs of cheap-press murder. He resorted to none of the carnival tricks, the mythmaking, or the excitation that had marked the coverage of the Jewett affair five years before. Rather than manipulating the details of the case, in fact, Greeley ignored them as much as possible. Although he agreed that Colt was undoubtedly a murderer and dutifully recorded each day's official revelations, he added nothing of his own discovering to those straightforward facts. Nowhere in his columns could readers find exhaustive dissections of the quarrel, lurid descriptions of the body, or imaginative speculations on the motive for the crime. He displayed absolutely no interest in acting as either investigative detective or agent provocateur.

The problem was not that the facts were inconvenient for Greeley. They were merely unimportant. His main interest was something much more metaphysical than blood or guilt; it was morality. Colt's career provided a classic example of Greeley's most constant theme: the dangers that could destroy a young man alone in the city without a concerned family or a close-knit community to help mold his character. From the moment Colt began his life of crime as a petty larcenist stealing from his employer's till, Greeley warned on 28 September 1841, the young man had steadily and inevitably slid into "a depth of horrid guilt and blasting infamy," demonstrating afresh "that Crime has a vital, growing power, which . . . thrusts downward deep into the heart its mighty roots, and overshadows the whole inner being with its death-distilling shade."

Colt's terrible end was just as inevitable as his second step into vice. The life of "this hapless being must afford a solemn warning to the Youth of our City and Land," Greeley preached on the day after the prisoner's suicide.

Of a respected and influential family, possessing good talents and a winning address, enjoying and profiting by liberal opportunities for mental culture, he might fairly have looked forward to a life of useful-ness, honor and happiness, closing at ripe maturity in a death-bed soothed by the attentions of loving and sorrowing hearts. This *might* have been, but for the canker in the heart — the selfishness, and pride, and recklessness, which entered deeply into his character — a disposi-tion to measure everything by the standard of personal interest or gratification. On this rock has he been wrecked.

The dry details of the case seemed so unimportant next to so urgent a moral message that, on 28 September, Greeley actually described the murder scene without divulging a single material fact about the room itself.

The imagination cannot avoid picturing to itself this terrible murder, nor can it dwell for a moment upon the scene without deep thrills of horror; that one human being, with the warm, bright sunlight stream-ing alike upon him and his victim, at the corner of two of the most thronged streets in our Metropolis, with the bustle of business and the voices of men sounding in his ears, should thus murder his fellow, with such aggravated atrocity, and then proceed with such cool, heartless indifference to remove the corse [*sic*] and to stifle the terrible voice which cried aloud, and all around him, for swift vengeance upon his most unholy act, seems almost impossible; and the mind half dreams — and rejoices at the delusion — that some fiend from the realm of guilt and woe has wrought this awful ruin.

The state of Colt's conscience was still preoccupying the editor during the trial three months later. Then, "the prisoner appeared perfectly calm and collected," Greeley reported on 21 January 1842, ". . . and to all appearances is as perfectly innocent of the terrible crime laid to his charge as any person in the room. What may be his thoughts and reflections no one but himself and his Maker can know." Nor was it just the prisoner whose peace was at stake. On 22 January Greeley grieved sincerely over the community's arousal "from a sleep of fancied security and repose, to a dread conviction that the security of human life is destroyed, the safety and even existence of social order and harmony put in fearful jeopardy and all the elements of discord and hate let loose to prey upon the vitals of the body politic."

The lessons of the crime for society were legion, in fact, and Greeley was eager to expose them all. On 19 November 1842, the day after the prisoner's wretched death, Greeley turned his attention to the folly of capital punishment. That issue of the paper carried a long and rather confused expression of his hope that the whole affair, "viewed in all its proportions," would help to do away with the death penalty. The general public, apparently, had been too eager for Colt's execution to take so rounded a view of the case, and Greeley's confusion undoubtedly stemmed from his desire to contribute to the moral well-being of the people without mortally offending most of them.

He acknowledged that the *Tribune* had not pressed for the mitigation of Colt's sentence because "if there ever was a case in which the public safety required a bloody expiation of crime, this was such a one." Nonetheless, he continued, capital punishment was never justified, and in this case the sentence had produced no moral effects. Would not any "reflecting" man agree, Greeley argued, that "the excitement and the concussion of the last five days, as to whether Colt would or would not, should or should not, be hung, has been prejudicial to that filial regard for the laws and their administration which all ought to feel?

"If the punishment of murder had been solitary confinement for life," he continued, "without chance of pardon, would not the acquiescence of the community have been hearty and universal, and the moral influence far more salutary than now? And here at last we see the gallows cheated of its prey, and the culprit hurried out of existence by his own deadly hand, in a manner which may well throw doubt on the sincerity of his professions of penitence. . . . Not from compassion to criminals but from regard to the community — whose sympathies and whose feelings are so unhealthily excited by public executions — . . . we demand the abolition of the Punishment of Death."

His argument sparked a spate of emotional letters to the editor continuing the public debate, as well as a sarcastic private comment from George Templeton Strong. It was just as well, wrote Strong in his diary, that Colt had not been hanged, because "there would soon have been a strong feeling of sympathy got up for him, for he would have protested his innocence under the gallows itself, and great use would have been made of the case by the silly people who are seeking the abolition of capital punishment."[5]

Thus Greeley's coverage of the Colt story was less an account of a crime than a dissertation on public morals. He transformed the sordid murder of a tradesman into a general plea for an end to the death penalty, an exhortation to young men to avoid the snares and pitfalls of the city, and an implicit invitation to his readers to reconsider the quality of urban life.

Yet although such a dissertation might seem tailormade for out-of-town readers fearful of the city they knew only by evil reputation, and naive if not offensive to cosmopolitan readers averse to *isms,* it did hold an inherent appeal for one particular group of New Yorkers. In fact, the *Tribune's* subscription list was reported to have gained "several thousand" new names around this time, and the respectable sixpenny *Commercial Advertiser* even printed excerpts from the *Tribune's* reporting in its own venerable columns.[6]

These New York readers, few of whom, probably, had ever read a penny paper before, were members of an important group highly characteristic of the antebellum city: the mostly Protestant, mostly middle-class moral evangelicals and reformers. And the *Tribune* was doing for them in a more secular vein what the great antebellum reform organizations like the American Tract Society, the American Sunday School Union, and the American Female Moral Reform Society were trying to achieve for the same citizens. Both newspaper and organizations were giving readers a voice to decry the horrors of city immorality as well as a supporting chorus to reinforce and ratify their efforts.

Spurred initially by the militant religious enthusiasm of the Second Great Awakening and by their increasing fear of urban disorder, evangelical Protestants founded hundreds of voluntary associations in the 1820s and 1830s to distribute tracts, establish Sunday schools, and stamp out prostitution, gambling, drunkenness, Sabbath-breaking, and a host of other vices that tended to cluster most alarmingly in the huge cities. Most of these societies were narrowly focused, typically devoting themselves to eradicating a single vice or to advocating one kind of reform, and they operated with little coordination. Nearly all of them, however, shared a common larger goal: to establish in the cities what they rosily painted as the "traditional" moral order of the rural village, in which the entire community shared responsibility for overseeing each citizen's behavior and ensuring his or her conformity to a generally accepted code of conduct.

Such associations, however, were often less help to their professed quarry, the mostly urban underclass, than they were to the middle-class volunteers who banded together for the cause. The societies provided men and women, many of them young and new to the city, with healthy companionship, moral guidance, a feeling of self-worth, and a shared sense of purpose in an unexceptionable crusade, besides a means of affirming their own identities and their own social cohesion in the midst of a strange and chaotic urban environment. Even if the volunteers did not manage to imbue paupers and immigrants with middle-class morality, still their very struggle to crystallize and transmit this morality reinforced their own commitment to it.[7]

The early optimism of these evangelical single-issue organizations was already beginning to fade by the 1840s. The city masses — especially the increasingly Catholic immigrant population — were often hostile to the Protestant reformers' mission; the volunteers rarely won the governmental support they needed to validate their efforts; and not even the most dedicated activists could deny that their exhortations and tracts, however sincere, were making little headway against the city's vast and complicated problems. Some frustrated reformers were slowly beginning to make changes in their focuses and methods — to secularize, organize, and professionalize their efforts.

But with the establishment of the *Tribune* and Greeley's emergence as the voice of the city's conscience, reformers of every stripe, from the teetotaler to the abolitionist, could at least and at last begin to savor the comforts of belonging to a larger community of social critics and activists. Here, finally, was an alternative to both the disturbing moralism-of-convenience as practiced by James Gordon Bennett and the equally disturbing amoralism of the *Sun*.

Greeley's "indispensable New York condition" that new things and ideas be made available, the trait that so diverted his dinner companion Ralph Waldo Emerson, ensured a measure of public recognition for all the numerous crusades of various reform groups and helped to dispel their uneasy fear, grown positively disconcerting of late, that no one was paying their work any attention. The editor's firm, public, and militant stand on the side of virtue and morality was a novel but refreshing encouragement of the reformers' endeavors and a credible certification that what they were doing was important.

Citizens of Arkansas could measure themselves against New York and feel virtuous, but New Yorkers who wished to feel virtuous themselves had a harder time. Greeley helped. For those city readers who disliked capital punishment, feared for the souls of the young, and quailed before the restive city underclass, reading Greeley's paper and admiring Greeley the man provided the secure feeling that many other people felt exactly the same way. Together they could divorce themselves from the public perception of general New York degradation and corruption and declare themselves to be a wholly different kind of New Yorker, a species hitherto nearly invisible in the press. The *Tribune's* anguished sermons against crime and moral pollution in the city served the classic function of helping its readers to mark the outer edges of their group and to reinforce their shared cultural identity. The city readers of the *Tribune*, simply by reading the *Tribune*, were celebrating themselves as a separate population, a community of the earnest, virtuous, and genteel.

They were also pronouncing themselves superior. In the wake of the weaknesses, frustrations, and failures of most the reform actions in which any of the *Tribune's* readers had been involved to date, the paper's lamentations may in fact have served as even more than an aid in identifying kindred spirits. They could also have acted as a sort of self-benediction. Anguish over declining social standards has always gripped most coldly those who would be most discommoded by social chaos, who have property or standing or face to preserve. It troubles most deeply those city dwellers who wear as a badge of honor their own hopeless ineptitude in the seamy and fraudulent arts of street survival. It is, in short, a preoccupation for the privileged.

By lamenting New York's moral laxity and the humiliating image of the city that most of the penny press projected abroad, *Tribune* readers told the world that they themselves were better than all that. In fact, acknowledging their failure to achieve reform was in its own way a celebration of their superiority to the poor souls who had never even bothered to try. Even if the city did not respond to their efforts, still the reformers could feel, consciously or unconsciously, that their very failure to change evil conditions reinforced better than anything else the difference between themselves and their inferiors. Any readers whose activism was confined entirely to lamentation would also have found comfort in lamenting along with the *Tribune*. "The exhortation to a reformation which never materializes," writes a historian of the Puritans, who understood both moral superiority and guilt as well as anybody, "serves as a token payment upon the obligation, and so liberates the debtors."[8]

THE HUMAN RACE ADVANCES

Bennett loved the Colt affair. "There is nothing like going the whole figure in a thing," he wrote on 7 May 1842 in unconcealed admiration of the prisoner's insouciant turpitude, "even in that which startles and terrifies — men who have killed their wives, and committed other such every-day matters, have been condemned, executed, and are forgotten — but it takes a deed that has some of the sublime of horror about it to attract attention, rally eloquence and energy, and set people crazy, in addition, to see the lion that perpetrated it."

This particular deed certainly rallied Bennett's own eloquence. As he had during the Jewett affair, the editor devoted column after column to examining every possible aspect of the case, issued a blizzard of extras, loudly proclaimed that his paper had the only true and complete coverage, ridiculed anything the other penny papers said, airily dismissed complaints of sensationalism, and asserted repeatedly that all of his reporting was dedicated to serving the legitimate interests of the people. This time around Bennett professed himself convinced of the prisoner's guilt, and referred to him frequently — even before his trial — as "Colt, the Homicide."

The editor soon relieved his readers of any lingering fears that the Moral War had made a mollycoddle of him; his style was as brash and lurid as ever. On 6 October 1841 he described a courtroom encounter in which the victim's widow faced Colt with "such [a look] as few ever received from mortal," and the prisoner in turn "glared upon her like Macbeth upon the ghost of Banquo."

> No mimic tragedy ever came up to that scene in real life. It was a calm, bright Sabbath evening, the sun shining in the blue heavens, and the deeply verdant foliage of the Park, was in a glow of beauty; yet in its midst was the dead house, with the mangled and decaying corpse of the murdered man, and close by the man accused of the crime in all the remorse of discovered guilt, and the widow in her pale and tearless agony! And all around, filling the atmosphere, filling the lungs alike of prisoner and witness, was the horrible effluvia of the mouldering dead. Can it be wondered that that woman is now a maniac? Warned as she was — three times, did she dream that her husband was murdered. . . . Her reason is a shattered wreck, and it is probable that she will soon lie peacefully beside her husband in the quiet grave.

She actually did no such thing. In fact, when she testified later in court, her reason was so unshattered as to prompt a complaint from Bennett on 23 January 1842 about her "cold, unfeeling, and . . . flippant manner. We are deeply sorry that such should be the case," he sniffed, "but it is a fact."

Nor was the *Herald*'s editor so chastened as to descend to false humility or simpering modesty. "We are, beyond the possibility of a doubt," he trumpeted on 7 November 1842,

> the Napoleon of the press in both hemispheres. The New York Herald is unquestionably the greatest and mightiest intellectual institution of civilized society in the present country. . . . Steam and the press, applied by skilful engineers, are attaining their legitimate position as the combined power of the age — higher than governments, sects, creeds, or

systems. In the age of the French revolution, a master spirit, capable of wielding the energies of war, was absolutely necessary — in the present age, a master spirit to wield the energies of the press, is the potent charm to call humanity back to honor, to principle, to morals, to religion and to intelligence.

Yet although the brashness of the style carried Bennett's unmistakable brand, in other respects the story could have been written by an entirely different person from the man who had caused such a hubbub in the penny press less than six years before. The Colt murder case was the most extravagant public drama to come along since Jewett was found axed in her fiery bed, but Bennett's treatment of it all but abandoned some of his most successful earlier devices.

It was no morality play, hypocritical or otherwise: whereas Bennett had previously taken great pains at least to appear morally outraged, loudly bewailing the shocking corruption rampant in the city and demanding a wholesale reform of public virtue, this time he seemed quite uninterested in justifying his reporting with any pious claims to moral superiority. It was no maverick frolic: rather than assuming the role of an independent investigator and contentiously championing the unlikely cause of the underdog in the case, Bennett led the community in calling for the accused man's blood. And it was no humbug: it featured no knotty but amusing deceits for readers to test their wits on, no faked interviews, no invented letters confessing all, no fictional forays into exotic pasts, no teasing hints of dark secrets that remained forever dark — and no choice about which version of the crime and the society to believe in. Bennett had found something that suited both himself and his audience far better than all of that. Bennett had discovered verisimilitude.

The *Herald's* reporting on the Colt case was a veritable carnival of minutiae, a massive accumulation of miscellaneous but concrete facts. Throughout the whole long affair, Bennett fed his readers thousands of evocative details that added up to a vivid and convincing picture of the proceedings. Colt's office, where the crime occurred, was "on the second story, facing Chambers street, and the second room from Broadway." The attorneys interviewed exactly three hundred and thirty-six talesmen before finally managing to settle on twelve jurors. The jury was sequestered in the Knickerbocker Hotel on Park Row. Caroline Henshaw had a straight nose, a round forehead, and "a very beautiful and small mouth with lips like a sleeping infant's in their shape."[1] Colt himself, as the *Herald* told its

PORTRAIT OF JOHN C. COLT.

The *Herald*'s woodcut portrait of John C. Colt
is clearly attempting to be true to life.
(*Courtesy of the American Antiquarian Society*)

fascinated readers on 28 September 1841, "is well made, but very slim,
although full of nerve and sinew. He is about 5 feet 9 inches high. His hair is
dark brown and curly, and he has largish whiskers. He would be good
looking but for his eye, which is one of those brown colored class of eyes
that cannot easily be read, and that are generally found in the faces of all
scoundrels, schemers and plotters."

To help his audience understand the story, Bennett even included some
large woodcut illustrations, still an expensive and time-consuming rarity
in a daily newspaper. Aided by a sketch of the building where the crime
took place, a floorplan of Colt's office, and a portrait of the prisoner that
clearly appears to have been drawn from life, even distant readers could
envision the surroundings with as much as clarity as any loafer in City
Hall Park saw them.

Sometimes Bennett's facts were rather less than concrete, but never did
his conviction waver. He floated prophecy, speculation, and ostentatious

displays of "inside knowledge" alike with the same air of cool omniscience. "What the defense in this case will be," he commented on 23 January 1842, "it is impossible to say. Some think an *alibi* will be proved; but we think that the counsel for Colt will admit the killing, and attempt to show it was manslaughter or homicide. One thing is remarkable: Adams never called out or groaned. And the lid of the box with the direction on it, (by which the carman identified Colt with that box) — *has been lost, and cannot be found anywhere.*" In this case Bennett did turn out to be correct in his prediction about counsel's plea. The box lid, however, about which Bennett was so emphatic, was never found — nor, apparently, did anyone ever care.

The eighteenth of November, the day set for Colt's execution, was perhaps the most exhaustively documented twenty-four hours of the city's history. Bennett issued edition after edition offering moment-by-moment, you-were-there commentary. The regular morning *Herald* described the preparations for Colt's hanging and quoted the latest official statements on the prisoner's appeal. An "evening edition," issued at two o'clock, contained an update on the appeal as well as a meticulous description, by a vigilant reporter stationed right at the scene, of every move in Colt's cell: he was shaved at eleven o'clock by Deaf Bill Dolsens of Centre Street, was married at noon to Henshaw, who was dressed in a "claret colored cloak trimmed with red cord," and bade the prison guards a last farewell at twelve-thirty.

"It is now one o'clock," the reporter continued in a new paragraph, "and Colt has just ordered a quart of hot coffee, which has been brought in and himself and wife are drinking it." The extra issued around four o'clock included a pathetic picture of Colt's last goodbyes to his brother and his new wife, who "sobbed convulsively as though her heart would break." It also quoted, carefully, Colt's speech of forgiveness to "one gentleman connected with the press," who he knew had "a good heart."

Finally came the thrilling climax, and the omniscient *Herald* man was still right there on the scene. "We had written the above at a ¼ to 3 P.M. this afternoon," the nameless journalist reported.

At that time Colt was alive. No one entered his cell till precisely 5 minutes to four o'clock, at which time Sheriff Hart and Westervelt dressed in uniform with Dr. Anthon [the clergyman], proceeded to the cell, on the keeper opening the door, Dr. Anthon who was first, drew back, threw up his hands and eyes to Heaven, and uttering a faint ejaculation, turned pale as death, and retired.

"As I thought," said the keeper. "As I thought," said we. And going into the cell, there lay Colt on his back stretched out at full length on the bed, quite dead, but not cold. A clasp knife, like a small dirk knife, with a broken handle, was sticking in his heart.

The enterprising reporter then stepped up close enough to feel Colt's temples, and with a physicianly detachment he examined the bloody wound in the chest. The prisoner, he reported, "had evidently worked and turned the knife round and round in his heart after he had stabbed himself, until he made quite a large gash."

Bennett's choice of hero for his new kind of story was also novel. During the Jewett affair the editor had concentrated mostly on the fabulous lives of the prostitute and her high-living lover. In the Colt episode, his reports featured a character much more real to readers — and dearer and more important, too. His hero was the *Herald's* readership itself, the dense, tumultuous, excited New York crowd that gawked at the proceedings from beginning to end.

The crowd rampaged through almost every issue of the *Herald.* It milled around the dead house, blocked the streets around the courthouse, spread wild rumors about the jury's deliberations, tried to burst into court on the day after the trial ended "under a vague and confused notion that Colt would be present," and made bets under the gallows about whether he would actually be hanged. Two weeks after the event, the crowd was still a palpable phantom, a departed acquaintance too fascinating to forget. On 30 November 1842, Bennett presented a reprise of the crowd's role in "The Extraordinary Scenes Connected with [Colt's] Last Hours and Death." It dripped with nostalgia for the exciting times just past.

> In Colt's cell all seemed still as death! Three o'clock came — the suspense was terrible — half past three — the excitement was of a frenzied character — quarter to four, and the mob seemed about to break into the jail — the sheriffs put on their death livery — five minutes to four — the time's up — bring him out — now he's coming — where's the cap and rope? — the cell door is slowly unfastened and opened — in stepped the parson, and, merciful Providence, what a sight met his glazed vision — there lay Colt, stretched out on his back on his cot, weltering in his blood — warm, but dead! . . . The excitement resembled madness.

Bennett's embrace of fact was obviously not entirely new either for himself or for his readers. He had always declared himself dedicated to truth and accuracy; during the Jewett affair six years earlier, the *Herald* had been spiced with piquant details, ostensibly derived from the editor's own investigations and observations, about Helen Jewett's possessions, her life, her letters, her marblelike bust. The great difference this time was that he actually did what he had always professed to do. He and his reporters actually did base their descriptions on investigation and observation rather than imagination and popular tradition.

As new as the role of fact collector was for Bennett, it was no less crucial or public spirited than his old ones. Or so the editor argued, loudly and often. Nor was his self-defense any less necessary now. Complaints from defendants, lawyers, and other citizens that the press in general, and the *Herald* in particular, were meddling in the course of justice had by now become as inevitable and futile an accompaniment to notorious trials as Dr. Brandreth's pills were to gout or dropsy. Retorts from editors that they were actually serving the public interest were no less inevitable but — supported by the public's special interest in murder — much more effective.

During the Colt case, however, Bennett took the idea of an editor's civic duty further than it had ever gone before. It became the animating spirit behind the *Herald*, the rationale for all his reporting and the excuse for all his excesses. It was based on a single premise: no fact was a bad fact. Just as no scenic detail in the drama, from the color of the bride's cloak to the doomed man's taste for coffee, was too small to merit attention, so no secret about victim or defendant was too lurid or sensitive to keep from his deserving public. Bennett constantly reassured his readers that they were entitled to know every last fact and conjecture connected with the case, and that only he could provide them.

As always, it could be a harrowing duty. On 22 November, after Colt's suicide, the editor avowed his reluctance to add to the "misery" of the murderer's bereaved family with further reporting. "With his surviving and highly respectable relatives," Bennett noted, "we can profoundly sympathize." Yet as a public servant he could not allow himself to be swayed by pity. "But this is not all. We have a sacred duty to perform to the public, that is paramount to all other considerations. . . . If hereafter a Sheriff intends to allow a desperate criminal, under sentence of death, to have every facility for obtaining knives, scissors, poison, &c. for committing self-murder . . . why the sooner the public are aware of it, the better for all parties."

In the same issue, Bennett also published Dr. Anthon's description of his last meeting with Colt. The clergyman reported that he had urged Colt to bury his bitterness against the penny editors; "they probably meant well," Dr. Anthon said, "even if they had wounded his feelings." Yet even so temperate a reproach nettled Bennett. In his own commentary on Anthon's remarks, the editor passed from carefully modulated compassion to out-and-out belligerence in his ardent defense of an editor's duty. "Every criminal makes it a point to rail against the press," he wrote bitterly.

> They are all victims of the press. When the fact is, that the press simply narrates facts, as in Colt's case, and leaves the public to judge till the trial is over. . . . one of the great errors committed by his counsel, Dudley Selden . . . [was that] instead of confining himself to the best means of defending his client, he launched forth invectives against the press, and wanted the Judge to commit some one or more for contempt. Contempt of what? Why, simply of telling the truth. Out upon such trifling with a court of justice and the rights of a client. Every whipper-snapper two-penny lawyer now-a-days, thinks he is accomplishing a great feat if he can have a fling at the press. And it, therefore, astonishes us to see a man like Dr. Anthon following in the wake of such persons.

Bennett continued to maintain that a newspaper ought to hold all public officials accountable and responsible for their actions. After the prisoner's suicide, on 19 November, he reported confidently that "the public will demand a full investigation of the circumstances through which such a catastrophe was permitted. . . . We have every reason to believe that Governor Seward will order an investigation into the facts." He himself suggested by name one particular candidate for that investigation. "How came Colt to ask for religious consolation from a clergyman, and yet to commit suicide? The prayers said over him by the Rev. Mr. Anthon, seem to have had little influence on his mind."

Demanding an inquiry into the inefficiency of a clergyman's prayers is hardly the mission one would expect a hard-hitting investigative journalist to embrace. The call for a "full investigation" was more likely Bennett's excuse for indulging in two of his favorite pastimes: pointing fingers and naming names. Obviously the hapless Anthon was paying for having riled Bennett in some way or other. Or perhaps the notoriously irreligious editor found the clergyman's profession provocation enough.

Bennett found other uses for the rhetoric of public duty. On 20 January, the first full day of trial testimony, he published an afternoon extra containing a grotesque three-column woodcut of a naked, battered, huddled body that represented, according to the caption, "Samuel Adams, the Printer, Before He Was Cut Up and Salted." Colt's enraged counsel demanded Bennett's immediate arrest for contempt of court. Judge Kent, however, while deploring "the contagion of public manners" by this sort of publication, refused to apply the contempt statutes to a newspaper editor. The law was clear: "contempt" applied only to the actual physical disruption of judicial proceedings within the courtroom.[2]

Bennett professed himself delighted by this official sanction, however lukewarm. It tended, he said on 22 January, to unite "the administration of the press, and the administration of the laws . . . in the same great progressive advancement of the human race." Indeed, the editor's disputed report was certifiably memorable to some members of the human race. More than forty years after the murder, New York's chief of police recollected some of the malefactors who had first turned his interest to crime. Among them was Colt, who, "after braining Adams with a hatchet," then "cut up the body and salted it down in a box." Still later, at century's end, a venerable citizen recalled in his memoirs the discovery aboard ship of a box containing "detached portions of a human body. . . . It had been dismembered, salted, boxed, addressed, and shipped to a fictitious address in St. Louis *via* New Orleans."[3]

Yet that famous description of Bennett's was also certifiably and grotesquely exaggerated. The printer's body had indeed been rudely handled, and throughout the trial the attorneys had argued vigorously but inconclusively over whether the white powder, variously described as either salt or chloride of lime, had been sprinkled on the body by Colt before he nailed up the crate or by the officials in the ship's cargo hold when they opened the box on the noisome, week-old corpse. But the printer's body had never been either cut up or dismembered. It is difficult to discern a contribution to the progressive advancement of the human race in an overwrought assertion that the murdered printer had been butchered into bacon.

Despite such monstrosities, or perhaps because of them, Bennett's message about the sacredness of fact was getting through to his readers. "Editor on public duty," the wishful title he had once bestowed on himself because no one else would, was becoming his by acclamation. In fact, the penny press's insistence on its role as the fount of information and the

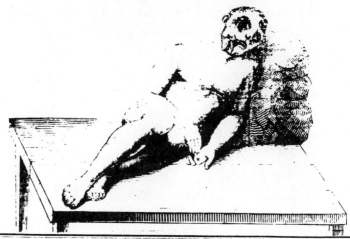

Samuel Adams, the printer, was never cut up and salted.
(*Courtesy of the Library of Congress*)

defender of liberty was beginning to earn the supreme public ratification: its opponents' satire.

This satire arose chiefly from a predictable quarter, the city gentry — those well-to-do, sophisticated, and cosmopolitan gentlefolk who were embarrassed by the crassness of hustling New York and its deficiency in the gentler pursuits of literature and art. Some of them had dedicated themselves to forging a distinctive national literature, preferably something urbane and witty. They were quick to realize that Bennett was clearly a distinctive and recognizable national possession. He was also, as they made plain, a vulgar and ludicrous one, the sort of creature who gave New York its bad name — the sort who richly deserved a slash of their rapier wit.

In 1839, the sharp-tongued *Knickerbocker* writer Charles Frederick Briggs — best remembered now for having inspired Herman Melville on the metaphysical nature of chowder — found room for a Bennett lampoon in his picaresque *Adventures of Harry Franco*. The young hero, a bewildered country innocent engulfed in misunderstandings and brawls the moment he arrived in the city, at one point made a naive mistake in a hotel dining room and was dragged off into another room to settle the matter. "Somebody on the outside knocked and kicked very hard against the door," the hero went on, "and demanded entrance on the score of his being one of the gentlemen of the press. But the man who was guarding the door refused to move, and the gentleman of the press on the outside gave another savage kick, and swore that the public should be informed of the outrage it had suffered, in the disrespect shown to his person."

The next morning Franco was distressed to find in that gentleman's paper a scurrilous and utterly fantastic story about the "late disgraceful outrage at the City Hotel." The gentleman of the press himself reported that he had gone to great pains to get the particulars, "feeling the full weight of the responsibility which rests upon our shoulders, as public journalists, to furnish our subscribers, — who, we are proud to say, are daily increasing, having added more than two thousand to our lists within the last week, which we happen to know, is more than the entire subscription of any of our cotemporaries [*sic*], — with the latest and most correct information."

Franco, the poor, green country boy who had "always believed implicitly every thing which I saw in print," was distraught over the newspaper's abusive portrait of him. "I could hardly persuade myself that I had not been guilty of the outrage of which I saw myself accused," he mourned. "I felt all the shame, at least, of a real culprit." But he was comforted by a wiser and more experienced New Yorker.

"Don't be alarmed, young man," he said, "abuse and misrepresentation are the unavoidable penalties of newspaper notoriety. . . . Dont [*sic*] care a fig about them; there's not a bit of danger; nobody cares any thing about a newspaper, for although there is nothing which men read more eagerly, there is nothing which they heed so little, not even their Bibles. However, to make all sure, I will take it upon myself to see the Editor, who is a personal, as well as a political friend of mine, and to-morrow you shall see that he will contradict every word he has said to-day in relation to you."[4]

In June 1841 another sophisticated gentleman took a fling at Bennett. Cornelius Mathews, New York's most inexhaustible — and intolerable — evangelist of literary nationalism, in that month began publishing *The Career of Puffer Hopkins* in serial form in the short-lived "Young American" magazine *Arcturus*. The work was a labored political farce spliced to an ersatz Dickensian tale of yet another young innocent learning his way around the great mysterious city; in Perry Miller's judgment, "it was and is unreadable."[5] Yet even though Mathews confused an accumulation of local color with the display of native genius, still some of the local color he heaped up is useful for insights into the New York of the 1840s. The hero, Puffer, was aided in his task of interpreting the city by a majestically omniscient guru called Halsey Fishblatt, who at one point discoursed on the importance of the cheap press.

Give us plenty of newspapers! . . . The press, sir, the press is the palladium of liberty, and the more palladiums we have the freer we are — of course. See here, sir, here's a big palladium and here's a little pal-ladium. . . . This people can never be free, Mr. Hopkins, thoroughly and entirely free, till every man in the country edits a newspaper of his own . . . in which he's at liberty to speak of every other man as he chooses. The more we know each other, the better we'll like each other — so let us have all the private affairs, the business transactions and domes-tic doings of every man in the United States, set forth in a small paper, in a good pungent style, and then we may begin to talk of the advancement of the human race. That's what I call the cheap diffusion of knowledge; a penny-worth of scandal on every man's breakfast table, before he goes to business.[6]

The urbane humorists who turned their rapiers against Bennett were obviously hoping to demolish the nasty creature. Yet although their slashes doubtless earned the gentle applause of their small circles of like-minded associates, they actually drew little blood. Bennett and his *Herald* were fully as gritty, vulgar, and hustling as the satirists painted them. They were also apt reflections and keen observers of the city they inhabited. The thousands of New Yorkers who preferred the urban to the urbane did not need to *read* about a Halsey Fishblatt. They had a majestically omniscient guru of their own in the flesh.

16

THE NEW, IMPROVED *HERALD*— MISSES A STORY

If we compare the Jewett affair of 1836 with the Colt case of 1841 for clues as to why James Gordon Bennett treated the second murder so much more straightforwardly, we are immediately tempted by a straightforward explanation: the nature of the murder itself. Perhaps Bennett reported the Colt affair as fact because he could not make it work as a humbug. Perhaps he felt the story simply could not inspire and support the sumptuous scaffolding of illusion and allusion that had grown so naturally about the Jewett episode. "Ruined girl dead for love" conformed to a formula and accommodated formulaic explanations. "Tradesman bludgeoned for a picayune debt" was harder to manipulate.

Indeed, the facts of the Colt affair displayed none of the theatricality, the panache, the poetic potential of the prostitute's murder; it was petty and sordid, a crime more of petulance than of passion, with overtones of penury rather than of privilege. The chief players in the Colt drama were, by and large, humdrum characters. The suspect in the case had influential friends but no claque of like-minded supporters to whoop and cheer him in court. As the undistinguished teacher of an unlovely art, he never garnered much public interest, and his hard sullenness while on trial invited no sympathy. Nor were his attorneys either brilliant or provocative; their personal lives were unremarkable, their political and professional histories commonplace.

The murder victim, too, was no exotic being charged with myth and meaning, but rather an ordinary tradesman; character witnesses at the trial painted him as soft of voice, permissive toward his apprentices, and so mild-mannered that sharp words from a clergyman once drove him to tears. The scene of the crime was no elegant, fascinating haunt of the demimonde; Adams was killed in the Granite Building across from City Hall, a large office block inhabited largely by picture framers, bookkeepers, and scribes.

Nor did the Colt case seem to address with the same urgency pregnant issues of deep community concern. The raw class passions and moral questions that had stirred and confused the earlier affair were muted here. It is true that John Colt was a professional and his victim at least nominally an artisan. The master printer Adams, however, a respectable married man who habitually sported a gold watch on a chain, was paying off a mortgage on his own shop, and he employed a full complement of workers including a foreman and a number of boys. The philandering Colt, on the other hand, sublet half an office and was behind in his rent.[1] The killer and the victim between them present ample evidence of just how elastic and ambiguous the boundaries of the antebellum middle class actually were.

In the 1840s, furthermore, in the aftermath of the business panic of 1837, the social and economic atmosphere of the city had changed radically. Labor activism and agitation had come to a virtual standstill as most laborers concentrated their energies on scrambling for a living. Not even the *Sun* was prepared to carry the torch for artisanal power: very late, very mild, and very diffident was the only critique of the entire affair mounted by the apolitical new Beach regime. Up until the last month before Colt's death, the *Sun* seemed perfectly satisfied with the official handling of the case; on 27 September 1841 it had gone so far as to record its approval of the "indefatigable exertions" of the police officials in "placing [Colt] in a position to receive his deserts, as well as to satisfy the demands of the law, which has been violated by this terrible deed of blood and death."

The case was, to be sure, enlivened by a hint of illicit sex: the lovenest shared by John Colt and Caroline Henshaw was located at 42 Thomas Street — on the very block where Robinson sported and Jewett died. Yet no amount of embroidery could have lofted the surly bookkeeper, the death-bed bride who was "no prostitute except as regarded [Colt]," and their cheap third-floor furnished room into a tale as titillating as Rosina Townsend and her establishment had provided. Nor was there any mystery to the affair. Colt killed Adams, and no one could doubt it. When the wretched prisoner himself declined to argue for his own innocence and publicly confessed his guilt early on, what more remained to be said?

The simplicity of this explanation — that exotic stories require exotic treatment, straightforward affairs straightforward coverage — is beguiling. Yet if we were to succumb to this reasoning and examine the case no further, we would merely be repeating a favorite historical mistake: the uncritical acceptance of everything the penny papers said. The complexity of the penny-press organism demands that we consider another, more intricate explanation. Perhaps the Colt affair appears so simple to the modern reader, not because it *was* simple, but because the newspapers decided, for whatever reason, to smooth and streamline a complex story to *make* it simple. Perhaps we are humbugging ourselves if we believe that the story was too ordinary and too straightforward to have supported a humbug. Perhaps we are wrong to assume that the penny press got the story right at all.

A further examination of the circumstances surrounding the crime suggests that Bennett's choice was neither foreordained nor inevitable. The raw material of the affair that was known to the public was not actually as barren as it appears to us now in print. There was plenty of opportunity for an editor to challenge readers' loyalties, address social and political undercurrents, or create a humbug that supported an alternative reality — if he had chosen to try. There was even one crucial, hidden fact that could have completely changed public understanding of the truth of the case — if anyone had bothered to discover it.

The political climate alone offered an opportunity for creating a public controversy. The Colt case broke as New York was still attempting to recover from a particularly ferocious mayoral campaign rife with charges and countercharges of partisan corruption. In late 1840 Governor Seward and his fellow Whigs had accused city recorder Robert Hunter Morris of illegally entering a private house and stealing personal papers. Morris, a Democrat, countered that he was justified in seizing the papers because they contained evidence of Whig electoral fraud. Seward fired Morris, whereupon the Democrats promptly nominated their martyr to run in the spring election for mayor. Horace Greeley launched his new Whig *Tribune* just in time to campaign hard against Morris; in his first issue of 10 April 1841 he slashed at the candidate's "criminal intent — a deliberate and daringly pursued purpose of prostituting the forms and powers of judicial investigation, to subserve the groveling ends of Party." Morris won anyway.[2]

The Adams murder posed an immediate challenge for the new mayor. Winning Colt's conviction was obviously important to him, and not just to prove himself a champion of law and order. The chief defense attorney, Dudley Selden, was a Whig, and the Colt family — sprung from old New England stock, friendly with the Reverend Anthon and Lewis Gaylord Clark — probably was, too. Also lurking in Morris's mind was doubtless the painful memory of his own loss of the state's case against Richard Robinson in 1836.

Morris dramatically underlined his concern by accompanying the three police officers sent to arrest Colt, and he appeared at the trial to testify about what he saw at the scene. The conviction in January 1842 may indeed have helped him politically, since three months later he won his second one-year term. Morris's personal popularity, however, could not prevent a generally frustrated electorate from sweeping a Whig majority to power on the Board of Aldermen, ushering in a painfully divided administration that presided throughout the long and arduous appeals process.[3]

Yet this seething undercurrent of political hostility and grudge never boiled over into the reporting on the trial. No paper ever charged political manipulation; no hint ever arose of partisan protest, attack, barb, smear, or whine. Whig and Democratic editors alike joined in condemning the criminal and celebrating the prosecution's victory.

Some New Yorkers did think differently. Notwithstanding the virtual unanimity of the newspapers' coverage, some dissent did register in other quarters. And notwithstanding the penny press's rejection of the humbug option, some New Yorkers did mount humbugs in other media. One of these was tentative and stemmed in part from habit; another was deadly serious and was spawned from desperation.

The first humbug was launched in pamphlet form by the sire of the genre, the *Sun*, and reflected concerns both philosophical and financial. Throughout most of the case, the *Sun* had agreed with the conduct of the investigation and trial. The murder had been "certainly one of the most cold-blooded and atrocious ever perpetrated," the paper reported on 31 January 1842, after the verdict of murder was announced, and confessed itself "at a loss to conceive" how anyone could possibly have argued for manslaughter. "The community now feel relieved upon finding that no such injustice has been done. . . . Had the result been different, the moral atmosphere would have seemed tainted."

In the last week or so before the date set for the execution, however, the *Sun* began to express some doubts. The "very general and growing repugnance to capital punishment," as well as some recent reports by medical professionals arguing that Adams might indeed have fought back, argued for delay, deliberation, and perhaps even a new trial, the paper commented on 18 November. Yet the protest was temperate, the argument passionless, and the *Sun* also took pains to state that the governor's refusal to grant clemency was strictly legal and strictly correct.

Although the paper's change of heart may well have reflected the prickings of conscience, it also conferred a clear economic benefit. The new argument made good copy — much too good to be squeezed into the overstuffed columns of the daily *Sun*, which still sold for only a penny even though both the *Herald* and the *Tribune* went for double that price. For a ripe story like Colt's, nothing would suffice but a special sixteen-page EXTRA SUN!!! pamphlet, bargain-priced at six cents a copy. In fact, since the basic text was continually updated — at various times incorporating fresh trial news, the latest on the appeal process, a description of the suicide, and the inquest report — the six-cent pamphlet could be sold over and over again.

The story it told was highly romanticized. Leaving unmentioned every one of the more awkward details of Colt's history — including his gambling career, his octoroon mistress, his propensity to sneak thievery, and his sorry record with the United States Marines — the pamphlet emphasized the pathos of the accused man's life. Poor little John, it said, had suffered a grim childhood under a harsh father and a cruel stepmother who had hounded his fragile sister to an early grave.

The pamphlet's version of John's childhood did contain a grain of truth. John's stepmother had indeed been unable to handle her husband's children and eventually farmed most of them out to other relatives. She was no ghoul from the pages of Grimm, however — merely a woman faced with the challenge of winning over a houseful of resentful stepchildren grieving for a mother who had, by all accounts, pampered and indulged them.[4]

Yet for all its pathos, the pamphlet seemed intended more to comfort Colt's mourners than to protest an injustice. The two centerpieces of the booklet were among the time-honored staples of the crime-pamphlet genre: a selection from letters supposedly written by Colt from his cell and a "last conversation," in both of which he expressed himself prepared for his fate. "Death hath no terrors for me," the prisoner allegedly wrote after the sentence of death was passed. "There is a world above this, and I believe a just one. Man, at the worst, can only destroy the body." The conversation and letters seem another humbug, homage to the long and comfortable tradition of the criminal's deathbed repentance — and, perhaps, solace to any purchaser who shared the "growing repugnance" to capital punishment.

A second humbug also came out in pamphlet form, but this version was not squeezed out of the press; it was for the most part barred from it. It was, like Bennett's embrace of Robinson's cause in the earlier case, an alternative position. The prisoner's attorneys realized they could never make a convincing argument for his innocence. Yet in one last attempt to save him from the gallows they encouraged and nursed a groundswell of support from people who believed that Colt had acted in self-defense and thus should pay only a milder penalty for manslaughter.

This support was in fact considerable enough to trouble Governor Seward himself. On the day before the scheduled hanging, the beleaguered governor wrote to his wife:

> It will never be known, and cannot be conceived, how much I have heard, read, thought, and felt, on that painful subject. . . . When the judges refused [Colt] a new trial, his friends came with Willis Hall and delivered me several letters. . . . Then Judge Spencer came into town, and called to inform me that Colt was unjustly condemned. . . . The next day Robert Emmet, David Graham, Willis Hall, and Samuel Stevens, appeared with witnesses newly discovered. . . . On Monday I listened to

appeals from wandering philanthropists without knowledge; and with especial attention to a phrenological professor who demonstrated that Colt was a murderer, but he was so because society had cultivated the wrong bumps; and therefore society ought to be hanged, not he![5]

As troublesome as this opposition was to Governor Seward, however, it apparently burdened the newspaper press not at all. Despite both the scent of money and the stirrings of popular support, the press and its readers — with the exception of the *Sun's* gentle, last-inning demur — were virtually united in condemnation of Colt. Nothing the prisoner's friends could do seemed to shake the general conviction that he had committed cold-blooded murder.

Soon after his arrest, in late October, Colt's friends had sent his confession statement directly to the *New York Express* in the hope of making his case for self-defense. The statement was copied in many other papers, including the *Herald*, but most were noncommittal at best, if not downright skeptical. Even the *Express*, a staunchly Whig and business-oriented paper that Colt's supporters had hoped would be sympathetic to a man from a family both commercial and Whig, would say only that without the presence of witnesses, no one but Colt and God would ever know the truth.

After the failure of this venture in spin control, the prisoner's friends apparently decided to circumvent the newspapers entirely in order to get their message out. Their cheap pamphlet recounted what they called the "authentic" version of Colt's life and letters from prison. Not surprisingly, it emphasized the prisoner's "gentleness," his "amiableness," and his frequent "deeds of liberality and benevolence." His character as a child had been "joyous, active, benevolent and confiding," but "by a fatal mistake . . . of those intrusted with the management of his early years," it had not been turned "to proper account." This version, too, gave Colt an evil stepmother and supplied him with several extra sisters who also encountered tragic deaths. This version, too, was silent about the awkward details of Colt's misdeeds as a young adult. Yet this pamphlet was much more pointed and argumentative than the *Sun's*, and even though it claimed to be making an impartial investigation of the case, its advocacy was clear.

The anonymous pamphleteer, who said he had visited Colt accompanied by two of the prisoner's friends, claimed to be a neutral observer searching only for truth. "Those who reflect and wish well to their fellow creatures," he commented, "will not censure this attempt to exhibit a career fairly." He had, the putative visitor continued, formed an "impression," based on careful observation of the prisoner, "that there must be something in the man's character, and in the event for which he is condemned, not yet understood. . . . I desired to judge of him with my own eyes and mind." Yet this impartial observer was lucky enough during the visit to hear Colt cry out: "The newspapers! *they* are the true mischief-breeders; *they* are the really unprincipled and remorseless murderers!"[6]

Nothing in the nature of the Colt case itself, therefore, made it resistant to treatment as a humbug. If Bennett had truly been looking for a maverick and attention-grabbing stance, he could have joined forces with Colt's friends. If he were really interested in challenging his readers with another humbug, he could have anticipated the *Sun* by moving faster and earlier to propagate the latest incarnation of an old favorite, the crafted biography. If he had seen profit in promoting Colt's cause, he would have known from his experience with Robinson's unlikely case how to camouflage the holes in his story with a righteous belligerence. So practiced a fantasist as the *Herald*'s editor could easily have turned "Tradesman bludgeoned for a picayune debt" into something on the order of "Poor friendless youth abused and falsely accused." That particular classic formula, in fact, was certainly working well enough for Charles Dickens, who right in the midst of the excitement over Colt's case had followed poor friendless Oliver Twist, poor abused Little Nell, and poor falsely accused Barnaby Rudge to America's shores, there to meet with an idolatry nearly hysterical.

Bennett's rejection of so hospitable an invitation to the humbug is irrefutable evidence that something — or more likely some things — had changed between 1836 and 1841 to make circumstantial fact a more rewarding specialty for the *Herald*.

Obviously, we cannot ignore the possibility of simple evolution. Perhaps Bennett was growing more skilled at fulfilling the requirements as well as the forms of journalistic inquiry as they are generally accepted now. Clearly, he had always understood that a newspaper *ought* to sound credible, sincere, and authoritative. We need only recall his creative insistence during the Jewett affair that Judge Weston's letter corroborated his own story, an insistence apparently based on his belief that his story *deserved* corroboration. In 1841, furthermore, Bennett would have found facts much easier to gather. He had managed to bully, cajole, charm, and threaten his way to an assured entrée virtually anywhere in the city, even the exclusive private balls of the wealthy, and with a stable of reporters like the invaluable Attree at hand to go out and find the facts, Bennett would have been less tempted to invent them.

Yet although a larger staff and improved access around the city doubtless had some effect on the *Herald's* development, they fall short of an adequate explanation. To argue that Bennett grew better at the generally accepted skills of journalism still begs the questions of why those particular skills were accepted instead of others, and why people had been so demonstrably content with so "inferior" a version of those skills in 1836.

Like any dealer in anything from words to red flannel to mutton, Bennett prospered at every stage only by managing to satisfy the needs of the *two* parties that counted: not just himself but also his public. Yet as we have seen, the public he wanted was being wooed simultaneously by scores of other dealers in print, in fields ranging from fiction and romance to political activism, from how-to-do-it articles and science to religion and even filth. Bennett made a logical choice to leave those genres more and more to others and to concentrate instead on what a newspaper did best and what a readership hungry for direction and distinction needed most: the immediate publication of information about daily life. Even that choice, however, was not without contest and risk. Horace Greeley had just announced his candidacy to win the "active and substantial middle class," exactly the newspaper readership Bennett had marked out for himself. Bennett, pressed and squeezed on yet another front, had to distinguish himself from that dangerous new rival, too.

The *Tribune* did not steal away the *Herald's* audience forthwith. As we have seen, the active and substantial middle class received the eccentric Greeley with decidedly mixed feelings; his oddball enthusiasms struck many as too radical, too extreme, while his deep-seated traditional Whiggishness bothered many others. Viewed alone, the city circulation figures of the *Tribune* should have been a comfort rather than a threat to any of Greeley's rivals. Yet Horace Greeley was succeeding, instantly and resoundingly, in two crucial middle-class arenas. To out-of-town readers and to readers interested in moralism and reform, Greeley was becoming a god. In those two areas in particular, Bennett was only too human.

In the case of his old favorite claim of moral divinity, the answer for Bennett was easy. He recanted. Even though the Moral War had not required him actually to improve his morals — even though it had ended by freeing him to behave almost as badly as ever — still he had delightedly taken the occasion to trumpet his purity. Now, however, even Bennett could see that Greeley was usurping the role of moral standard-bearer — and doing it much more convincingly. *His* moralism was sincere and pervasive, *his* readers genuinely distressed by injustice and sin. In the face of the *Tribune's* earnest crusades against capital punishment, abortion, tobacco, city squalor, strong drink, and the spread of slavery, not even Bennett could maintain the fiction of his own superior devotion to virtue.

Suddenly, therefore, moralism was admirable no longer in the columns of the *Herald.* Suddenly a concern with upright behavior was exactly the sort of contemptible aberration to be expected of that milquetoast Greeley. Bennett staked out his position at the very outset of Greeley's venture. When the week-old *Tribune* blasted Bennett for his unholy glee in reporting every detail of the shovel-murder of the banker, Bennett responded in kind the following day. "HORACE GREELY [*sic*] is endeavoring, with tears in his eyes, to show that it is very naughty to publish reports of the trial, confession and execution of Peter Robinson. . . . No doubt he thinks it equally naughty in us to publish a paper at all; and if we would stop the Herald, he might condescend to thank us. 'A marvellously proper man!'

"Now this Horace Greeley, BA and ASS, is probably the most unmitigated blockhead connected with the newspaper press. Galvanize a large New England squash, and it would make as capable an editor as Horace."

With provincial readers, on the other hand, the *Herald* editor's problem was more acute. By 1841 Bennett had progressed from declaring he did not want them at all to needing them very badly. Although he had earned his first fame by ridiculing anyone who lived outside his "dear, delightful, enchanting New York," the improvements in technology that were opening more and more of the country to penetration by the penny press soon made clear to Bennett the narrowness of his vision.

As early as the fall of 1836 he had started a weekly edition of the *Herald,* a compilation from the dailies designed for distribution beyond the reach of the city edition. It was very nearly a dud. The weekly *Herald* did arouse some interest, and Bennett boasted constantly of its success. But the Moral War provided convincing proof of the weekly's weakness. Although the daily *Herald's* local circulation remained more or less secure in the city even under pressure, nearly seven thousand of the nineteen thousand country buyers — more than a third — obediently deserted the weekly edition. Non–New Yorkers obviously felt so much less intimately served by the *Herald* that they gave it up without fuss even when their persuasion came from a distance, from strangers, and without surveillance. Greeley's success soon thereafter in serving country readers so well could only have exacerbated Bennett's problem.

So, too, did the tradition of the journalistic humbug. That posed a serious dilemma for the editor of the *Herald.*

The difficulty with the penny-press humbug was mainly a practical matter. Such humbugs worked only when a compact and cohesive group of readers shared the recognition that facts in a newspaper were elastic things, entertaining toys to be manipulated by knowing players. That presented no problem in 1836, when the limits to technology ensured that most of the New York papers stayed right at home in the New York community. As improvements in production and transportation helped to swell the circulation of the city papers, however, their facts lost their elasticity as inevitably as an old garter taxed by a thickening thigh. The perplexity, disgust, and disapproval of the occasional reader in outposts such as Indiana or Arkansas, insignificant to the circulation of 1836, became a matter of grave importance to editors of the 1840s, who wanted the broadest possible reception.

The penny press was clearly traveling far, clearly becoming a regular source for editors across the country and even a familiar companion to those rural and small-town Americans whose reading used to be confined to the local paper alone. The stiff-necked and defensive *Arkansas Gazette* had never been shy about unearthing and reporting New York crime in its ongoing campaign to prove that the city was even more hideous than the frontier. But even the *Vincennes Western Sun* of Indiana, which five years earlier had struggled hard to get news from Texas and had barely noticed happenings farther east, referred to the 1841 Colt case in terms so casual and offhand as to suggest that its readers were receiving regular, timely, and complete news stories about it from other sources. "Colt, the murderer of Adams," read one report in its entirety on 12 February 1842, "has been found guilty of murder in the first degree." Down in the Shenandoah Valley, the *Virginia Free Press* actually specified its other source. Its tiny excerpt of 24 November 1842 on the *"Preparations for His Execution — Marriage — Suicide"* came directly from Bennett's *Herald* itself.

The evidence must have been suggestive to Bennett. Horace Greeley was not perpetrating humbugs, and his *Tribune* was succeeding wildly among out-of-town readers. Beach of the *Sun* was, and although Beach's city circulation was huge and ever increasing, his paper was virtually unknown outside New York; the weekly *Sun* he dutifully produced made only minuscule inroads into the country. Because the *Sun* was definitively a working-class paper, moreover, Beach's continued embrace of the humbug may also have begun to taint it with the odor of class: anything the *Sun* liked was probably too "common," too egalitarian, for separatist middle-class readers.

Still, choosing between the humbug and the country readership must not have been easy for Bennett. Giving up his license to manipulate a story for the particular pleasure of a select audience was a gamble, and it raised again the very risk that Bennett was already working so hard to elude. Virtually every other newspaper in the city was also branding Colt a cold-blooded murderer. By declining to invent a contentious stand or to champion a crafted cause, Bennett fell again into the serious danger of merely blending in with the crowd — a fate the proud and ambitious editor had always considered worse than death. Clearly Bennett, by joining the rest of the press, was giving up his trademark renegade status. Clearly he would not have done so had he not gained an equally distinctive new status in return.

Thus obsessed with the drive for a huge circulation, buffeted by competition from a myriad of other peddlers of print, striving to make himself unique and conventional at the same time, the *Herald* editor responded to these various pressures and dilemmas by gradually substituting authenticity for humbug. Yet his embrace of authenticity did much more than merely feed his subscribers interesting tidbits about the shape of the prisoner's lover's mouth. The transformation had far-reaching consequences for his readership as well as for his circulation.

It had even more far-reaching consequences for John Colt. In an ironic twist, at the same time the *Herald* decided to devote itself to fact, it entirely overlooked one crucial fact, one simple but entirely transforming piece of the puzzle.

John Colt did have blood on his hands. He did try to cover up a crime. But he also had real competition from another Colt for the label of cad. Although no one in New York seemed to know it, the murderer's notorious liaison with Caroline Henshaw was actually a deed of rare generosity and their deathbed marriage both bigamous and semi-incestuous. For Caroline was the abandoned wife of Samuel Colt.

The inventor had met and married the very young and unschooled Caroline some years earlier in Europe. Soon, however, he decided that so humble a bride was no worthy partner for him. He brought her back to America with him but never acknowledged her as his wife, and finally, out of either pity or duty, the rakehell John took the pregnant Caroline in. The child she bore just before the trial, to such universal scorn, was Samuel's legitimate son. Her marriage to her own condemned brother-in-law on the day of his death had been arranged by her legal husband in an attempt to legitimize her and extricate himself.

Samuel then made sure he remained extricated by arranging for Caroline to disappear immediately after the suicide. He rechristened her Julia Leicester, packed her off with their infant son to her native Germany, and supported them there on condition that they pass as his niece and nephew. The appealing young Miss Leicester eventually eloped with a Prussian officer of noble family despite determined opposition by the young man's suspicious father. With good reason, the old baron was demanding to know why, "if Colonel Colt loved Julia as a ward, or if she was worth loving and caring for," the rich American inventor had nonetheless left her to make her way alone overseas. Even after the stern father disinherited the couple, Samuel refused his "niece's" desperate pleas to come back home.

Samuel himself went on to make — and acknowledge — a much more brilliant marriage and lived another twenty years after his brother's death. The first inkling the inventor's widow had of her husband's shady past apparently came when the "bastard orphan," grown to manhood, turned up to request his patrimony.[7]

The best that can be said about Samuel's disposal of Caroline is that it may not have been *technically* criminal. John, however, was plainly dealt a bad hand. It is clear that the deeply prejudicial reports that circulated about his cold, heartless callousness and the scandalous irregularity of his domestic relationship were entirely based on a gross misunderstanding of his private affairs.

The truth *could* have come out at the time. Intriguing evidence survives of inklings, half-truths, hunches, and shots in the dark about the secret marriage. George Templeton Strong privately recorded a tidbit from his friend George Anthon, who had heard it from his father the clergyman, who in turn had gotten it from someone whose name Strong later crossed out in his diary. This anonymous tipster said John had been under pressure to "spare his family," but in his version it was the suicide, not the bigamy, that was supposed to redeem the honor of the Colts.[8] On the day after the suicide, Bennett reported hearing an unsubstantiated rumor that Caroline had already been married by the time of the trial. He managed to incorporate the item into the official story, however, guessing in print that she had married John earlier but kept it secret because a wife was not permitted to testify about her husband in court.

Then there was the suggestive fact that Henshaw christened her child Samuel Colt, Jr. And there was even some documentary evidence. Twenty years later, when young Sam claimed his two million dollars under his true father's will, he was able to present his parents' marriage certificate as proof of his identity.

Various explanations spring to mind for the apparent failure of the *Herald*, flush with its new devotion to fact, to unearth the vital fact of Samuel's marriage and John's benevolence. The craft of investigative reporting was still new, its practitioners learning their way; they may have been too green to understand the significance of the hints and clues afloat. Doubtless, too, the Colt family worked extraordinarily hard to keep its secret. And if anyone *had* come too close for comfort to the truth, the parties would have had plenty of precedent for reaching an understanding through the medium of a little bribery.

But another possible explanation is this: Bennett had already chosen the facts that would add up to the most congenial Truth about the murderous John Colt, and neither he nor his readers saw the slightest need for any more.

IN SEARCH OF
JAMES GORDON FISHBLATT

Bennett's coverage of the Colt murder was a double boon for his readers. Not only did his choice of fact over humbug render a sensible account of the crime; he also chose the *right* facts to make the best sense of the larger questions of life in New York. He had a particularly demanding audience to satisfy.

Horace Greeley had appealed to a substantial readership whose faith in New York was absolute: they believed absolutely that the city was a cesspool of corruption and catastrophe. Many New Yorkers and other Americans, however, had a much more conditional and complicated relationship with the city, and to them, Greeley's alarmed righteousness seemed not merely sanctimonious; it was also simplistic. Although New York could indeed be cruel to the poorest, the most desperate, and the most different, nonetheless many in the middle class, the near middle class, and the would-be middle class actually regarded the city with a measure of affection, interest, hope, pride, even exhilaration. New York was a city rich in variety, stimulation, energy, and possibility. It offered a heady sense of opportunity, potential, and liberty. It was a place where things could *happen*.

The urban reformers' greatest anxiety was, in fact, part of the city's greatest allure. Greeley and his fellows feared that the young and adventurous who came to the city without family or community supervision would fall into evil ways. Yet the unique possibility of freedom from supervision was precisely what drew many of those young and adventurous souls to the city in the first place — freedom from constraint and the shackles of tradition, and freedom of action and choice. The large city may have been full of strangers, but strangers were unlikely to regulate each other's behavior, scrutinize each other's morals, or report to each other's minister.

The freedom of the city was also, clearly, the best avenue to economic reward. Many citizens were coming to realize that the nation's most cherished romantic ideal of itself as a republic of simple farmers was incompatible with another great American dream: prospering and getting ahead. Only the large and varied economic system of the city could offer a theater vast enough for truly spectacular success. New York, as a contemporary put it, "was, and is, a city of adventurers. Few of our eminent citizens were born here. It is a common boast among New Yorkers, that this great merchant and that great millionaire came to the city a ragged boy, with only three and sixpence in his pocket; and *now* look at him! In a list of the one hundred men who are esteemed to be the most 'successful' among the citizens of New York, it is probable that seventy-five of the names would be those of men who began their career here in circumstances that gave no promise of future eminence."[1]

But the appeal of the city was not merely its potential. For the young, rude, insecure, boastful, striving American nation, New York was also a treasure it could actively grasp and fondle. Everything about the city was bigger, more extravagant, more noteworthy, more important. People who did not live there had to notice it, whether they liked it or not; often they had to admire it, whether they wanted to or not. Even the notoriously malcontent Mrs. Trollope, who had so adamantly refused to approve of anything American during her travels in the new country, had been seduced by the cosmopolitan air of the "lovely and noble city" on the Hudson. "To us who had been so long travelling through half-cleared forests," she remarked,

> and sojourning among an "I'm-as-good-as-you" population, it seemed, perhaps, more beautiful, more splendid, and more refined than it might have done, had we arrived there directly from London; but making every allowance for this, I must still declare that I think New York one of the finest cities I ever saw, and as much superior to every other in the Union, (Philadelphia not excepted,) as London is to Liverpool, or Paris to Rouen. . . . [New York] rises, like Venice, from the sea, and like that fairest of cities in the days of her glory, receives into its lap tribute of all the riches of the earth.[2]

Increasingly evident, in fact, was a sense that the provincial and the cosmopolitan were divided from one another by more than a difference in scenery. There was a gulf between their intellectual sensibilities as well, between their perspectives on the larger world and their willingness to integrate it into their own lives. One of the best descriptions of this gulf comes from a man who experienced both perspectives fully.

Henry Morton Stanley made a long leap from tending a shop in darkest Arkansas on the eve of the Civil War to become the archetype of the sophisticated world traveler and foreign correspondent. "Arkansas is sometimes known as the Bear State, and many of its people at that time were singularly bearish and rude," he recalled in later life, after his exploits for the *Herald* had made him famous.

> It is wonderful what trivial causes were sufficient to irritate them. A little preoccupation in one's own personal affairs, a monosyllabic word, a look of doubt, or a hesitating answer, made them flare up hotly. The true reason for this excessive sensitiveness was that they had lived too much within their own fences, and the taciturnity engendered by exclusiveness had affected their habits. However amiable they might originally have been, their isolation had promoted the growth of egotism and self-importance. This is the essence of "Provincialism," wherever it is met with, in country or in city life.[3]

The cosmopolitan city was becoming recognized as the natural habitat of the newest and most hustling segment of the middle class and the mecca for those from other parts of the country who liked to believe that at heart they belonged in that category too. Although some bourgeois Americans continued to cling to a more traditional understanding of their leadership roles in culture and morals, many who were newer to the possibilities of worldly success displayed much more interest in what Burton J. Bledstein has called "the advantage of being middle class" than in the responsibility. Such a person "in his heart" was typically "competitive, active, bold, brave, and even reckless. He mercilessly combated those who hated innovation. He agitated against complacency, he destroyed prescription, he invented means, he subverted monopoly, he opened doors of opportunity, and he multiplied the avenues for wholesome rivalry."[4]

City life nourished the hopes and desires of such Americans. It was gratifying to feel that they were living an important and envied life at the seat of commerce and the center of civilization. It was glorious to think they were somehow smarter, more experienced, and more enlightened than the ordinary American. It was novel and exciting to explore the infant germ of a new cosmopolitan sensibility that celebrated rather than censured the city's difference.

New Yorkers from this part of the middle class, and non–New Yorkers who hoped some day to join it, would have found little in the *Tribune* that was relevant to their lives — and a great deal in the *Herald.* Bennett's paper nourished their sense of excitement and importance. The editor actually seemed to like not only his city but even his readers. He put them into his stories; in his reporting of Colt's suicide, we recall, the crowd was almost as important and visible a character as the suicide himself was. He congratulated them for the taste and perception they showed in living in that fascinating city in the first place. "New York is the great central city of civilization for all future time," Bennett exulted on 7 November 1842. "It is the only city that possesses the elements, the soul, the originality, the enterprise. Placed in this city, we mean to perform our duty in our day and generation, and to leave to the present age and to all posterity to witness the issue, and to pronounce the verdict."

Yet as rewarding as New York could often be for its large-minded inhabitants, as much as they wanted to like and enjoy their city, they also faced a much more difficult task than the sort of person who preferred the *Tribune.* Whereas Greeley's readers only had to dislike everything, not even the most ardent urbanite could have painted New York a white as untinctured as Greeley's black. No one could deny that much of what made the city cosmopolitan in the first place also helped make it, at times, a trying and difficult place to live.

The Colt case clearly fell among those trying times. Since the murder of Helen Jewett in 1836, New Yorkers had repeatedly been stunned and sickened by flagrant acts of crime, brutality, and fraud. Sensational trials brought notoriety to some flamboyant characters: in 1841 the abortionist Madame Restell was indicted and tried for causing the death of a patient; a year later Colonel Monroe Edwards was found guilty of obtaining fifty thousand dollars through a clever forgery scheme.

Any New Yorker was vulnerable to petty crime or sordid urban indignity, and the moral and legal structure of the city seemed unable to cope with the problem. In the poorer wards, rival ethnic gangs with outlandish names like "the Faugh-a-ballaghs" staged vicious battles on election day, yet few arrests were made and even fewer charges filed. Seducers who deceived and ruined the innocent young paid no heavier penalty than the provision of child support.

For some offenses there seemed simply no recourse — except, perhaps, airing one's consternation to Bennett of the *Herald.* Unlike Greeley, who attracted correspondents seeking advice, aid, reform, and renown, Bennett drew the aggrieved. Typical of his correspondence was an undated, unsigned letter bringing to the editor's attention the "degrading" and "reprehensible" conduct of a man "who calls himself Doctor James R. Smith" and who had been caught in the middle of Broadway "ben[ding] his head into the face of a couple of ladies and making a disgusting noise with his mouth uttering some obscene language."[5] The crime did not go unpunished, since, as the letterwriter conceded, "Dr. Smith" was immediately apprehended and hustled off to prison. Yet the anonymous informant apparently believed prison too private a disgrace for so flagrant an outrage. Only public humiliation would suffice.

Murder was, of course, the ultimate indignity, but somehow New York murderers always seemed to get away unscathed. "In less than two years," Bennett's biographer later recalled, "from 1838 to the close of 1839, there were six murders and no convictions for the offences [*sic*] — a German girl was murdered on the Battery — a stevedore had his throat cut and his body thrown into the East River — a man, in broad day-light, was slain by negroes in Anthony street — Dr. M'Caffrey was knocked from his gig, and killed by some one, in the same street — Leuba, a watchman, was assassinated in the Bowery — an unoffending man was murdered in the Third Avenue, and another man in Cross street."[6]

The summer before Adams's disappearance saw the most baffling and heinous crime of all: the brutal killing of Mary Cecilia Rogers, a well-known beauty who had worked in a Broadway tobacco shop. Her battered body, bound with strips torn from her own garments, was found floating in the Hudson River near the Weehawken shore, and more scraps of her clothing were found amid signs of a struggle in a secluded thicket nearby. Shortly afterward her betrothed, Daniel Payne, who had been examined and released by the authorities, was found mysteriously dead in the same thicket. It might have been suicide.

Most New Yorkers at first believed Rogers had been kidnapped, raped, and strangled by rowdies. Evidence later emerged to suggest she had died at the hands of an inept abortionist. Neither scenario reflected much honor on the city — and the general failure to solve the case was even less admirable. So arrantly clumsy were the efforts of both the city newspapers and the city authorities that Edgar Allan Poe gallicized the characters and setting, set his fictional French sleuth to ratiocination, and came up with a much more convincing solution — and, as time would tell, a much more accurate one — in "The Mystery of Marie Roget."

Then there was the Adams murder. In broad daylight, in the busiest part of town, a perfectly ordinary tradesman went out to collect a debt and met violent death. Even that murder might well have gone unsolved had not the *Kalamazoo* been unexpectedly delayed at the wharf long enough for officials to trace Colt's suspicious crate there.

Thus New York presented special problems for its most cosmopolitan citizens and admirers simply because they were cosmopolitan — because they were in a position to see and experience the good as well as the bad, the promise as well as the crisis. In a city where murder stalked but freedom also beckoned, where confusion reigned but opportunity also flourished, who could sort it all out?

James Gordon Bennett assured his readers that he could.

Bennett chose to report the Colt case without humbug for many reasons of his own, chiefly having to do with circulation, distinctiveness, and self-aggrandizement. Yet all of his choices were encouraged and ratified by his readers' choice, for reasons of *their* own, to embrace the version he presented. They found much to satisfy them in Bennett's fact-laden account of the Colt affair.

First of all, they found a solution to the murder, a welcome gift indeed after so long a string of embarrassing, perplexing, and frightening crimes.

Citizens were clearly pining for a murderer caught, a penalty paid, and a case closed. On 31 January 1842, when Colt was found guilty, Bennett announced on behalf of the population of New York that justice had been served and the public satisfied.

> Now comes, then, the most exciting part of the drama; will he be hung — or will a new trial be granted? Will the Governor dare to pardon him? We think not. The verdict seems to give general satisfaction. The public have had their eye on Colt from the time of his arrest till this hour; and had the verdict not been "murder," we don't know what would have been the consequence. The public have been cheated so often, that Colt has to suffer for the sin of Ezra White [recently convicted on the mildest possible charge in a street-brawl stabbing], Robinson, and all who have escaped for the last ten years. It is a very unjust thing. But so it is.

Embracing fact also relieved readers of the increasingly onerous task of having to figure things out for themselves. No longer did readers have to worry about seeing connections, assigning causes, piercing through deceptions, or deciding between options. Replacing humbug with fact meant never having to make a choice.

During the Jewett affair, New Yorkers had explained the murder to themselves by weaving together bits of observation, assumption, and history that everyone knew. Much of it derived directly from their immediate environment: the well-known interest of the prisoner's patron in something that was either social manipulativeness or social improvement; the lingering bitterness of the defunct Working Men's movement; the ability of any street porter to view the corpse for himself; the opportunity for any college student to go and look Rosina Townsend in the eye. Based on their observations, readers could choose which of many alternative published versions best fit their own experience.

No alternatives distracted readers of the *Herald*'s reporting on the Colt affair. Gone were the wildly varying bits of information about the murdered woman's identity, the prisoner's history, the "real" perpetrator. Gone were the teasing hints and outright challenges for readers to craft a more congenial reality. Gone, too, however, was the danger of making a wrong choice, missing a crucial fact, or misunderstanding a playful deception.

In a world grown so large and confusing that many New Yorkers needed the same kind of explanatory guide to their own city as any Arkansan did, even those readers who prided themselves on their cosmopolitan sharpness would have been grateful for a few hints. In a world in which a Bowery loafer might have known no more than a Virginian about an accused murderer's home life or his supporters' politics, both would have been equally helpless to recognize and manipulate a full-fledged humbug. And in a world so often threatening and inexplicably violent, no one would have scorned a little direction toward an understanding of how violent murder happened.

Not only were readers freed from the burden of distinguishing fact from fantasy; they were actively discouraged from trying to do it by themselves. No longer were they assured that they had as much right and ability as anybody to express an opinion on public matters. All citizens may have had the right to know, but that did not necessarily mean they could be trusted to decide what was *worth* knowing.

This attitude was most evident in Bennett's treatment of rumor. Rumor was the very essence of humbug; the informal circulation of provocative but unofficial information was the backbone of the Jewett affair reporting. Now, however, Bennett was scrupulously careful to distinguish between rumor, grapevine, and hearsay — bad fact — on the one hand and verified information — good fact — on the other.

The *Herald* reported on "all sorts of rumors about the vote in the jury-room, but nothing certain"; it mentioned "a rumor . . . that an attempt would be made to impeach some of the [jury] panel, on the ground that they had previously expressed an opinion &c." but assured readers "nothing of the kind was attempted." The rumors that "a most extended system of bribery had been in operation to effect the escape of Colt" actually turned out to be true. "Last evening," the *Herald* asserted proudly, "[we] ascertained that the sum of $1000 had been offered to each of three of the deputy keepers."

The confirmation or denial of rumor had become the province of the press and the press alone. After the climax of the story, Bennett reported, "All sorts of rumors are in circulation relative to the suicide of Colt. Many of those who have not perused the city press, still doubt that he is dead." He was right. One of the disbelievers was George Templeton Strong. Visiting a fellow law student hours after Colt was supposed to be hanged, he reported himself "astounded" to hear of the suicide from a friend. "Didn't believe it, indeed," he told his diary, "till an Extra *Herald* confuted my *a priori* arguments against his views."

Readers were even starting to submit the rumors they heard directly to the press for verification. Three weeks after the suicide, the *Herald* printed a pseudonymous letter to the editor that passed on a "strange story which has been whispered in some circles for the past few days." According to the whisperers, two years earlier a Detroit man visiting New York had disappeared mysteriously just after he was seen in Colt's company at the Bowery Theater. Soon thereafter, a gang of New Orleans stevedores unloading a ship just in from New York had found a box containing a human body that was never claimed or identified. The correspondent wrote Bennett "to ask you whether there is any grounds for such a rumor — and whether you are able to throw any light on this strange story." The *Herald* contentiously called upon the district attorney to do so.[7]

So Bennett did the hard part for his readers. He became a Halsey Fishblatt in the flesh — an omniscient guru who could explain all. He had a stable of reporters at hand who could go places most people could not — the ballroom of the wealthy lawyer, the prison cell of the sentenced murderer — to ferret out facts for his readers and to specify them precisely, without guile or subterfuge. His detailed descriptions of Colt's appearance and Henshaw's wardrobe left nothing to the imagination, but neither did they require of his readers any special knowledge or previous acquaintance to comprehend. No longer did he assume that they held common understandings or perceived hidden undercurrents. By treating New Yorkers the same as Hoosiers, he ensured that New Yorkers and Hoosiers read the same story in the same way.

Yet Bennett's factual recounting of the crime did more than simply offer his readers a clear, satisfying, and authoritative resolution. It also presented that resolution free of all ambiguity, responsibility, and guilt and encompassed the death of Samuel Adams and the trial of his murderer into the ongoing morality play that the penny press made of daily life in New York.

Actually, Bennett's greatest contribution to New York's morality play was to *substitute* fact for morality. Simply by embracing it *instead* of moralism, he and his readers avoided the unpleasant possibility of having to consider New York immoral. Greeley was blaming Colt's fall on the evil rampant in the city; Bennett, in his earlier incarnation, had moaned that *"we are all guilty alike,"* even while he fingered Townsend. Both viewpoints had the disturbing and confusing consequence of implicating readers themselves in the crime. The *Herald*'s new tone, however, made clear the criminal's guilt while keeping readers safely distant from responsibility for it. It was not that Bennett was emotionally dispassionate; his evocation of the "horrible effluvia" of the dead house, his grisly portrait of the printer's butchered body, and his detailed exploration of the suicide's death wound certainly raised frissons of horror, revulsion, perhaps even sympathy or remorse. Yet by justifying this sensationalism in terms unburdened by moral didacticism, Bennett freed his readers to contemplate sin without atoning for it.

It was, furthermore, a wholesale absolution, not the special indulgence he had afforded his targeted audience during the Jewett affair. Then, he and the other editors had worked out together with their readers their own ideas of why evil happened and who was ultimately responsible for so ugly a crime. Each group had ended up laying the guilt at the door of someone else — a rival, a threat, an oppressor.

Now, however, Bennett laid the guilt at the door of the only culprit who could neither resist nor resent the stigma: Colt himself, the cold and remorseless killer, the reprobate who, by seducing a pure and innocent girl into a life of degradation, had already proved he was capable of any monstrosity. The prisoner came to his "untimely end," wrote Bennett on 28 September 1842, just after the death sentence was passed, "by a want of moral and religious culture — by entertaining mistaken notions of honor and respectability." On the day after the suicide, Bennett again attributed the murderer's fate to "a false system of morals — a perverted sense of human honor — and a sentiment that is at utter variance with the mysterious revelations of Christianity or the sacred institutions of justice in civilized society." This time, in other words, everyone was innocent except Colt himself.

Bennett's cool and untroubled moral detachment is all the more striking in the light of developments in another sensational genre. The 1840s also marked the high tide of the "urban-exposé" novel devoted to endless lurid dissections of big-city scandal, vice, and depravity. Most notorious was George Lippard's *Quaker City: Or, the Monks of Monk Hall*, which took the true story of a seducer shot by his victim's brother in Philadelphia and elaborated it into a riot of perversion and evil. Other cities from New York and New Orleans to Fitchburg and Nashua all had their muckrakers, too.

Like Bennett, these authors alleged that their information was based on truth and that they were forced to probe their unpleasant subjects so deeply only in order to put a stop to them. Yet their exposures had something Bennett's did not. They had moral ambiguity. Lippard presented a "topsy-turvy moral world, [where] goodness and virtue remain powerless before the forces of darkness, while religion and social respectability are mere masks hiding inexorable evil. . . . An understratum of doubt runs through the novel and becomes especially visible in numerous instances when disillusioned characters question God's existence and man's goodness. . . . *The Quaker City* shows how the mixture of dark-reform themes can carry the popular novelist toward troubled philosophizing."[8]

Bennett was kinder to his readers. He kept the exposé but dispensed with the ambiguity, philosophy, and doubt. No extraneous information about sin or accountability would be allowed to complicate readers' understanding of the affair or to compromise their admiration of their city. And no inappropriate questions about Colt's false and perverted sense of morality could be allowed to disturb their calm conviction that he deserved to pay the ultimate penalty. For this theory to work, Bennett and his readers *needed* a cold, heartless beast like Colt to take the fall.

Thus Bennett, whose reputation still stands, a century and a half later, as the pioneer of objective reporting — who did indeed in the Colt case present an objective-sounding story, full of verifiable facts vetted by experts and intended to convey the same meaning to whoever read them — was in crucial ways still the same old Bennett of the Jewett affair. And the maturing penny press was still bearing, clearly visible, the impress of its roistering youth among the moon voyages, debauched nuns, and withered nannies.

Both Bennett and his latest rival, Greeley, perceived their public duty in the same way as the earliest penny-press editors had. And at bottom they achieved the same thing with their coverage of the Colt murder as Bennett and the other earlier editors had accomplished during the Jewett affair. They told their readers what they wanted to hear.

They, too, appealed to different communities, but both were encompassed within the vast new middle class. The moralistic Greeley used antiurban moralism to tell reformers and country readers that they were correct to fear the city and virtuous to fight its filth. He comforted them with solidarity and rewarded them with notice. Bennett, on the other hand, assured hustling, ambitious New Yorkers and would-be New Yorkers that the nation's largest city was its finest treasure. He congratulated them for their enterprise and canniness and helped them over the rough spots of urban life without compromising their overall appreciation of it.

Yet while Bennett and Greeley carried on the penny-press tradition of telling congenial truths, they went about it in a very different fashion from the earliest penny editors. Even though the great social and economic changes of the preceding six years had not altered the function of the press, they did force editors into finding new ways of confirming the social vision their readers preferred. The penny editors, seeking the large readership that technology made possible and economics made imperative, substituted factual revelation for literary interpretation, open explanation for tacit understanding. Rather than liberating an assortment of possible truths from which their readers could choose, they instead endorsed the truths they knew their readers would like. One staked out as his own the sphere of moralism and reform, the other championed the sometimes amoral but always thrilling hubbub of New York — but in their different ways they were equally emphatic. They set the standards, they interpreted the reality, they quashed the rumor, they held the keys to truth and validated it with their own weight. In short, they replaced humbug with authority.

Yet the success of the penny-press idea was not without its problems. The massive broadening of the press's readership, which helped to inspire and define the role of authority in the first place, also plagued some of those authorities with special difficulties. And Bennett, whose dedication to massiveness was much more single-minded than Greeley's, found himself much more plagued by the demands of massiveness than Greeley was.

Greeley won his vast readership and his equally vast camp of enemies on the principle of never compromising his principles. He was antiwar, antirum, and antiseduction, and all knew it; the farmers who believed he wrote every word of the *Tribune* himself and the sharp middle-class New Yorkers who considered him a milquetoast both knew exactly which truths he would espouse. Bennett, on the other hand, clung to a different principle: that his newspaper ought to make money. To that end he accumulated a mass of sensational details in his coverage of the Colt murder, while ultimately drawing the most conventional, even commonplace, moral from them. He was known as the man who, "without any particular convictions or fixedness of principle himself, gives no one else credit for them; and therefore thinks the best thing is to render his paper acceptable to the largest class of people possible."[9] Yet if one is looking for the most broadly acceptable truths, one has only a severely circumscribed area in which to look for them. That may have had something to do with how Samuel and John Colt managed to keep their dark secret intact.

Bennett considered himself, and was widely considered by others to be, the duly constituted authority on official reality for mainstream middle-class New York. The position did not, however, convey license to feed his readers any truths he chose; having attained the status of authority by sounding sufficiently authoritative about the questions that mattered most to his readers — by respecting and reinforcing the rigid limits of mainstream middle-class experience and belief — he ran the risk of losing that status should he challenge the limits too forcefully. If his expert version of the truth were to succeed as the only acceptable version, it must therefore be noncontroversial enough and psychically satisfying enough to please an immense spectrum of readers.

Thus, with public pressure so intense for Colt's conviction, Bennett chose not to consider any other label for the prisoner except "Colt, the Homicide." With public disdain so pronounced for Colt's personal life and character, the editor chose not to heed the pressure of a small minority for conviction on the milder charge of manslaughter. With a readership so broad, he chose not to risk blaming anyone in particular for the troubling presence of evil and sin.

Bennett's assumption of authority had an even more problematic consequence: it choked off public debate. Once the editor had established uncontroversial truths for his readers and backed them with his own tremendous clout, he discouraged the public expression of private opinion. His official choice of one particular reality to explain Colt's crime, and his amused, even contemptuous dismissal of other versions as mere rumor, kept him from examining possible alternative solutions himself. It also kept his readers from deciding for themselves the validity of such solutions. Readers cannot consider, debate, accept, or reject options they do not know about. Readers bobbing gently atop the froth and scum cannot readily sound the eternal sea.

And readers pacified with a sufficiently congenial and authoritative truth do not easily rise to the challenge of reconsidering its justice. The real reason that the story of Samuel and John Colt's marriages went undiscovered in New York may well have been that it was unimaginable. The press and the public alike may simply have been unprepared to entertain the prospect of an exculpatory wrinkle in a story that was already so clear, comprehensible, and satisfying.

The very idea of investigative reporting probably never occurred to Greeley, but ironically, Greeley's devotion to moralistic sermonizing rather than factual detail caused him to overlook evidence of the actual moral decay embodied by Samuel Colt. And the very possibility of alternative truths seems never to have bothered Bennett. His dedication to journalism that his readers would like, and his readers' obvious hunger for a criminal caught after so long a string of unsolved murders, together militated against the editor's discovery of the deeper truth of the story.

All of this leaves us with an intriguing what-if. What if the editors had approached the murder of Adams, not as authorities, but in the same feisty, argumentative spirit that had animated their coverage of the Jewett murder? What if their readers had again been willing to challenge authority instead of accepting it? Gadfly *Sun* editor Benjamin Day might well have been much more aggressive and rebellious than his cautious successor Moses Beach about rooting into the odd floating rumors in order to embarrass or challenge his rivals. The old struggling *Transcript* might conceivably have chosen for its special audience the community of protesters who harassed Governor Seward for mercy on Colt's behalf and sought a truth more congenial to them. The old bumptious *Herald* itself, headed by a Bennett still desperate to seize attention for himself, might plausibly have cast the affair into something less carefully innocuous than the easy formula of a cold-blooded killer's comeuppance.

And if the truth about John Colt's living arrangement with Caroline Henshaw had indeed been made public before the trial, it may well have prodded and pricked the public out of its complacent contemplation of just deserts and into open debate about his character and motives. It could have raised in the jury such serious questions about Colt's alleged coldness and heartlessness as to have led to his conviction only on the lesser manslaughter charge after all. It could have led to a successful appeal or sparked overwhelming public pressure for a pardon.

We will never be able to prove that John Colt was unjustly condemned or that the cause of his death was bad journalism. Nor can we convincingly argue that much of what the *Sun* and the *Transcript* did in the Jewett affair was good journalism. It is noteworthy — it is tolerable even — only because the truths preferred by their community of readers also happened to be an accurate depiction of reality. But truths made too congenial can be lies. The *Herald*'s false but ringing assertions of Robinson's innocence — which have rung down the ages and still reverberate to this day — were *also* a product of humbug.

Yet what the *Herald* did during the Colt affair was not good journalism, either. Bennett's narrow-minded support of a conventional story ended up enshrining one official version of events and muzzling the discussion of all others — including a more accurate one. Truths made too universal can also be lies.

Journalism is important. It catches events on the cusp between now and then — events that may still be changing, developing, ripening. And while new interpretations of the past can alter our understanding of lives once led, new interpretations of the present can alter the course of our lives as we live them.

Understanding the news properly is important. The way a community receives the news is profoundly influenced by who its members are, what they hope and fear and wish, and how they think about their fellow citizens. It is informed by some of the most occult and abstract of human ideas about truth, beauty, goodness, and justice.

All the more troublesome is it, then, that so many Americans today are so dissatisfied with the course and practice of modern journalism. All the more unsettling is it that so many Americans have so misshapen an idea of how to read, hear, watch, and understand the news.

EPILOGUE

A good many problems plague the modern mass media, but looming large among them is this: we still expect journalism to tell us the Truth. Our Truth.

More than a century and a half after the founding of the penny press, we still grapple with problems and dilemmas that budded during the Jewett and Colt murders. The argumentative spirit of the humbug, at its best, can inspire the sort of lively debate that draws citizens to participate in public life, brings about a fair consensus on matters of public interest, and helps mold a population into a responsible society. Too often, however, we succumb to the Jewett syndrome, the tendency for each and every community to declare victory for its own truth, whatever that happens to be. Objective, authoritative reporting, at its best, can lead to the free and fearless investigation of public questions, the exposure of public wrongs, and the dissemination throughout a large nation of a common body of understanding and knowledge. Too often, however, we fall prey to the Colt syndrome, the easy triumph of the most inoffensive and orthodox of truths.

Too much of the time, in other words, news executives and news consumers collude to drape the vestments of journalism gently over their own chosen vision of the way the world ought to be.

For most of the history of the modern mass media, even before the term *objectivity* came into general use, mainstream journalists and their public found that both the news and the Truth appeared to best advantage garbed in the sort of authoritative voice that had distinguished the *Herald*'s coverage of the Colt affair. Barely two years after John Colt's death, the many advantages of the morally unambiguous, carefully unchallenging brand of reporting pioneered by Bennett were confirmed by one of the seminal events in the history of communications.

In 1844 news of the first successful transmission of a message by telegraph — the "lightning line" — hit the nation like a thunderbolt. For the first time in human history, communication could be virtually instantaneous over distance — at least the distance between Baltimore and Washington, where Samuel Morse had run the first wire; and soon after his stunning demonstration, cables began snaking out across the continent at furious speed. Now a message could fly to its recipient entirely liberated from the messenger; now a few taps of a key could outpace even the swiftest twenty-four-horse relays. Immediately, immediacy became the paramount value for news.

The proprietors of the New York press realized early what a prize the new invention could be — *if* they could get it under control. Newsgathering by telegraph, they soon realized, was not only highly expensive, but also deeply frustrating. Unseemly wrangles often erupted when reporters from different papers converged all at once on a single telegraph office, each scheming and clamoring to use the wire first. Discerning editors quickly understood that cooperation might serve their interests better.

In 1848 six New York daily papers, including the *Sun*, the *Herald*, and the *Tribune*, agreed to combine in a cooperative newsgathering venture that became known as the Associated Press. Its strength and power increased year by year as it consistently outorganized and outspent feebler competitors while inviting the participation of more robust journals, among them one formidable new entrant. The *New York Times*, founded in 1851 by Greeley's former lieutenant Henry J. Raymond, flourished, according to a contemporary, because of "three reasons: 1, it was conducted with tact, industry and prudence; 2, it was not the Herald; 3, it was not the Tribune."[1]

In 1867 the big city papers tightened their grip on the news still further when the AP, faced with a stiff challenge from the Western Associated Press, defused the crisis with more cooperation. The two agencies worked out a news-sharing agreement that gave each free rein on its own designated turf. Then both agencies together forged an agreement with Western Union, which at that point had absorbed enough of its competition to emerge as the indisputable leader of the telegraph business. The news agencies contracted to use no wires other than Western Union's; the telegraph company promised them special rates and pledged to stay out of the newsgathering business itself.

This trend troubled many Americans — and not just frustrated would-be editors who could be left newsless if the local AP group decided to block their papers from membership, as the San Francisco chapter did to progressive reformer Henry George. Yet despite widespread sentiment that the telegraph, as a public good, should not be under private control, the companies managed to maintain their interlocking and mutually reinforcing monopoly and soon came to wield almost complete control over the gathering, transmission, and marketing of foreign and domestic news in

America.[2] Together, the companies made news into a commodity to be bought and sold, and themselves into the arbiters of which news could be sold and who could buy it. Together, they made journalism into big business.

The typical country paper, meanwhile, remained closest in spirit to a lemonade stand hit by sugar rationing and was challenged by daily indignities undreamed of by the New York press. The telegraph did not even reach Little Rock until 1861, when the line from Memphis was finally finished, arduously strung from tree to tree to post-oak pole through terrain that was "almost impenetrable . . . the habitat of every species of wild animal and reptile indigenous to Arkansas."[3] The *Virginia Free Press* constantly had to cajole, beg, and bully readers to pay their bills. "IN EARNEST, AND NO MISTAKE!" ran one such message on 7 September 1848. "WE WANT MONEY AND MUST HAVE IT! We have been laboring for many long years for a large number who have never paid us a solitary picayune, and we cannot stand this game any longer." And the *Vincennes Western Sun* often had to confess, as it did on 13 March 1847 in type so ancient and battered it would have been scarcely more legible even *with* enough *e*'s, that "w 'run short' of type this week, and ar forced to draw upon our adv rtising columns to h lp us out. We are looking for th balanc of our n w typ ev ry hour."

In response to the ever-increasing reach, wealth, and power of the urban press, the country papers more and more devoted themselves to the only news the city papers could never scoop them on. Their columns brimmed with chronicles of daily life at home: the arrival of the new instruments for the German brass band; the colonel's plans to build three new houses in the upper end of town; Mrs. Nancy Porter's fall on the sleet-slickened pavement.[4] Even as they concentrated on hometown news, few editors and readers were ready to entirely abandon the newspaper's traditional fare, the news of the nation and the world. Yet for these larger tidings the provincial papers were utterly dependent, not on the telegraph, but on the telegraphic news services monopolized by the city press. The heavy responsibility of forging a link to the wider and wilder world no longer fell on the hometown editor — on proud and conscientious Elihu Stout or good old H. N. Gallaher, who was known to have carried a hatter's unpaid subscription for nineteen years. Now it was carried out by faceless institutions operating far away in places few Hoosiers or Virginians had ever seen.

In the weeks following the capture of Fort Sumter, the *Western Sun* proudly filled its pages with column after column of reports from Washington, New York, Richmond, Montgomery, Indianapolis, Chicago, Nashville, and dozens of other cities around the nation, all of it "By Telegraph Expressly for the Sun." The range and variety of the news were no tribute to reportorial enterprise, however; the *Vincennes Western Sun's* hometown competitor carried virtually the same news items — expressly for the *Vincennes Gazette*. Both of them got their items expressly from the same source: the urban-based wire service.

This is how the telegraph was truly revolutionary; this is how a technological invention not only overcame time and subdued space, but rearranged the nature of language. The *Western Sun* was staunchly Democrat, the *Gazette* firmly Republican; that the two could ever show any similarities would have been unthinkable throughout the early days of their political rivalry. Yet the telegraph made this congruence perfectly natural.

In their editorial columns, most of the New York papers did continue to express the politics and prejudices that had helped make them famous. During the Civil War, the *Times* was largely pro-Lincoln; the *Tribune* was often bitterly critical of the president's leadership and his generals' skill; the *Herald* championed the secessionist cause until the southern states actually went and seceded, then it reversed itself to support the war; and the *Sun* favored McClellan as both military commander and presidential candidate.

The telegraphic news gathered by the New York papers' wire services, however, was quite different in style and tone. First of all, the high per-word tolls made a financial burden of the adjective and the opinion and turned a lean, streamlined prose style into an economic asset. Yet the wire-service reporters and editors were, like Bennett during the Colt affair, also confronted with the challenge of attracting the largest conceivable number of readers while offending as few of them as possible. They recognized the necessity of a writing style both authoritative and neutral enough to be credible to the Democratic *Western Sun* as well as to the Republican *Gazette*, to tiny rural Charles Town as well as to cosmopolitan Princeton, to midwestern Vincennes as well as to southern Little Rock. That meant more than merely banishing partisanship; it also meant "rework[ing] . . . the nature of awareness itself," as a scholar of journalism has written.

The wire services demanded language stripped of the local, the regional and colloquial. They demanded something closer to a "scientific" language, one of strict denotation where the connotative features of utterance were under control, one of fact. If a story were to be understood in the same way from Maine to California, language had to be flattened out and standardized. The telegraph, therefore, led to the disappearance of forms of speech and styles of journalism and storytelling — the tall story, the hoax, much humor, irony, and satire — that depended on a more traditional use of language.[5]

Yet trouble was already brewing. The wire services were developing the special grammar and style of objective reporting at a time of unprecedented turmoil, bitterness, and rage in America. Just as the wires were sending their standardized news in flattened language to readers from Maine to California, readers from California to Maine were disagreeing ever more violently about the meaning of the news they all read. And sometimes the cool, distant authority of the AP served not as oil poured on troubled waters, but rather as fuel cast on flickering flames.

After the nervewracking standoff at Fort Sumter, for instance, the *Arkansas Gazette* of 20 April 1861 approvingly quoted a complaint from the *St. Louis Republican*. "We respectfully suggest to the telegraph that it is making a fool of itself," the *Republican* scowled.

We thought at first that it had only gone crazy, but that which we took to be lunacy turns out to be a bad case of idiocy. . . .

We pay that mythical corporation called the "Associated Press," for news — for facts. Instead of facts, it keeps continually poking at us nonsensical batches of owlish speculation, furnished by the cheap-panic-correspondents of the New York papers. If there were the least probability of these speculations proving true, of approaching truth in the remotest degree, perhaps we might feel disposed to submit without a murmur. But there is not.

When the *Republican* went on to list examples of the wire service's owlishness, it reserved special ire — expressed in the scorching indignation of italics — for the AP's report that "If the secessionists fire on [the supply ship], *they will initiate whatever trouble follows.*" Yet this was neither speculation nor panic on the part of the AP; it was a not unreasonable rendering of Lincoln's strategy to place the burden of action on the Confederates. The president had announced that he was sending an armed ship to supply the besieged fort with food — and food only; and he had pledged that the ship would offer no violence until and unless it were attacked. Lincoln's action was manipulative, of course, and as southern sympathizers the *Republican* and the *Gazette* were bound to resent it; but the wrath they heaped on the idiocy of the telegraph was more properly the deserts of the Yankees. It would not be the last time that, in superheated matters of politics and identity, readers found that flattened news simply could not rise to the occasion.

The penny press and the telegraph were only the beginning. Like Alice after she devoured the cake marked "EAT ME," the big news organs were continually challenged to adjust to sudden and disorienting spurts of growth. As new developments in technology and new business arrangements made feasible a wider and wider audience for news, executives continually had to face the perennial question of how to attract and satisfy yet another new pool of readers without losing the readers they already had. Sometimes they tripped over their own feet; often their elbows pressed where they were not welcome. Again and again, they embraced tried-and-true techniques: cooperation when profitable, privatization when possible, monopolization when permissible, and standardization when feasible. Again and again, news executives recognized that, in addition to whatever philosophical virtues they might bear, the ideals of authority and impartiality also possessed a unique compatibility with these tactics.

Toward the end of the century, well after telegraphic news had made manifest both the mechanics and the rewards of impersonal, authoritative reporting, its philosophical virtues also became apparent enough to begin earning the distinction of a label. At that point nearly all of the established New York papers were going through a period of change, mostly for the worse. The generation of pioneering penny editors had all but died out, silencing some of the most personal and distinctive voices in journalism. Raymond died in 1869, leaving the *Times* in the hands of undistinguished successors. After Bennett died of apoplexy in June 1872, the *Herald* passed to his son, James Gordon, Jr., a volatile, willful, egocentric, often nasty man best known for his appreciation of a good stunt, both public, like sending Stanley to find Livingstone, and not quite private enough, like the time he used his fiancée's grand piano for a *pissoir* in front of her assembled guests. The engagement was broken off.

Greeley, too, died in 1872, not implausibly of a broken heart; already shaken by his wife's recent death, he survived by only three weeks his crushing loss to Ulysses S. Grant in the presidential election. His successor at the *Tribune*, Whitelaw Reid, drifted steadily rightward, especially after marrying the daughter of one of America's richest men. Only the *Sun*, which the talented Charles A. Dana took over in 1868, seemed firmly on an upward road — but at that point the sadly sagging paper had absolutely nowhere to go *but* up.

Into this morass stepped a young first-generation German American, the owner of the well-regarded *Chattanooga Times*, who was eager to make the move to New York. When Adolph Ochs bought the *New York Times* in 1896, it was nearly moribund. When he died nearly forty years later, it had become the avatar of objectivity, its goals embodied in a godlike creed: "To Give the News Impartially, without Fear or Favor."

Ochs's journalistic strategy was in large part a genuine effort at civic service and a natural outgrowth of the intellectual climate of the 1890s. It was a time when scientific method was revered, when the role of the specially trained "professional" was exalted in careers from teaching to politics, and when empirical observation was considered the only true path to knowledge, reckless interpretation the road to hell. Just gather enough facts, the belief went, arrange them sensibly, exclude emotion and eschew speculation, and they would explain themselves. "We want nothing more to do with the approximations of hypotheses, useless systems, theories as brilliant as they are deceptive, superfluous moralities," one eminent scholar told the opening session of the First International Congress of Historians at the Paris Exposition of 1900. "Facts, facts, facts — which carry within themselves their lesson and their philosophy. The truth, all the truth, nothing but the truth." Borrowing a term from the Germans, some American historians began referring to the cool unbiased assemblage of facts, facts, facts as *objectivity*.[6]

Ochs was not the only newspaperman to apply these ideas (and, more slowly, their label) to journalism. E. L. Godkin of the *New York Evening Post* required of his writers a detachment so glacial that Lincoln Steffens never forgave him for it. "Reporters were to report the news as it happened," Steffens recalled about the *Post* job he took in 1892, "like machines, without prejudice, color, and without style; all alike. Humor or any sign of personality in our reports was caught, rebuked, and, in time, suppressed. As a writer, I was permanently hurt by my years on the *Post*."

Yet through a combination of skill, luck, a fine staff, and a keen business sense, Ochs succeeded in making his paper the city's — and eventually the nation's — premier authority in matters of fact. The *Times* strove to be more than merely nonpartisan; it also wished to be seen as calm, dignified, and decent, a public trust dedicated to the public welfare. Ochs "view[ed] himself not as the keeper of the flame of any political faith or social creed but as a builder of a never-ending monument to public enlightenment. . . . He was a public-spirited businessman selling a commodity — information — in abundance, with high-quality ingredients, untainted by partisanship, free of self-aggrandizing additives, all plainly wrapped and delivered at a low price."[7]

Public-spirited as Ochs was, he was indeed a businessman, too, and his devotion to objective reporting filled not only an intellectual niche but a market niche as well. As Horace Greeley had done a half century earlier, Ochs flourished in part because of his integrity and in part because he perceived in New York a decency gap that a new kind of paper could profitably satisfy. The *Times* was distinctive as much for what it repudiated as for what it represented, as another of its contemporary slogans makes manifest. The paper that "Does Not Soil the Breakfast Cloth" was clearly standing up in splendid contrast and silent rebuke to the excesses of another type of newspaper — a type that was selling even more successfully in 1890s, though its spirit derived little sustenance from the prevailing intellectual climate of science and reason.

Again like Greeley, Ochs perceived his opening in the midst of another mammoth circulation war. In 1883 the immigrant Hungarian Joseph Pulitzer had come to New York hoping to repeat the success he had already earned in St. Louis with his popular *Post-Dispatch*. Pulitzer bought the flagging *New York World* from financier Jay Gould and recast it to appeal to the sort of reader he knew well: the working family, the immigrant family, the new urban American. The revitalization was so swift, so splendid, and so successful that it soon attracted an envious rival in the person of the hungry California mogul William Randolph Hearst, who purchased the *New York Journal* in 1895 as a direct challenge to Pulitzer.

The two relied on new ploys as well as old familiar circulation builders: lots of crime, scandal, and sensationalism, lots of self-promotion, lots of gaudy pictures, lots of comics in color (notably yellow), lots of screaming banner headlines, lots of stories about life in the city and how to live it; attention-grabbing stunts like Nellie Bly's voyage around the world in seventy-two days; crusades against targets ranging from Standard Oil and cruel insane asylums to white slavers; and of course the Spanish-American War, America's first media conflict. Even if they did not ignite the nation's war fever all by themselves, the battling papers fueled it assiduously with jingoism, agitation, and excitement. As many as three hundred correspondents from around the country showed up to cover the brief, ill-matched conflict.

The sensationalism was finally tempered by its own excesses: Hearst's relentless campaign of vituperation against the "spineless" President William McKinley, capped by an editorial and a doggerel verse that hinted at assassination, provoked an appalled backlash when Leon Czolgosz soon thereafter seemed to have taken the hint.[8] Cycles of sensationalism continued to recur, of course, and doubtless always will, but the dispassionate and respectable authority of the *Times* became the model for an increasing number of newspapers.

As the twentieth century dawned, new marketing developments stretched the newspaper's embrace further. Not only were individual papers growing bigger than ever before; they were beginning to look more like each other than ever before. The modern newspaper chain made its debut shortly after the Civil War, when the Scripps family, soon followed by Pulitzer, Hearst, Ochs, and others, began buying up or starting newspapers in cities often far distant from their home bases. These pioneer chains were modest enterprises. In 1900, 10 chains controlled just 32 dailies that claimed some 12 to 15 percent of the nation's total circulation. By 1933, however, 63 chains owned 361 dailies responsible for more than a third of the total weekday circulation and nearly half of Sunday's. At present, nearly two-thirds of the nation's dailies belong to chains, with Gannett alone boasting over 80 peas in its pod.

Not only did the huge size and reach of the chain papers soon make them "America's *mightiest advertising force*"; it also gave new might to America's advertisers and placed subtle new pressures on America's media.[9] For most of the nineteenth century, publishers could afford to be cavalier about their advertisers, whose coffers contributed perhaps one-third of a paper's revenues. By late in the century, however, booming Gilded Age businesses, fully conscious of the potential rewards of nationwide marketing, began to forge new relationships with the national media. Manufacturers of such brand-name products as bicycles, soap, phonographs, and cereal were developing large followings, and huge department stores like Wanamaker's and Macy's made huge demands for space, sometimes buying a whole page at a time. Advertising was becoming a big business, with its own agencies and associations, its own "scientific" market analyses, and its own monster budgets. Soon newspapers were earning three-quarters or more of their revenue not from their readers but from their advertisers.

A publisher as prickly and powerful as Hearst could obviously get away with rejecting ads for Mae West's movie *Klondike Annie* purely to avenge a "slighting remark" West had made about his inamorata, the constantly aspiring actress Marion Davies. An editor as principled as Lincoln Steffens could tell an advertiser who called his *Commercial Advertiser* to demand special treatment in the news columns that "you have the wrong number. This is the news department. We have a business department that attends to business." A firm as courageous — for the moment — as Alcoa could refuse to withdraw its name from Edward R. Murrow's scathing television documentary "Report on Senator Joseph R. McCarthy," even in the face of McCarthy's threats to unleash the IRS on the company's books.

From the Gilded Age onward, however, many advertisers (and, in the case of public radio and television, many politicians brandishing their power of the purse) have been and are just as willing and just as able as a publishing magnate to wield their own clout in ways either overt or subtle, giving news executives another incentive to keep their news as uncontroversial as possible. A recent survey of newspaper editors reveals that nearly every one of them — nine out of ten — had felt pressure from their advertisers. More than one-third acknowledged giving in.[10]

The development of radio followed a familiar pattern. In the early 1920s, AT&T, Westinghouse, RCA, and General Electric, all of which had been competing for dominance in the new field of wireless transmission, decided, as the AP papers had before them, that cooperation might serve their interests better. They pooled their resources in a complicated cross-licensing agreement that ensured access for each company to all the parts, patents, and services it needed — in effect an interlocking monopoly.

At the same time, AT&T's experiments in what it called "toll broadcasting" laid the foundation for the commercial sponsorship of the airwaves. It was a controversial move. Some Americans were arguing that the new medium should be supported by a tax or government licensing scheme of some kind; they believed, as Commerce Secretary Herbert Hoover put it, that if an advertiser attempted to sell "some brand of shoes or anything else over the radio you'll have no radio audience. People won't stand for that." But many people did. For listeners and advertisers both, radio advertising "represented a substantial victory for the ideology of consumption in American life."

Soon internecine disagreements among the cross-licensing companies, along with a threatened federal antitrust suit, forced them to reconsider their arrangement. Out of this reappraisal grew a new subsidiary company that came to be known as NBC and a new concept for radio programming — the network of affiliated stations. Like a newspaper chain, a radio network brought the same news in the same voice, sandwiched between the same advertising messages, to Americans all across the country. When the three major radio networks ventured into the new technology called television, Americans everywhere quickly learned to recognize the same faces along with the familiar voices.[11]

In 1842 James Gordon Bennett had discovered untold economic and social advantages in the apparently objective reporting of a printer's murder. Exactly one hundred years later, objectivity had become so enthroned as a desideratum of journalism that CBS radio asked for the resignation of its correspondent Cecil Brown for inserting a personal opinion into his report on a summit meeting between Churchill and Roosevelt.[12]

Recent history has been tough on faith and ideals. The calm confidence of the nineteenth century — the easy belief that with enough facts one could explain anything and everything — has been cruelly ravaged by the insults, tragedies, and uncertainties of the twentieth. Yet even as art, literature, music, and historiography turned more and more to nihilism, relativism, or skepticism, in the mainstream journalism of the Big Media — the network and cable newscasts, the national wire services, the pacesetting newspapers — the enthronement of the objective voice survived. It also survived the periodic alarms and diversions of such rebels as Upton Sinclair, who raged that journalism was only as objective as the capitalists and vested interests allowed it to be; Henry Luce, who saw no reason to suppress his opinion just because he wrote for a newsmagazine; and assorted "New," alternative, and gonzo journalists who cultivate distinctive personal voices and styles. It even survived the careful forays made by some of the Big Media themselves into opinion, always rigidly segregated into the op-ed pages and the Sunday talk shows, although the meticulously labeled two-minute "commentary" on the evening news now seems to have been merely a passing fancy.

The question for journalism now is: will the enthronement of the objective voice also survive the public's growing conviction that true objectivity is not actually possible?

Whether reporters, or any human beings for that matter, are in fact capable of putting aside bias, preconception, and personal experience to describe events according to some pure standard of truthfulness is of course a valid question, one with which many responsible news organizations and reporters continue to struggle daily. Whether people really *want* reporters to be purely, magisterially, nonjudgmentally objective is a question both more delicate and less popular.

Clearly, people want the press to *appear* objective. The best proof of that lies in their frequent complaints that it doesn't. Americans perpetually express themselves surprised, aggrieved, or embittered over yet another abysmal failure by the press to achieve its most basic and traditional goal. "Media watchdog" has become a full-fledged, full-time profession; a lush array of groups, centers, and institutions ranging the entire ideological spectrum now constantly scans the media and carries out all sorts of surveys, analyses, and investigations, vying to shout "gotcha" at the slightest hint of "bias." The single most common reaction to news coverage these days seems to be the cry "Unfair!"[13]

Nothing arouses ire like political news. After the 1992 election, the Times Mirror Center for The People and The Press surveyed people's feelings about the season's campaign coverage. The center found that although 36 percent of its sample was largely satisfied with the media's job, almost as many respondents — 31 percent — gave the press an overall grade of either D or F. More than one-third of the poll group also felt the press had been unfair to George Bush. Smaller percentages complained of unfairness to the winner, Bill Clinton, and the eccentric Ross Perot.[14]

In a less scientific poll, the weekly ABC newsmagazine "Prime Time Live" invited viewers to comment about the coverage of the campaign. The results, as described in a segment aired on 11 March 1993, were not pretty. Most of the viewers who responded were angry and dissatisfied; most of their dismay could be summed up in the two words "biased reporting." Not just ABC but all the media, they felt, had entirely failed in their duty to present the news objectively. Tales were told of opinionated headlines, unflattering photographs, hostile debate moderators. "If I could see the front-page editor of the *New York Times*," commented one New Jersey man, "I would look the person straight in the eye and say, 'Listen, pal. Keep your opinions to yourself. Just give me the facts, ma'am. Just the facts.'" Facts, facts, facts.

Coming in for particular criticism was the "Prime Time Live" program aired during the last week of the campaign, in which combative correspondent Sam Donaldson conducted separate interviews with George Bush and Bill Clinton. Some viewers thought Donaldson had been much harder on Bush and, as evidence, pointed out that he had interrupted the president much more often than he had Clinton. Other viewers complained that Donaldson had been much harder on Clinton and, as evidence, observed that he had interrupted Clinton much more often than he had the president.

In fact, the program reported, Donaldson had interrupted Clinton fifty times and Bush fifty-three — a negligible difference. Not even Marlin Fitzwater, Bush's own spokesman, could be goaded into blaming the president's loss on unfair press coverage. "The fact is, we should have run a better campaign," Fitzwater told a "Prime Time" reporter, "and we should have made changes during our four years that would have allowed us to win."

Certainly the press can be guilty of misjudgments and prone to feeding frenzies. Certainly headlines can be skewed and reporting slanted. But another familiar dynamic is at work here as well. It seems fair — objective and fair — to suggest that the respondents who complained of bias against Bush were rarely the ones wearing the Clinton buttons. It seems fair to say that, like readers of the *Sun* and the *Transcript* during the Jewett affair, many of the disgruntled were unhappy not because their abstract sense of fairness was betrayed, but because their own specific idea of truth was ignored. A large part of the reason many Americans are so dissatisfied with the "fairness" of the media stems from this fundamental misunderstanding. They want the *appearance* of objectivity, all the trappings of Olympian authority and validation, in a press that does not challenge their own vision of truth. They seem to believe that the definition of objectivity is "agreement with me."

The historic and happy congruence between growth and objectivity perhaps made the confusion in terms unavoidable. The mass media got where they are today largely by trying to be all things to all people. From the Colt affair onward, consumers have been programmed to expect cautious and respectful treatment in the mainstream press — something dependably amiable and amenable. Small wonder it is that when the inevitable failure comes — when readers or viewers see the press contradicting, or merely failing to ratify, some cherished ideology or conviction — they can feel as resentful or even betrayed as the nagging child slapped by a normally doting uncle. Small wonder that when so much of what has always passed for "objective journalism" has striven to be bland and inoffensive, reporting that actually does try to dispassionately examine questions of public interest — those spirited interviews with candidates, those investigations into controversies from My Lai to Watergate to Iran/Contra — can seem so patently offensive.

Given this evident public dissatisfaction, it should be no surprise that few defenders dare rise up anymore in support of traditional journalism. When *Rolling Stone*'s media critic dismissed what he called "Old News" as "pooped, confused and broke" and lauded the "new culture of information, a hybrid New News — dazzling, adolescent, irresponsible, fearless, frightening and powerful," he was also making a case for the dazzling power of *Rolling Stone* itself. But many executives of the "Old News" press seem to agree that they are growing superannuated. A former president of both NBC News and PBS recently inquired whether "our long-unquestioned standards of balanced, dispassionate reporting have made television news bland, dull, and largely unimportant in people's lives." And a staple item on the agenda of virtually any gathering of newspaper executives seems to be a panel on how to reverse the public perception that traditional newspapers are irrelevant, dull, and difficult to read.[15]

In recent years we have been seeing an explicit backlash against all this, a trend away from the mass media and toward something we may have to call personal media. More and more editors, publishers, and press executives are dedicating themselves to making the consumer, viewer, or reader feel unique, noticed, and involved. In a move that recalls the style and tactics of the Jewett affair and the penny-press humbug, many media are now reversing a decades-old trend and inviting the consumer to feel like part of a smaller, more cohesive, more distinctive community, not a larger one.

The increasing specialization of media — niche marketing to smaller and smaller niches — is one sign of this trend. Whatever one's aspiration, hobby, interest, passion, or vice, it is somewhere chronicled in a magazine, newsletter, or homemade, home-published "zine," from *Classic Cycle Review* and *Chocolatier* to *Gorezone*, for fans of splatter movies, or *The Optimistic Pezzimist*, which no collector of Pez candy dispensers can be without.

Cable television channels, too, multiply so fast that some critics have been conjuring up images of the wretched viewer reduced to quivering indecision when confronted with a choice among five hundred programs at any given moment. Yet the viewer who has been tormented by an unslaked thirst for vintage Betty Boop cartoons, or cooking programs, or golf games, or real-life criminal trials, or travelogues, or Korean drama, or documentaries about history, does not see forty dozen channels; she sees the One of them that is just for her.

Technology is also helping to foster the illusion that we are all an audience of one. Coming soon, we are told, is the electronic newspaper, with one's chosen sections beamed directly to one's home computer. Video on demand, allowing the subscriber to view virtually any entertainment on the home television screen at any time. A vast fiber-optic "information highway," connecting every home with an even more dazzling array of resources: data bases, any book in the Library of Congress, financial services, travel reservations. Already here are cybertext novels, interactive pornography, and movies that pause to allow viewers, by pressing coded buttons at their seats, to vote for the plot twists they prefer.

The ultimate example of the personalization of communications was the 1992 presidential campaign, in which both the underdog candidate who upset the incumbent and the third-party candidate who tergiversated his way to a historic vote total virtually ignored the Big Media. Bill Clinton and Ross Perot took more calls from John Q. Disgruntled than from Tom Brokaw; their campaigns featured appearances on popular radio and TV talk shows with Arsenio Hall, Don Imus, and Phil Donahue, chats on MTV with the very youngest voters, questions from callers on Larry King's phone-in show, and televised "town meetings" in which they conversed directly with members of the selected audience. Their mandate was E. M. Forster's: only connect.[16]

This return to the more personal style of the humbug, however, is turning out to be just as problematic as the depersonalization of journalism that provoked it, and for the same basic reason: too many consumers chasing too many personal truths. The feisty, gabby, disputatious spirit of the humbug, which according to theory ought to galvanize citizens into productive debate about questions of public interest, has nearly been quashed by the harsh realities of American society in the late twentieth century. What we have now is not a public; it is a great noisy swarm of competing publics. What we have now is not discussion or argument; it is a food fight. The crowded, expensive, high-stakes open bazaar that is modern America has rendered nothing short of wistful the old tenet that the best test of any truth is its ability to get itself accepted in the marketplace of ideas.

We are a nation struggling to come to terms with an eyepopping diversity, a nation where citizens so often define themselves — voluntarily or not — on the basis of race, gender, economic status, national origin, religion, activist ideal, sexual orientation, health, age, or shared obsession. We have a business community preoccupied with protecting its profits, a political establishment obsessed with its own perpetuation. For all of these Americans, passively entrusting to the invisible hand of the market the truths that define their very purpose and being is just too risky. The trick now, as many of them see it, is to get the idea into the marketplace by whatever means necessary — and then claim that its very presence there must mean it *has* been accepted.

Sometimes, of course, attempts to manipulate the news are purely and merely mistakes. The recent and celebrated spate of evening-news fiascoes — the unlabeled "reconstruction" with actors impersonating spies, the accident-prone pickup truck rigged with sparking devices to burst into flames on cue — were driven by nothing more or less sinister than journalistic sloppiness, stupidity, or zeal. Much more significant, much more dangerous, however, are those cases when accuracy is hijacked by desire, when truth becomes a matter of just deserts.

Examples of this sort of hijacking abound. Burgeoning armies of consultants, public relations specialists, and spin doctors spend their lives, their fortunes, and sometimes their sacred honor persuading the media to persuade us of what no schoolchild ever knows: that white-collar crooks aren't really crooks or religious frauds frauds; that instant coffee can buy us love; that "smart bombs" kill only bad guys and nobody ever *dreamed* it was arms for hostages. Men argue that women journalists are biologically incapable of doing justice to sports, and women claim they know, not *more* truth, but *better* truth about peace and environmentalism simply because they are not men.

Incidents like the Jewett murder case that are particularly meaty or resonant to the public mind can still inspire the most baroque efforts to uncover the right truth. A recent "Helen Jewett affair" in reverse — the case of a Long Island high-school prostitute who shot and wounded her lover's wife in the head — aroused a frenzy of attention in press and public both. For months, the chief protagonists in the drama retailed their various truths to media that begged and implored them to appear — and often paid them when they did.

The expression of personal opinion has become so touchy a matter that an outraged demand for a gag order is the automatic and inevitable response to unflattering public comments about anything from race and religion to vegetables. George Bush's disrespect of broccoli inspired a ruckus, Colorado has proposed a fruit-and-vegetable antidefamation bill, and when Hillary Rodham Clinton, behind the scenes on a children's TV show, allegedly slighted the green pea, the president of a New York produce cooperative immediately sprang to its defense. "We're very sensitive to any statement that is derogatory to produce," he said. "We don't see why anyone's personal preference towards vegetables should be voiced." (Not even if Mrs. Clinton had publicly announced that she *loved* green peas?)

And some media are so fiercely determined to rewrite historical or social reality that they persist even in the face of overwhelming evidence to the contrary. Sometimes the motive is frankly aggressive, as when several black-run newspapers worked to keep alive Tawana Brawley's accusations of rape by a gang of white men long after exhaustive investigation had discredited her; they wanted to "prove" that racial justice is impossible in America. Sometimes the motive is something gentler, as when, over the objections of dozens of experts and eyewitnesses, a 1992 PBS documentary insisted that black American soldiers had taken part in the liberation of the Jewish inmates of Dachau and Buchenwald; the producers wanted to "prove" that racial harmony is possible for America. Even as the protests and challenges were raging, the film was nominated for an Academy Award for Best Documentary.[17]

There is nothing wrong with ideas that are wrong, or misguided, or stupid, or weak; there is nothing wrong with them, that is, that a little free and honest trade in ideas won't address. But this is not free trade. The personalization of the media has given rise to rampant protectionism, fought out with weapons ranging from determination, pressure, and unrelenting din to rabbit punches and weighted gloves. This is the humbug run amok: a personal truth for everyone who wants one. As a result, this kind of journalism is less and less about informing, enlightening, challenging, or engaging people and more and more about bonding with them. We know who you are, the media's subtext goes, we hear your concerns, and we want to make you happy. Message: we care.

"He is an editor — he is on public duty," James Gordon Bennett quoted (or imagined) a policeman telling the envious crowd that tried to follow the newspaperman into the elegant brothel still reeking of smoke and spattered with Helen Jewett's blood. The public duty of the penny press, as Bennett and his fellow editors developed it, turned out to be something new and different for America. In one decade the *Sun*, the *Tribune*, the

Transcript, the *Herald,* and the other cheap papers imagined and created a wholly new public, or rather a group of new publics. Their editors brought together communities of people, many of them unaccustomed to the habit of reading, and showed them they had something in common with other readers: a shared consciousness, a common way of viewing and understanding the world.

The enduring appeal of both styles of penny-press journalism — the disputatious humbug of the Jewett coverage and the authoritative fact-finding of the Colt case — lies in the continuing capacity of each to generate publics willing to stake their identities on its own particular truths. Changing times, changing technologies, and changing social structures have favored one or the other style of journalism as more responsive to public needs, but both have managed more often than not to deliver the ultimate product of journalism — its audience.

And that is the root of our ongoing difficulties and disillusionments with the news coverage we read and hear. We tend to confuse the product of journalism with its processes. Journalism itself is essentially a process, a way to search for truth, not a tool to ratify it — a conversation, not a lecture. Throughout history and among all peoples, communication has always been more than the mere exchange of words; it has been a kind of ritual, "a process through which a shared culture is created, modified, and transformed. [As ritual, it is concerned with] the maintenance of society in time (even if some find this maintenance characterized by domination and therefore illegitimate) . . . [and] the creation, representation, and celebration of shared even if illusory beliefs."[18]

Various methods serve the process of journalism. Humbug itself is a method, not a conclusion; it was the arduous task of working through truths, comparing them, debating them, and judging them that allowed readers to form their *own* conclusions about Jewett's death and Robinson's guilt. Objectivity is a method, not an outcome; it was the painstaking work of examining, investigating, and observing that allowed the *Herald* to paint such vivid descriptions of Colt's last day that readers in Little Rock could see the scene with as much clarity as any denizen of Broadway.

Yet while journalists have gotten more and more skilled at the methods of finding things out, in the end their work will always be directed by the public's need to fashion out of these discovered things a comprehensible drama that adequately explains human suffering, injustice, anger, or want.

Whether the press chooses to trust the will of its audience to pursue truth wherever that might lead, or to publish only the truths it believes its audience will accept, is, finally, the choice of those of us who read, hear, watch, and buy the news. It is we who ultimately decide whether Thoreau was a curmudgeon or a prophet.

NOTES

1. Although journalism historians generally accept the argument that the penny editors recognized objectivity as an important news value, they disagree violently about why this new view of news took hold. In *Discovering the News*, Michael Schudson advances a market interpretation. He argues that the rise of the penny press clearly symbolized the replacement of gentry rule with "a new way of being in the world which we awkwardly summarize as 'middle class.'" This new kind of society was characterized by mass democracy, egalitarianism, and, most important, "a culture of the market [as] a more pervasive feature of human consciousness." The political independence and mass appeal of the penny press, he writes, "expressed and built the culture of a democratic market society, a culture which had no place for social or intellectual deference. This was the groundwork on which a belief in facts and a distrust of the reality, or objectivity, of 'values' could thrive" (pp. 57, 58, 60).

Dan Schiller, on the other hand, explicitly rejects Schudson's emphasis on the role of the market economy for a more Bailynesque interpretation of the penny press as a crystallization of deeply held political and social ideas. Its success, according to Schiller, "stemmed largely from its remarkably fluent use of the idiom and ideology prevalent among its public of tradesmen." He posits an explicit practical application of the Working Men's ideology: the cheap press used the traditional ideals of egalitarianism and enlightenment to justify its role as a watchdog of equal justice and a defender of equal rights. By investigating and exposing public vice and "the corruption that connived at permanent class divisions," the press "claimed to play a powerful remedial role in redressing" it (*Objectivity and the News*, pp. 10, 54.)

In a similar vein, Alexander Saxton argues that the early penny papers were not as politically neutral as they claimed. Their artisan editors, he suggests, actually transmitted "egalitarian messages about class and social values" that "propagated elements of the Jacksonian legitimizing synthesis" ("Problems of Class," p. 234).

Examining the interplay and conflict of social, economic, and political needs in the strange brew of Jacksonian America can indeed suggest richer and more provocative explanations of the development of the penny press than the traditional technological determinist view. And all three authors get some of it right: the rhetoric of egalitarianism did inspire and undergird some reporting in some of the papers, and market forces were clearly critical in shaping the direction of the press.

All three, however, take too narrow and rigid a perspective. Each has chosen a pet class as the exclusive mover and shaper of the penny press and has blithely consigned all other classes to invisibility. None seems to recognize any normal, ordinary interaction between various sectors of society, or the ambiguity and fluidity of class divisions in the Jacksonian era in particular. And all start with the premise that their favored class of penny-press readers made up one great undifferentiated mass, one great *Lumpenproletariat* united by a single longing that only the cheap press could satisfy.

Schudson bases his argument solely on Bennett and his *Herald*. While speculating convincingly that the *Herald* was intended for a better class of reader, he dismisses as irrelevant the development and influence of the papers aimed at readers on the lower rung of the social ladder — including the *Sun*, the singlehanded inventor of the entire genre. He also completely — and mystifyingly — ignores the special characteristics of the *Tribune*, which openly acknowledged that it was intended solely for the "active and substantial Middle Class of our citizens" while at the same time declaring itself the antithesis of the middle-class *Herald*. How two such wildly different papers could pursue and attract readers from the same class is a question Schudson never addresses.

Schiller and Saxton, on the other hand, paint the penny-press readers as a solid phalanx of like-minded and liberal-minded artisans whose single greatest interest was class solidarity. Sean Wilentz, however, specifically disavows the thesis that the antebellum working class was anything like "a single entity . . . never to change or to be changed, ever bound by a unity of sentiment across the shifting barriers of trade, region, race, sex, or ethnicity, autonomous and eternally resentful of all other classes. This Working Class never existed, least of all before the Civil War" (*Chants Democratic*, p. 18). In the penny press, furthermore, the language of Thomas Paine, Robert Owen, and Fanny Wright occupied a tiny and often dubious proportion of columns more enthusiastically modeled on the voice of Balzac, the ultimate *flaneur*.

2. Thoreau, *Journal*, 4:486–87 (entry dated 24 April 1852).

CHAPTER ONE

1. O'Brien, *Story of the "Sun,"* pp. 61 (circulation figure for January 1836), 79. O'Brien is quoting the *Sun*'s 19 April 1837 edition, in which the paper reported a net return of $12,981.88 for the six months from April through September 1836. After the murder, in August 1836, daily circulation was reported at 27,000 (p. 69).

2. On the changing economic basis of the newspaper press during this period, see Baldasty, "Nineteenth-Century Origins."

3. Benjamin Rush, "The Influence of Physical Causes upon the Moral Faculty," in *Selected Writings*, p. 206, and "Directions for Conducting a Newspaper, Addressed to Mr. Brown, Editor of the Federal Gazette," ibid., p. 397.

4. On developments in early American crime literature, see Williams, "Rogues, Rascals and Scoundrels" and " 'Behold a Tragic Scene' "; Papke, *Framing the Criminal*, chap. 2; Eberhard, "Mr. Bennett Covers a Murder Trial"; Jaffe, "Unmasking the City."

For a British journalist's account of the working methods of sellers of street literature in London, see Mayhew, *London Labour and the London Poor*, 1:213–26. The "patterers" interviewed by Mayhew found that an account of "a stunning good murder" was always a best-seller, even when, as one seller cheerfully reported, the tale included "'*a sorrowful lamentation*' of [the murderer's] own composing, which I'd got written by the blind man expressly for the occasion. On the morning of the execution we beat all the regular newspapers out of the field; for we had the full, true, and particular account down, you see, by our own express, and that can beat anything that ever they can publish; for we gets it printed several days afore it comes off" (p. 223).

5. On the connection to the *Daily Sentinel*, see Saxton, "Problems of Class and Race," p. 215; on the GTU, see Wilentz, *Chants Democratic*, pp. 219, 224n.

6. For a detailed discussion of the Working Men's platform, see Hugins, *Jacksonian Democracy*, chap. 3.

7. Wilentz, *Chants Democratic*, pp. 189, 206–7. See also Hugins, *Jacksonian Democracy*, pp. 11–23.

8. Wright, *Course of Popular Lectures* (1834), quoted in Wilentz, *Chants Democratic*, p. 177.

9. *Sun*, 9 June 1836; *Transcript*, 13 June 1836. On the question of public education, see Wilentz, *Chants Democratic*, pp. 177–83, 187–88; Hugins, *Jacksonian Democracy*, pp. 131–35; Pessen, *Jacksonian America*, pp. 62–63. On the mechanics' institutions for self-improvement, see Bender, *New York Intellect*, pp. 78–88.

10. On Bennett's life, see Francke, "James Gordon Bennett"; Crouthamel, *Bennett's "New York Herald"*; Carlson, *Man Who Made News*; and [Pray], *Memoirs*.

11. Crouthamel, *Bennett's "New York Herald,"* pp. 16–18; Hudson, *Journalism*, pp. 411–15; Francke, "James Gordon Bennett," p. 34; Crouthamel, *James Watson Webb*, pp. 30, 209n (citing numerous sources).

CHAPTER TWO

1. On Robinson's character and connections, see the sixpenny *New York Courier and Enquirer* for 11 April. For his birth date, see Fowley, *History of Durham*, p. 418. Robinson was the eighth child and oldest son of eleven children by his father's two wives (see Fowley, pp. 418, 429).

2. Hone, *Diary*, 1:211.

3. Most of the New York papers published daily "verbatim" transcripts of all or part of the trial proceedings; their accuracy and completeness vary widely. For the

most coherent transcript, see Lawson, ed., *American State Trials*, 12:426–87, from which I quote here: the testimony of Frederick W. Gourgous, the druggist's clerk (4 June, pp. 461–62); the wrangling over the letters (6, 7 June, pp. 479–81); the prosecution's description of Stevens's death (p. 468); Price's summation and Judge Ogden Edwards's charge (7 June, pp. 483, 485).

4. Citing the pressure of the "constant call" for the *Herald* on the day after the murder, Bennett reported on 12 April that his press had broken down the previous day, leaving many readers bereft of copies. For days thereafter, he reprinted the articles from 11 April along with new material.

CHAPTER THREE

1. *Sun*, 14 June 1836; *New York Herald*, 30 April 1836.

2. There is some suggestion that Attree not only knew Jewett in 1834 but pursued her actively and publicly. On 13 April the *Herald* printed what were supposed to be extracts from the correspondence found in Jewett's room, including one letter, full of purple passages of extravagant admiration and coyly interlarded with asterisks, signed "Wandering Willie" — a person, said the *Herald*, "well known last summer to have been connected with certain prints of this city, now going into 'the sere and yellow leaf.' "

Willie, it is clear from the *Herald*'s hints, was Attree, who was then enjoying a temporary sojourn from journalism in Texas. See also Horace Greeley's letter replying to a query by a friend: "You enquire — Who is the Wandering Willie of Bennett? I presume he is a scribbler of whom you have heard little or nothing. His name is Wm. H. Attree, a Londoner by birth, and a Police, Law and Speech Reporter by profession, but known here as a shrewd, active and unprincipled penny-a-liner, mainly for the small dailies" (Greeley to B. F. Ransom, 9 May 1836, Horace Greeley Papers, New York Public Library). Extracts from other alleged Attree letters appeared in various newspapers and pamphlets.

Yet the authenticity of the letters is unverifiable and highly suspect. Bennett's lush Wandering Willie "excerpt," published the day after the *Transcript*'s scoop, reads less like a lover's outpourings than a concoction designed to embarrass Attree and diminish his former paper's triumph. On 19 April the *Sun* joined the game. It printed what it called "A Leaf from the Diary of Ellen Jewett," which described the young woman's encounter with "a queer looking, cross-eyed man who represented himself to be the editor, proprietor and publisher of a penny paper printed in Nassau street. Said he was smitten with my beauty yesterday as he met me walking in Broadway — represented his paper as in a flourishing condition, and himself the very paragon of editors." Bennett proposed to Jewett, the diary went on to say, and when she refused him he asked to borrow money for his newspaper.

Whereas the *Herald*'s Wandering Willie letter and the *Sun*'s diary leaf were obviously faked for comic effect, the authenticity of the other supposed letters that floated about are harder either to confirm or to disprove. We know from the trial that Coroner William Schureman did indeed seize some letters from Jewett's room (Lawson, ed., *American State Trials*, 12:453, 477), and we know that during the trial the prosecution did try to introduce as evidence fifteen or so letters to Jewett from Robinson, along with his "private diary."

But because Joseph Hoxie and his head clerk, appearing as defense witnesses, blocked the use of virtually all the documentary evidence by professing themselves unable to swear that every page was in Robinson's own hand, only one of Jewett's letters was ever transcribed in any official source. (At one point in the trial, Hoxie marked several diary pages and picked out one letter of which he was certain [ibid., pp. 460–61]; another witness marked twelve diary pages as Robinson's but denied the others and, upon being shown seventeen letters, swore to eight of them [ibid., pp. 462–63]. Later, Phoenix attempted to read "the four" authenticated letters in court, but after a great deal of dickering only one was admitted into evidence and read aloud [ibid., pp. 479–81].) Dated 14 November 1835 and signed "Frank Rivers," the transcribed letter broke off Robinson's relationship with Jewett because "I am no longer worthy of you" and promised to return a miniature to her that evening. The prosecution argued that this was the miniature he would retrieve from her room when he killed her.

A flourishing business in humbugged documents was going on at this point outside the penny press. At least nine different cheap pamphlets touching on the killing appeared within a few years (see McDade, *Annals of Murder*, nos. 812–14, 816–21); others appeared as late as 1880. Of these, only two presented actual excerpts from the trial proceedings. The other seven purported to include "conversations" with Robinson in prison or en route to Texas, "extracts" from the letters or diaries of killer or victim, and even selections from Jewett's own poetry. Three days after the acquittal, the diarist George Templeton Strong confessed to buying a pamphlet version of Robinson's journal from a street hawker, but dismissed it as "no more his diary than it is mine" (Strong, *Diary*, 1:24 [11 June 1836]).

Without further verification, we cannot assume that any of the documents in either pamphlets or papers were any more real than the "dying words" that sounded the popular grace note of the traditional chronicle of crime.

3. An account of one of the Portland riots, taken from the *Eastern Argus* of 11 November 1825, is reprinted in Hofstadter and Wallace, eds., *American Violence*, pp. 447–50. According to this account, Portland was embarrassed as much by the presence of the whorehouses, which were "tenanted by the most loathsome and vicious of the human species, and made a common resort for drunken sailors and the lowest off-scouring of society," as by the riots themselves, perpetrated by a mob of "idle roaring boys and raw Irishmen."

On Jewett's life, see, for instance, the *Eastern Argus*, 15–19 April; the *Kennebec Journal*, 20 April; and the *Portland Courier and Family Reader*, 22 April. The report on her moral obtuseness comes from a *Boston Post* article reprinted in the *Transcript* of 18 April and the *Courier and Enquirer* of 23 April.

4. See P. C. Cohen, "Helen Jewett Murder," for a survey of various versions of the truth about Jewett's life that supplements the newspapers' reporting with information from other, more convincing sources. On the daughter's divorce suit and on Dorcas's father, see p. 386. When the famous traveler Anne Royall visited the Weston home in 1827 and remarked on the poise, sweetness, and accomplished airs of the young girl who attended the door, Mrs. Weston claimed credit for the raising of the poor orphan (pp. 385–86, quoting Royall's *Black Book* for 1828 [pp. 269–70]). Interestingly, none of the many reports of her birthplace was accurate. Young Dorcas was actually born in Temple, a tiny town some thirty-five miles from Augusta (letter to author from Cohen, 23 July 1991).

5. Leo Braudy calls Byron one of the world's first "public personalities," a person more valuable to his audience as an embodiment of their fantasies than for any talent of his own. The brooding poet who craved fame while publicly disdaining it, who titillated his readers with careful hints of deep secrets and dark passions greater than those of ordinary mortals, was celebrated for "the literary display of 'himself' . . . in which his audience might glimpse an image not of their public selves so much as those desires and aspirations that had seemed socially unfit or irrelevant." Like a high-class prostitute, Byron stood above the social order and symbolized the possibility of escape from its trammels (Braudy, *Frenzy of Renown*, p. 401).

Porter Van Nest testified on 4 June: "Heard of the murder of Helen Jewett about seven or eight o'clock on the morning of [Sunday,] April 10th; went to the house and saw the corpse. . . . [Saw] the corpse a second time, on Monday morning" (Lawson, ed., *American State Trials*, 12:455).

6. Strong, *Diary*, 1:15.

CHAPTER FOUR

1. Bennett's summing up of the case appeared in the *Herald*, 8 June. The "indicted thief" charge refers to a January 1836 episode in which Webb of the *Courier and Enquirer* hired an express messenger to rush him the text of Andrew Jackson's special message to Congress. Day waylaid the messenger, broke the seals, opened the package, and printed a summary of the text in his own paper a scant two days after the speech was delivered in Washington. Upon Webb's complaint, a grand jury indicted Day for theft, and the case was still pending at the time of Robinson's trial.

2. Strong, *Diary*, 1:23; Hone, *Diary*, 1:210; Marryat, *Diary in America*, pp. 328–29. Furlong's suicide was reported in the city papers of 14 and 15 December 1838.

3. Greeley to B. F. Ransom, 9 May 1836, Horace Greeley Papers, New York Public Library.

4. *New York Herald*, 8 June 1836, 8 June 1836 extra edition (also reprinted in the issue of 9 June).

5. Browne, *Great Metropolis*, pp. 303, 304.

6. [Pray], *Memoirs*, pp. 210–11; Marryat, *Diary in America*, p. 410. The black-mail charge was still circulating sixty years later. At century's end a venerable New Yorker recalled in his memoirs that "a person who had lately embarked in an enterprise requiring money to advance it" received $30,000 from a gentleman caught at Townsend's house on the murder night (Haswell, *Reminiscences of an Octogenarian*, p. 320).

Two bitter contemporary critics of Bennett also raised the blackmail charges. The anonymous writer of the vituperative 1844 pamphlet *Life and Writings of James Gordon Bennett* outlined many of the *Herald* editor's sins, including his "disgusting" coverage of the Jewett affair (pp. 12–21). The bibliographer Joseph Sabin notes, without elaboration, that this pamphlet "is said to have been suppressed" (*Bibliotheca Americana*, no. 4728). Critical of the penny press in general was L. A. Wilmer, who dissects the Jewett incident (*Our Press Gang*, p. 231).

7. See, for instance, the *Sun* and the *New York Evening Post* of 4 June; Lawson, ed., *American State Trials*, 12:447–48.

8. Allusions to Robinson's life bobbed up occasionally in the national press for years after the trial. On 25 March 1848, the *National Police Gazette*, refuting a rumor that Robinson had died, reprinted a brief outline of his life from the *New Orleans Crescent*. The piece gave his alias and remarked on his marriage, his job, and his "flourishing" circumstances.

Official records of Nacogdoches County, Texas, bear out most of the *Crescent's* facts. A Richard Parmalee does indeed appear as clerk of the district court in the county records, and "Parmalee" would have been a plausible alias for the fleeing youth: along with Richard's own ancestor David Robinson, a Joel Parmalee was one of the original patentees of Durham, Connecticut, and in Richard's time Parmalees were still almost as numerous as Robinsons in the Durham records. Also suggestive was Richard's middle initial "P," although the full name seems never to have been recorded. See Fowley, *History of Durham*, pp. 21, 349, 418; for Parmalees in the vital records, see, e.g., pp. 409, 416–17, and 422; and for mention of a cousin of Richard's, Henry Parmalee Robinson, see p. 424.

The 1850 Nacogdoches census, furthermore, lists Parmalee's birthplace as Connecticut and his age as thirty-two; Robinson would have turned thirty-three in April of the census year. He died in Sabine Parish, Louisiana, in 1855 at the age of thirty-eight, leaving a widow and a stepdaughter.

See Murrie, comp., *Early Records of Nacogdoches County*, p. 96; Ericson, ed., *People of Nacogdoches County*, p. 79, and her *Nacogdoches — Gateway to Texas*, p. 113. On Robinson's father-in-law Archibald Hotchkiss, a pioneer settler, land agent, engineer, and active Mason, see Murrie, *Early Records of Nacogdoches County*, p. 72;

on his slaves, see Ericson, transcriber, *1847 Census*, p. 2; on the duties of clerk, see McDonald, comp., *Inventory of Court Records*, pp. 3–5.

CHAPTER FIVE

1. Poe, "Raising the Wind (Diddling)," in *Collected Works*, 3:869.
2. Poe, "MS. Found in a Bottle," in ibid., 2:146; Jackson, "Poe Hoax," pp. 47–48; Silverman, *Edgar A. Poe*, pp. 137, 143.
3. Barnum, *Struggles and Triumphs*, p. 13; on his career generally, see this autobiography and also Harris, *Humbug*.
4. Barnum, *Humbugs of the World*, pp. 8–9, 11.
5. Halttunen, *Confidence Men and Painted Women*, p. xv.
6. Trollope, *Domestic Manners of the Americans*, p. 302. On Melville's work and its genesis, see Bergmann, "Original Confidence Man," p. 201. Peddlers from Connecticut were so renowned for their skill with the nutmeg that they gave the state its nickname — and a particularly nasty reputation. When Gouverneur Morris was growing up in New York, his father specified in his will that the youth not be sent for his education to Connecticut, "lest he should imbibe in his youth that low Craft and cunning so Incident to the People of that Country" (will of Lewis Morris, 19 November 1760, quoted in Mintz, *Gouverneur Morris*, p. 15).
7. For details of the Moon Hoax, see O'Brien, *Story of the "Sun,"* pp. 37–57; Poe, "The Literati of New York City: Richard Adams Locke," in *Essays and Reviews*, pp. 1214–22; and Barnum, *Humbugs of the World*, pp. 193–203. The full text of the hoax is reprinted in Maverick, *Henry J. Raymond*, pp. 273–317.

On Clark's involvement, see Moss, *Poe's Literary Battles*, pp. 87–89 (quoting Benson J. Lossing, *History of New York City* [New York: 1884], pp. 360–62). Lossing and Moss cite this episode as the root of the long feud between Clark and Edgar Allan Poe, who always felt that the Moon Hoax had been a plagiarism of his own spoof "Hans Pfaal," published in the *Southern Literary Messenger* several weeks earlier.

CHAPTER SIX

1. Bok, *Lying*, pp. 20, 22.
2. Harris, *Humbug*, pp. 77 (quoting J. E. Hillary Skinner in *After the Storm: Or, Jonathan and His Neighbors in 1865–66* [London, 1866], 1:9), 73, 77.
3. Buckley, "To the Opera House," pp. 523–29, 472.
4. Dana is cited in Park, "Natural History of the Newspaper," p. 285; Thoreau, *Walden*, p. 52.
5. Carey, "Press and the Public Discourse," pp. 10–11 (drawing on Robert E. Park — see particularly his *Crowd and the Public*).

6. Compare Walter Lippmann: "The hypothesis, which seems to me the most fertile, is that news and truth are not the same thing, and must be clearly distinguished. The function of news is to signalize an event, the function of truth is to bring to light the hidden facts, to set them into relation with each other, and make a picture of reality on which men can act. Only at those points, where social conditions take recognizable and measurable shape, do the body of truth and the body of news coincide. That is a comparatively small part of the whole field of human interest" (*Public Opinion*, p. 358).

CHAPTER SEVEN

1. The quiet disregard of aberrant detail is a common phenomenon in the encounter between real-life person and living tradition. In one typical example documented by a student of folklore, an inconveniently pregnant Indiana girl was murdered by her lover. Her sad and familiar story soon set her neighbors to singing mournful ballads about the fate of poor Pearl, but none of them mentioned what should have been the most memorable aspect of the case. Pearl Bryan had been beheaded, and despite her family's pleas her murderer never produced the head. The reason for the odd distortion of detail is simple. In the classic girl-murdered-for-love ballad formula already at hand to explain Pearl's story, there were no stanzas about headless heroines (A. B. Cohen, *Poor Pearl, Poor Girl!*).

2. Stansell, *City of Women*, p. xii; Carroll Smith-Rosenberg, "Davy Crockett as Trickster: Pornography, Liminality, and Symbolic Inversion in Victorian America," in *Disorderly Conduct*, p. 90; Welter, "Cult of True Womanhood."

3. Quoted in Gilfoyle, *City of Eros*, p. 60.

4. Lawson, ed., *American State Trials*, 12:436.

5. The number of working prostitutes was often overestimated for shock value. Since New York's population of women between sixteen and thirty-six numbered some 70,000 at the time, we can believe either that one in every seven women was a prostitute or that McDowall was exaggerating. Gilfoyle estimates that "probably 5 to 10 percent of all young nineteenth-century women in New York (between fifteen and thirty years in age) prostituted at some point" and, for the decade of the 1830s, posits a total of from 1,850 to 3,700 working prostitutes (*City of Eros*, pp. 57, 59, 344 [n. 7]).

6. Ibid., pp. 76–91 (for "illusion of power," see pp. 81–82); P. C. Cohen, "Helen Jewett Murder," p. 375, quoting the *Journal of Public Morals* 1 (1 May 1836): 1, on the twenty deaths in three months.

7. Carroll Smith-Rosenberg, "Beauty, the Beast, and the Militant Woman: A Case Study in Sex Roles and Social Stress in Jacksonian America," in *Disorderly Conduct*, pp. 109–28; Berg, *Remembered Gate*, pp. 176–222. For a minority perspective on the Jewett affair, see the coverage throughout the spring in the reformers' *Advocate of Moral Reform*. The women criticized the "most unrighteous

distinction between the guilty man and woman," and denounced as gross injustice the fact that "the same degree of guilt which sinks a female beyond all hopes of redemption makes the young libertine a *hero*, who has manly courage enough to throw off the shackles of virtue, and dare to think and act for himself" (15 June 1836).

8. Hart, *Popular Book*, pp. 53–54.

9. Brooks, "Mark of the Beast," p. 131.

10. Rowson, *Charlotte Temple*, pp. 119, xiii–xiv.

11. Davis, *Homicide in American Fiction*, p. 156 (quoting Neal).

12. The novel *Charlotte Temple* made a similar argument about the inequities of the social order. Cathy N. Davidson points out that the heroine's story was characterized by its "quintessential injustice, its disappointed promises, its sense of being betrayed by the liberal and republican ideal that posited a correlation between merit (in a woman, read 'virtue') and reward. Charlotte was recognized as just such a victim by even the first reviewer of the novel" ("Life and Times of *Charlotte Temple*," pp. 169–70).

13. *New York Herald*, 14 April, 19 April (twice) 1836. Kai Erikson calls this strategy for handling deviance a "deployment pattern." Deviant persons "often supply an important service to society by patrolling the outer edges of group space and by providing a contrast which gives the rest of the community some sense of their own territorial identity." A community that relegates its deviants to a separate and incurable "category of misfits who would normally be expected to engage in unacceptable activities and to oppose the rest of the social order," therefore, grants itself in the process a permanent pool of scapegoats for all unpleasant, messy, or embarrassing social ills (*Wayward Puritans*, pp. 196–97).

14. Reynolds, *Beneath the American Renaissance*, p. 59.

CHAPTER EIGHT

1. Fowley, *History of Durham*, p. 239.

2. On Price, see Lawson, ed., *American State Trials*, 5:360–62 (quoting various sources, including Philip Hone on his violence); it is Lawson who judges Price the "foremost" trial lawyer and points out that "no lawyer has or will appear so often" in his seventeen-volume compendium of trials. He is bemused by Price's absence from most standard reference works, which he says is testament to the "ephemeral notoriety of a member of the bar." It may also be testament to Price's clientele — accused bigamists, libelers, murderers, procurers, larcenists, and blasphemers — and to his death in 1846 in a silly duel with his colleague Maxwell's brother.

In the murky and convoluted story of the failure of the Life and Fire Insurance Company, Bennett and Hugh Maxwell, who were both Democrats at the time, figure together in a suggestive and unflattering light. One of the defendants, Jacob Barker, maintained his innocence in an outpouring of articles and letters over the next thirty-seven years, and another, Henry Eckford, went so far as to challenge Maxwell to a duel to protest the district attorney's improper "intrusion" into the grand jury room during its vote against him. The case apparently had been brought to trial in the first place mainly through the relentless efforts of M. M. Noah, then the editor of the *Morning Enquirer*, who had been nursing a grudge ever since Eckford had beaten him two years earlier in a power struggle for control of another sixpenny paper. By the time of the fraud trial, Noah had hired as a reporter for his new *Enquirer* none other than James Gordon Bennett.

Bennett's biographer Isaac C. Pray later singled out for special notice the Scotsman's reporting "during all the trials brought forward by the energy of Hugh Maxwell, the district attorney," during "this dark period" of "corruption, bribery, and temptation." Pray reported that Bennett maintained his integrity even though "money flowed like water to convert truth into a lie." Yet Pray also noted that Maxwell privately believed Eckford innocent, a "victim of the base conduct of others" — but did not allow his private convictions to affect his public duty. If Maxwell had indeed tried to influence the grand jury against Eckford anyway, some other reward could well have compensated him for subordinating his private moral sense to his public prosecutorial zeal ([Pray], *Memoirs*, pp. 72–75, 81–84; Carlson, *Man Who Made News*, pp. 70–71; *Dictionary of American Biography*, s.v. "Jacob Barker"; and Barker, *Conspiracy Trials*.

3. On Hoffman, see Lawson, ed., *American State Trials*, 1:540; *Dictionary of American Biography*, s.v. "Josiah Ogden Hoffman," "Ogden Hoffman." In the ward-by-ward election returns for 1836, Hoffman won about two-thirds of the vote in four of the five wards with the highest per-capita wealth (Hugins, *Jacksonian Democracy*, p. 211). On Edwards, see Lawson, ed., *American State Trials*, 2:512; Schiller, *Objectivity and the News*, pp. 61–64; and Wilentz, *Chants Democratic*, pp. 291–93.

4. The indefatigable Hoxie also supported the abolitionist cause (Wilentz, *Chants Democratic*, pp. 202, 207n, 263n). Maxwell was a manager and Edwards a vice president of the new society (see New-York City Temperance Society, *First Annual Report*, p. 52).

5. On the motives and methods of these evangelical businessmen, see Wilentz, *Chants Democratic*, pp. 145–53, and Johnson, *Shopkeeper's Millennium*. The profitability of total abstinence comes from Joseph Brewster, master hatter and temperance leader, writing in the Temperance Society's first annual report and quoted in Wilentz (p. 148). Stuart Blumin points out that most of the temperance leaders in the big cities were comfortable or wealthy professionals and merchants. In New York's Temperance Society, he writes, "businessmen and professionals undertook the task of eliminating alcoholic drink from the city by associating with each other in an organization designed to reach downward, in a distinctly hierarchical fashion, into the various neighborhoods and trades.... [I]f the NYCTS had any influence at all in shaping the social contours of New York, it was to sharpen the growing divide between the business and working classes" (*Emergence of the Middle Class*, pp. 198–99).

6. Wilentz, *Chants Democratic*, p. 202.

7. *New York Herald*, 10 June, 8 June 1836. In 1833 Day had paid his first assistant, an unemployed printer, four dollars a week to report on the police court — or about two hundred dollars a year. When Horace Greeley first arrived in New York in 1831, he set type for a complicated and maddening polyglot Bible with such speed that he earned six dollars a week — or about three hundred dollars a year (Parton, *Life of Horace Greeley*, p. 125). A journeyman shoemaker complained in 1835 that with constant work he could earn some four hundred dollars a year, yet he required six hundred and fifty dollars to support his family (*National Trades' Union*, 6 June 1835, quoted in Wilentz, *Chants Democratic*, p. 231). Fifteen hundred dollars was also three times the sum Bennett had expended to start up his *Herald*.

8. Bennett was, according to Mitchell Stephens, a "proto-investigative reporter . . . [who] did in fact do his best to bring to justice the person responsible for Jewett's death" (*History of News*, p. 245). He was "an active news-gatherer rather than a news-receiver," argues Warren Francke; "he observed and he questioned. . . . His remarkable use of the observation technique clearly played a central role in the popular excitement over the *Herald*'s murder coverage" ("Investigative Exposure," p. 46). He "assembled the raw materials for a detective story," cheers Thomas Leonard, "and prompted citizens to think like criminal investigators" (*Power of the Press*, p. 148). See also Mott, *American Journalism*, p. 233; Carlson, *Man Who Made News*, pp. 166–67; and even O'Brien, *Story of the "Sun,"* p. 67. Richard Kluger (*The Paper*, p. 36), and John Stevens (*Sensationalism and the New York Press*, pp. 42–53) express doubt about the trial outcome but accept uncritically all Bennett's claims of journalistic enterprise, including the visits to the house and the interview with Townsend. All are silent on the charges of bribery and blackmail, Bennett's subsequent change of heart, and the affair of William Gray's letters.

Steven Jaffe does explore the journalistic ramifications of the charge that George Wisner, who worked for the *New York Evangelist* before joining the *Sun*, had used his position with the first paper to blackmail owners of gambling dens and to threaten merchants with ruinous adverse publicity because of grudges that were purely personal and perhaps unfair ("Unmasking the City," pp. 172–75). Jaffe does not, however, address the considerably more serious potential consequences of blackmail by a paper as popular and influential as the *Herald*.

Dan Schiller warrants particular recognition for the doggedness of his bedazzlement with Bennett. He pounces on any bit of rhetorical evidence for Bennett's "unbending . . . defense of all men's natural rights," while ignoring or discarding all the contradictions, lapses, distortions, and sophisms that gnarled and twisted the rest of the *Herald*'s reporting of the affair. The subtler but more firmly grounded radicalism of the *Sun* and the *Transcript* also escape him completely (*Objectivity and the News*, pp. 57–65; quote, p. 65).

CHAPTER NINE

1. The *Virginia Free Press* of 16 August 1866, for example, reprinted from the Philadelphia papers a graphic item about the stabbing death of Mary Kearney, a "woman of the town." The headline read: "A 'Helen Jewett' Affair."

2. *National Police Gazette*, 24 January 1846, 16 May 1846, 1 November 1845, all quoted in Schiller, *Objectivity and the News*, pp. 105, 108. The *Gazette*'s pamphlet version appeared in 1849 under the title *The Lives of Helen Jewett and Richard P. Robinson*.

3. Riis, *Making of an American*, p. 340; Byrnes, *Criminals of America*, pp. 341–44.

4. Lawson, ed., *American State Trials*, 12:426–27. Robinson, too, continued after death to inspire wild "true-life" stories of his own. Nearly twenty years after Jewett's former lover died in Louisiana, the warden of the Tombs prison recounted, in his memoirs of famous criminals, an elaborate tale of ongoing machinations by various lawyers in a suit arising from Robinson's will. The property at issue was a valuable parcel of land in Hyde Park that Robinson supposedly had either given to Hoxie outright after the trial or had merely put up as security for the repayment of the "defalcations" he had committed against his employer. The parties to the dispute were Robinson's named heirs, a family named McKay "who had been kind to him in his exile," and the murderer's sister Mrs. Still, a "professed spiritualistic medium" in St. Louis who had been cut out of the will (Sutton, *New York Tombs*, pp. 134–36).

Although it is quite possible that the warden was describing a genuine suit, somebody was humbugging somewhere: Robinson's will (listed in Murrie, *Early Records of Nacogdoches County*, p. 96) clearly names first his wife and stepdaughter and then a sister named Coe and his wife's brother, Rinaldo Hotchkiss, as his heirs. Sutton was a bit of a humbug himself. The Tombs did not open until 1838, and Robinson was incarcerated in Bellevue. Sutton derived much of his account from the *Herald* and various cheap pamphlets about the murder.

5. Tocqueville, *Democracy in America*, p. 185; Trollope, *Domestic Manners of the Americans*, pp. 92–93. Allan Pred has collected and evaluated various official statistics on the number and circulation of nineteenth-century newspapers. He lists 861 papers in print in 1828, 1,258 in 1835, and 1,404 in 1840; but there were undoubtedly many more (*Urban Growth*, p. 21). As late as 1937, the bibliographer Winifred Gregory searched American libraries and found surviving copies of 1,469 different newspapers in print at some time in 1840 (see *American Newspapers, 1821–1936*; Gregory's bibliography is arranged geographically, and the count for 1840 is mine). How many more had already disappeared without a trace is impossible to conjecture.

6. Gallaher Family Papers, William R. Perkins Library, Duke University, Durham, N.C.

7. "The fact is that regular local news columns — a regular feature of the eighteenth century English provincial press — became a standard part of Ameri-

can newspapers only gradually over a long period of time, appearing here and there in the 1840s, somewhat more regularly in the 1850s, and typically by the 1860s and 1870s" (Russo, *Origins of Local News*, p. 4). See also below, Epilogue.

8. Caroline Danske Dandridge, "Henry Bedinger [III] and Old Bedford," typescript, pp. 86 (28 October), 82 (18 April), Bedinger-Danske Papers, William R. Perkins Library, Duke University, Durham, N.C.

9. Whittington, *Letters*, pp. 5–6 (2 July 1828).

10. Whittington, *Letters*, pp. 1–2 (21 April 1827), 17 (29 September 1830). On the early history of Arkansas and its first paper, see Ross, *"Arkansas Gazette."*

11. Émile Durkheim suggests that shared opposition to crime is an especially strong force for cohesiveness in a community. "Since . . . the sentiments which crime offends are, in any given society, the most universally collective that there are; since they are, indeed, particularly strong states of the common conscience, it is impossible for them to tolerate contradiction" (*Division of Labor*, p. 99). In a raw young frontier society, the *Gazette*'s public anguish over the prevalence of crime and its public reproofs of ruffians and blackguards would have helped crystallize and express a sense of heightened social solidarity in the face of crime. It also provided the community a useful reference point against which to measure and define its public self by marking and ratifying, as Kai Erikson suggests (see above, chap. 7, n. 13), the outer edges of acceptable behavior.

CHAPTER TEN

1. Melville, "Bartleby the Scrivener," p. 36.

2. On the lives of Samuel and John Colt, see Rohan, *Yankee Arms Maker* (which is uncritical and should be used with care), and Edwards, *Story of Colt's Revolver.* The estimate of the lawyers' fee comes from Rohan, p. 141; they also received a cash payment of at least two thousand dollars. On Selden, see Lawson, ed., *American State Trials*, 1:458, and *Biographical Dictionary of the United States Congress, 1774– 1989 . . . from the First through the One Hundredth Congresses, March 4, 1789, to January 3, 1989, Inclusive,* 100th Cong., 2d sess., S. Doc. 34 (Washington, D.C.: Government Printing Office, 1989), p. 1789. On Emmet, see Lawson, ed., *American State Trials*, 1:63; on Morrill's involvement in the Restell trial, see Browder, *Wickedest Woman*, pp. 35–37.

3. Clark, who adored Dickens above all other authors (see Miller, *Raven and the Whale*, pp. 34–35) sent his excuses to the committee on the grounds that he was "unexpectedly in a business maelstrom, made up of little currents of avocation which have provokingly converged upon me at this moment" (W. G. and L. G. Clark, *Letters*, p. 117).

4. Hone, *Diary*, 2:636. For the most coherent transcript of the trial, see Lawson, ed., *American State Trials*, 1:455–513, from which I quote here; most of the penny papers issued two or three editions a day and reprinted the best bits of testimony over the course of several days, making citation difficult.

See the following pages in Lawson: Selden reading aloud Colt's confession statement (pp. 475–83), his fear of the newspapers' lies (p. 479), and his standing on the corpse's knees (p. 481); Judge Kent's justification for including the press (p. 500); Samuel Colt demonstrating his pistol (p. 471); Judge Kent admitting Adams's head (p. 472); Selden describing Colt's relation with Henshaw (p. 474); Whiting pitying Henshaw (pp. 497–98); and Judge Kent instructing the jury (pp. 503, 506). The account of Samuel's reaction to the suicide, recorded by Lewis Gaylord Clark, is appended at the end of Lawson's transcript.

George Walling, who later became chief of police, was one of the many New Yorkers convinced that Colt had escaped: "I have heard it declared over and over again," he wrote years after the crime, "by those in a position to know, that Colt did not commit suicide; that the body found in his cell when the Tombs caught fire was only a corpse prepared for the purpose, and that he escaped in the confusion. The coroner, it is said, was aware of the deception, and the jurymen were selected for their ignorance of Colt's personal appearance. Persons who know Colt well are positive they have seen him since the time of his alleged suicide in both California and Texas" (*Recollections*, p. 26).

On the rumor of the parcel for Poe, see, most recently, Wolf and Mader, *Rotten Apples*, pp. 49–50. Wolf and Mader also raise the reasonable question, "How could a man stab himself in the chest while resting supine on a bed — and afterward have the strength and will to cross his hands over his stomach?"

CHAPTER ELEVEN

1. On the panic of 1837, see Wilentz, *Chants Democratic*, pp. 294–300.

Defining so slippery a term as "middle class" is so fraught with peril that many historians adroitly avoid the task. I base this study on these assumptions. The member of the middle class was (and to some degree still is) economically and socially distinct from the lower-class worker in three important ways, as Burton Bledstein has written: He or she "owns an acquired skill or cultivated talent by means of which to provide a service"; enjoys "social prestige"; and follows "a life style approaching [his or her] aspirations" (*Culture of Professionalism*, pp. 4–5). Culturally, the antebellum middle class was evolving a distinctive "American Victorian" ethos and code of conduct based on "the belief in fixed moral laws, the emphasis on individual self-reliance, the faith in education and high culture, and the stress on economic security and social control" (C. E. Clark, *Henry Ward Beecher*, p. 4).

But I stress the word "evolving." As Richard Sennett put it, "a rising or developing class usually doesn't have a clear idea of itself. Sometimes a sense of its rights comes to it before a sense of its identity; sometimes the facts of economic power march ahead of appropriate manners, tastes, and morals. The appearance of a new class can thus create a milieu of strangers in which many people are increasingly like each other but don't know it. There is a sense that the old distinctions, the old lines between one group and another, no longer apply, but little sense of new rules for instant distinctions" (*Fall of Public Man*, p. 49). The middle class in antebellum America was discovering certain similarities — but slowly.

2. See Pessen, *Jacksonian America*, chap. 4 ("The 'Urban Revolution' and Other Social Developments"); Spann, *New Metropolis*, chap. 4 ("Poverty") and chap. 9 ("Wealth"); Wilentz, *Chants Democratic*, chap. 3 ("Metropolitan Industrialization"); and Diane Lindstrom, "Economic Structure, Demographic Change, and Income Inequality in Antebellum New York," in Mollenkopf, ed., *Power, Culture, and Place*, pp. 3–23.

Sean Wilentz, citing several sources, gives New York's population as 268,389 in 1835 and 515,547 in 1850 (*Chants Democratic*, pp. 109–100). By the mid-1850s, less than half the population of New York was native-born. For immigration statistics on the nation as a whole from 1820 to 1860, see U.S. Senate, "Immigration to the United States."

3. Quoted in Comparato, *Chronicles of Genius and Folly*, pp. 103–4. On the technological developments in printing, see Moran, *Printing Presses*; Lee, *Daily Newspaper*, esp. chaps. 5 ("The Physical Basis"), 6 ("Labor"), and 9 ("From Press to People"). On the earlier hand-press era, see Silver, *American Printer*; and for a highly detailed historical description of the entire publication process, from paper-making and typecasting to printing, distributing, and warehousing the stock, see Gaskell, *New Introduction to Bibliography*.

4. *Sun*, 3 September 1843; O'Brien, *Story of the "Sun,"* pp. 32, 71; Tucker, "History of R. Hoe," pp. 370–71. All contemporary circulation figures are suspect, as the penny editors routinely inflated their numbers. The judicious Lee gives the *Sun*'s circulation that year as 3,000 weekly and 19,000 daily (*Daily Newspaper*, p. 384).

5. Nichols, *Forty Years*, 1:322–23.

CHAPTER TWELVE

1. Quoted in [Pray], *Memoirs*, p. 267.

2. Hudson, *Journalism*, pp. 457–60; Carlson, *Man Who Made News*, p. 190.

3. [Pray], *Memoirs*, p. 266.

4. For details on Hone's life, see Allan Nevins's introduction to *The Diary*; for more on his disdain for and fear of city crime and lowlife in general, see Jaffe, "Unmasking the City," chap. 4. On the Knickerbockers, see Miller, *Raven and the Whale*, book 1. Hone describes the Brevoort ball in his entry for 28 February 1840 (*Diary*, 1:462–65); his comments on the Moral War are excerpted on p. 484.

5. Peter George Buckley describes the different spheres of public entertainment and presents a detailed case study of how a cultural war actually sparked a

shooting war — the Astor Place Riot of 1849. The proximate cause was a professional feud between the American actor Edwin Forrest, an ardent nationalist and Bowery favorite, and the orotund British tragedian William Macready. For months they and their supporters had been insulting each other's art and hissing each other's performances.

When Macready appeared as Macbeth before an audience of prominent New Yorkers at the smart new Astor Place Opera House, a great crowd of Forrest's supporters gathered outside to jeer, fling bricks, rush the building, heckle the assembled militia, and generally raise a ruckus. Finally the militia turned their guns against the crowd, killing more than a score, wounding dozens, and eventually arresting over one hundred.

The episode was more than merely a theater riot; it was "a riot *about* the theater — a contest for control over this 'public' place and the forms of behavior appropriate to it" (Buckley, "To the Opera House," p. 64). Yet it was a contest that no one really won. The rioters paid a high toll in casualties but the show nonetheless went on; the middle-class theater-goers, so far from "controlling" the place, had to be rescued by the militia.

6. Zboray, "Antebellum Reading," p. 79; on other aspects of the culture of reading, see also Charvat, *Profession of Authorship*, esp. chaps. 10 ("James T. Fields and the Beginnings of Book Promotion") and 15 ("The People's Patronage"); Hall, "Uses of Literacy."

7. Douglas, *Feminization of American Culture*, p. 9.

8. On the mammoth weeklies, see Mott, *History of American Magazines*, pp. 358–63; Barnes, *Authors, Publishers, and Politicians*, chap. 1. On the contractual arrangements with the magazines, see Charvat, *Profession of Authorship*, pp. 158, 288. On James's weakness for horsemen, see Hart, *Popular Book*, pp. 78–79.

9. Nord, *Evangelical Origins of Mass Media*, p. 8; Thompson, "Printing and Publishing Activities," pp. 88, 91 (citing Tract Society records, gives two presses in 1826); Silver, "Power of the Press," p. 6 (citing other sources, credits the society with four presses).

10. Richards, *"Gentlemen of Property and Standing,"* pp. 71–73.

11. The good tidings about the fining of the *Rake* traveled all the way to the frontier; on 17 August 1842 the *Arkansas Gazette* celebrated the news and suggested that the next indictment ought to be brought against "that prolific source of corruption, the New-York Herald." On erotic pamphlet literature, see Reynolds, *Beneath the American Renaissance*, pp. 211–24.

CHAPTER THIRTEEN

1. Greeley, *Recollections*, pp. 91–93; on Greeley's life generally, see also Parton, *Life of Horace Greeley*; Hale, *Horace Greeley*; Van Deusen, *Horace Greeley*; and Pfaff, "Horace Greeley."

2. Parton, *Life of Horace Greeley*, p. 189.

3. *New York Tribune*, 3 September 1842; McElrath to the *Tribune*, 24 December 1887, in scrapbook "Horace Greeley Clippings: Greeley's death etc.," ms. p. 109, Horace Greeley Papers, Library of Congress, Washington, D.C.

4. Greeley, *Recollections*, p. 137.

5. Emerson, *Letters*, 3:19–20 (letter dated 1 March 1842).

6. *New York Tribune*, 3 December 1845.

7. Greeley, *Recollections*, pp. 195, 199; on Hartley, see Boyer, *Urban Masses*, pp. 88–94.

8. Greeley was only the popularizer of the sentiment, not the coiner of the famous phrase "Go West, young man," but no popularizer was more indefatigable (Kluger, *The Paper*, p. 53n).

9. Greeley to H. Hubbard, 30 June 1845, 12 April 1844; Greeley to Ford, 15 September 1870; both in Horace Greeley Papers, New York Public Library.

10. On the farmers' adoration of Greeley, see Godkin, *Life and Letters*, 1:167; the anniversary lecture by George William Curtis, "Reminiscences of the Tribune," appears in *The Tribune, 1841*, pp. 19–21.

11. Congdon, *Reminiscences*, pp. 218–19; Durham to Greeley (16 January 1869), Edwin C. Parker to Greeley on behalf of his college's paper (14 November 1872), George Hoffmaster to Greeley requesting a loan (25 November 1872), Elnathan Davis to Greeley on the Eye Cups (22 November 1872), all in Horace Greeley Papers, Library of Congress, Washington, D.C.; J. Medill to Greeley asking for a Whig printer (4 November 1851), Kate Warrenton to Greeley looking for a friend of Greeley's to marry (21 October 1858), Holland to Greeley (29 November 1845), all in Horace Greeley Papers, New York Public Library.

12. Twain, *Roughing It*, pp. 152–53. The anecdote told how Greeley, in a rush to keep a lecture engagement, asked the stagecoach driver to hurry. The driver set off so fast as to jolt all Greeley's buttons off his coat and send his head shooting clean through the coach roof. But when Greeley begged him to slow down, the driver replied, "Keep your seat, Horace, and I'll get you there on time!" The punchline: "And you bet he did, too, what was left of him!"

13. Various circulation numbers are afloat. In the *Tribune*'s first year Greeley himself sometimes gave 10,000 or 11,000 for the daily and 15,000 for the weekly, but those figures seem inflated. Six years later, in 1847, an independent committee formed to settle a challenge between the *Herald* and the *Tribune* put the latter's weekly circulation at nearly 16,000 and its daily at 11,455. Soon thereafter, however, the sales did zoom. By 1860, on the eve of the Civil War, the weekly *Tribune*'s subscription list had passed the astounding figure of 200,000 even though many southern states had passed laws forbidding the mails to carry the abolitionist rag (Hudson, *Journalism*, pp. 526–29; Mott, *American Journalism*, pp. 268–69; Van Deusen, *Horace Greeley*, p. 54). In 1847 the *Herald*'s strength was precisely the opposite: its daily circulation was 16,711 and its weekly 11,455 (oddly, the same number as the *Tribune*'s daily).

14. Laborers suffered for years from the aftereffects of the panic and depression of 1837. Greeley himself estimated in July 1845 that a laborer earned about a dollar a day, and that at least half of the city's 50,000 employed women earned less than two dollars a week (cited in Spann, *New Metropolis*, p. 71). On the roughs, see Browne, *Great Metropolis*, p. 72. He was describing the situation in 1868, which could have been no worse than that of twenty years earlier.

15. Godkin, *Life and Letters*, 1:167.

16. Parton, *Life of Horace Greeley*, pp. 205, 383.

CHAPTER FOURTEEN

1. Greeley to Obadiah A. Bowe, 2 February 1842, Horace Greeley Papers, New York Public Library.

2. On the bigamist, see the *Weekly Tribune* 20 November, 4 December 1841; on the impostor, see ibid., 4 December 1841.

3. "Personal Recollections of Horace Greeley," in *The Tribune, 1841*, pp. 14–15.

4. Maverick, *Henry J. Raymond*, pp. 34–35.

5. Strong, *Diary*, 1:192 (18 November 1842).

6. On the number of new subscribers, which McElrath attributed to the coverage of Colt's case and of the 1843 court-martial of Captain Alexander Mackenzie for hanging three mutineers, see Maverick, *Henry J. Raymond*, p. 35.

7. Boyer, *Urban Masses*, pp. 54–64; see also Berg, *Remembered Gate*, on the peculiar social and psychic uses of volunteerism for the middle-class urban woman.

8. Miller, *Errand into the Wilderness*, p. 9. See David Minter for a discussion of how the children and grandchildren of the first Puritans used the genre of the jeremiad, the lengthy lamentation over spiritual failure, as a way to proclaim that their very failure was "in a designation sublime. . . . In lamenting their sad decline, New Englanders subtly thanked their God and notified the world that they yet were not as other men, that they, despite all, were a chosen people dedicated to perfection" (*Interpreted Design*, p. 58).

CHAPTER FIFTEEN

1. *New York Herald*, 27 September 1841, 20, 22, 27 January 1842.

2. A federal statute passed in 1831 defined contempt of court very narrowly as "any misbehavior in the presence of the court or so near thereto as to obstruct the administration of justice." It was not contempt, in other words, if it did not impede the court officers, attorneys, or witnesses from doing their duty then and there. Publications circulated outside of court were not considered liable to punishment under this statute (Friendly and Goldfarb, *Crime and Publicity*, pp. 278–79).

3. Walling, *Recollections*, p. 26; Haswell, *Reminiscences of an Octogenarian*, p. 374.

4. Briggs, *Adventures of Harry Franco*, 1:40–41, 60, 63–64.

5. Miller, *Raven and the Whale*, p. 93.

6. Mathews, *Puffer Hopkins*, pp. 228–29.

CHAPTER SIXTEEN

1. For the testimony on Adams's character, see Lawson, ed., *American State Trials*, 1:466–69; for the Reverend John L. Blake confessing to making Adams weep, see p. 468; for Selden's comments on Henshaw's character, p. 474; for Asa H. Wheeler's testimony about renting an office to Colt, p. 459; for Emeline Adams's description of her husband's gold watch, p. 466; for the testimony of former foreman Monahan, pp. 468–69.

2. I. M. Leonard, "New York City Politics," pp. 3–5, 25–34, 50.

3. Spann, *New Metropolis*, pp. 53–56; Morris's testimony is in Lawson, ed., *American State Trials*, 1:463.

4. On the Colts' problem stepmother, see Rohan, *Yankee Arms Maker*, pp. 5–8. The extra edition entitled *Life, Letters, and Last Conversation of John C. Colt, Who Committed Suicide at the New York City Prison, Nov. 18, 1842, Just before the Time Appointed for His Execution for the Murder of Samuel Adams, Printer, on the 18th Sept., 1841* (New York: *Sun* Office, 1842) appeared in several editions that continually added updated material; a later edition, for instance, bears the title *Life, Letters, Last Conversation, Suicide, and Inquest . . . Together with Governor Seward's Reply*. In that edition, letter no. six appears on p. 8.

The *Herald* reprinted the letters and conversation from the *Sun* pamphlet in its issue of 21 November. While that may be a testament to their authenticity, it is more likely a tribute to their popularity, besides being a rare lapse into the fanciful for Bennett. At that point he was obsessed with the crime, filling column after column with frenzied descriptions and reminiscences of the entire course of the affair. In the week before Colt's death, Bennett several times reported that Colt seemed to be contemplating suicide. On 15 November, when his penknife and razor were confiscated, the prisoner allegedly told visitors in the sheriff's presence that "he could open a vein with his teeth if he desired, and thus bleed himself to death"; and the morning edition of 18 November revealed that he had requested books on anatomy. If these passages are as accurate as the rest of Bennett's on-the-scene reporting seems to have been, the resignation and placidity Colt displayed in his last letters and conversations are wonderful indeed.

5. W. H. and F. W. Seward, *Autobiography*, p. 632.

6. *Authentic Life of John C. Colt*, pp. vi, 67, 60–61, 3, 7. Although there is no hard proof that this anonymous pamphlet was written by a partisan of Colt's, the entire tone and message of the production suggest that it was intended to counter the united condemnation of the newspapers.

7. Edwards, *Story of Colt's Revolver*, pp. 181–83, 309, 340–42. Samuel Colt's ma-

nipulation of his family was, according to Edwards, "as close to true evil as Sam ever came, and the great good which he was to do in later life never erased the blot from his conscience — that still small voice was his silent drinking partner to his grave" (p. 182). Edwards offered no evidence for the existence of this drinking partner.

8. Strong, *Diary*, 1:193 (21 November 1842).

CHAPTER SEVENTEEN

1. Parton, *Life of Horace Greeley*, p. 119.

2. Trollope, *Domestic Manners of the Americans*, pp. 336–37.

3. Stanley, *Autobiography*, p. 155. Balzac, the great urban chronicler, expressed a similar view. A provincial, he wrote, "believes only in what he observes among those whom daily exposure makes familiar, while a cosmopolitan is willing to believe in what he can only imagine about ways of life and people he has yet to experience himself" (cited in Sennett, *Fall of Public Man*, pp. 40–41).

4. Bledstein, *Culture of Professionalism*, p. 27.

5. On the "disgraceful" election-day riot between two Irish factions in the "Bloody Sixth" ward, including an assault on Bishop Hughes's house, see the *New York Tribune*, 14 April 1842, and Hone, *Diary*, 2:596; on the stereotypical case of Julia Brewer, seduced and abandoned by a married man who was sentenced only to "give security for the support during infancy of the offspring of his guilt," see the *Weekly Tribune*, 11 December 1841. The unsigned and undated letter has the penciled librarian's note "1850?"; letter in James Gordon Bennett Papers, New York Public Library.

Charles Tilly suggests a cause-and-effect relationship between excessive change and excessive violence. "The state of the social order," he writes, "depends on the balance between processes of differentiation and processes of integration or control, with rapid or excessive differentiation producing disorder" (*Big Structures*, p. 50). Times of acute and painful social change tend to unleash a wide variety of deviant and disapproved behavior, such as madness, crime, suicide, and murder.

6. [Pray], *Memoirs*, p. 257.

7. Rumors reported in *New York Herald*, 31 January, 1 March, 18, 19 November (latest edition), 6 December 1842; Strong, *Diary*, 1:192 (18 November 1842).

8. Reynolds, *Beneath the American Renaissance*, pp. 82–84.

9. Browne, *Great Metropolis*, p. 303.

EPILOGUE

1. Parton, *Life of Horace Greeley*, p. 382.

2. Schwarzlose, *Nation's Newsbrokers*, 1:89–121, 169–209, 2:1–54; Czitrom,

Media and the American Mind, pp. 16–17, 21–29. Schwarzlose analyzes the conflicting stories about the relationship between the Associated Press and the Harbor News Association, which was not, as historians from Hudson onward have maintained, the forerunner of the Associated Press. The New York AP was founded in 1848 to coordinate various cooperative newsgathering efforts and gradually expanded to include formal partnerships for newsgathering by harbor boat and, by 1851, the telegraph.

3. Newton, "Coming of the Telegraph."

4. *Vincennes Western Sun*, 4 August 1860, 11 April 1857; *Virginia Free Press*, 2 January 1859.

5. Carey, "Dark Continent," pp. 164–65.

6. Peter Novick quotes Henri Houssaye at the Exposition (*That Noble Dream*, pp. 37–38); on the importation of the term "objectivity," see ibid., p. 25 (quoting George Bancroft).

7. Steffens, *Autobiography*, p. 179; Kluger, *The Paper*, pp. 184–85. See also Schudson, *Discovering the News*, pp. 106–20; Talese, *Kingdom and the Power*, pp. 6–7; Mott, *American Journalism*, pp. 549–51. Eric Alterman argues that the rise of the "punditocracy" — the sages of the Sunday talk shows and op-ed pages who tell us what it all means — was a direct consequence of Ochs's validation of the ideal of objectivity — and even though the *Times* was clearly an upper-class, conservative paper that only *appeared* to be objective, it was the appearance that counted (*Sound and Fury*, pp. 28–29). Once purely factual reporting, devoid of interpretation, became the ideal, pundits became necessary to explain everything the papers wouldn't.

8. See Mott, *American Journalism*, pp. 430–45, 519–48; Brown, *Correspondents' War*, p. 446 (on the 300 correspondents, revising the widespread estimate of 500); Swanberg, *Citizen Hearst*; and Swanberg, *Pulitzer*.

9. Lee, *Daily Newspaper*, pp. 215–18 (quoting *Editor and Publisher*, p. 218).

10. Fox, *Mirror Makers*, p. 16; Bagdikian, *Information Machines*, p. 207; Lee, *Daily Newspaper*, pp. 172, 336 (on Mae West); Steffens, *Autobiography*, p. 338; Sperber, *Murrow*, p. 453. The public reason for Hearst's distaste, expressed in an editorial in the *Los Angeles Examiner*, was the "immorality" and "indecency" of a movie that suggested a relationship between a white woman and a "Chinese vice lord." It was *Time* magazine (9 March 1936) that pointed out the Davies connection.

The survey of 147 editors by Marquette University found that 90 percent said advertisers had tried to influence stories in their papers; 37 percent said the attempts had been effective; and 55 percent said that pressure to accommodate advertisers had come from within their own papers (cited in "F.Y.I.," *American Journalism Review*, April 1993, p. 12).

11. Barnouw, *Tower in Babel*, pp. 58–61, 172–88; Czitrom, *Media and the American Mind*, pp. 69–71 (quoting Hoover, p. 76). Hoover in fact supported commercial advertising but recognized the widespread press and public concern about the prospect.

12. Bliss, *Now the News*, p. 140. As justification for firing Brown, CBS cited the FCC's recent decision in the case of the Mayflower Broadcasting Corporation that banned all editorializing from the airwaves. Criticism of CBS was nonetheless widespread; many writers and reporters, notably H. V. Kaltenborn, argued that "No journalist worth his salt could or would be completely neutral or objective. . . . Every exercise of his editorial judgment constitutes an expression of opinion" (ibid., p. 141). The Mayflower Doctrine forbidding opinions was soon replaced by another controversial effort, the Fairness Doctrine, which incorporated the "equal time" provision for political candidates and placed on broadcasters the "affirmative duty" of presenting contrasting viewpoints on public questions. Long opposed by broadcasters as government interference, this doctrine was repealed during the Reagan administration.

13. The conservative-leaning Center for Media and Public Affairs, for instance, has amassed statistics to prove that the national press corps is more liberal than the rest of the nation; the liberal Fairness and Accuracy in Reporting has done the same to prove that most television pundits and most guests on "Nightline" are markedly conservative. Neither group has ever addressed the ramifications of the proposition that *both* sets of statistics are true.

Another group, Accuracy in Media, ran full-page ads in several major newspapers to inveigh against "negative, one-sided, distorted news" that "den[ies] us one of our country's most precious and fundamental rights: the right to unbiased, fair, honest news." Yet the ad went on to complain that the networks promote "socialist, big-spending programs," air too many of the views of "irrational, inaccurate environmental alarmists, etc.," and never say "anything GOOD . . . about the FBI, the CIA, our ARMED FORCES or the POLICE" (*New York Times*, 14 February 1993, sec. 4, p. 14). Surely a press that called government spending programs "socialist," labeled environmentalists as alarmists, and actively celebrated the CIA would *also* be one-sided and distorted.

14. Times Mirror Center, *Press and Campaign '92*, pp. 1–2.

15. Katz, "Rock, Rap, and Movies," p. 33; Grossman, "TV News," p. 47.

16. President Clinton and his advisers continue to bypass the Big Media and work to reach the public more directly. Clinton is the first president accessible by e-mail (on Internet, tap in "president@whitehouse.gov") to anyone with access to a computer network. And during his first two months in office he met twenty-five times with reporters from local media but only once with the traditional Bigfeet of the Washington press corps. "You know why I can stiff you on the press conferences?" he asked them. "Because Larry King liberated me by giving me to the American people directly" (quoted in Blumenthal, "Letter from Washington," p. 42).

17. Teenaged Amy Fisher pleaded guilty to aggravated assault after wounding Mary Jo Buttafuoco in May 1992; Fisher claimed that Joey Buttafuoco was her lover and had encouraged her to become a prostitute, Joey denied any involvement (though he subsequently pleaded guilty to a charge of statutory rape and served a

brief prison term), and Mary Jo stood by her man. Media coverage was frenzied, reaching a peak of some sort during Christmas week that year, when all three major networks ran "docudramas" about the case, one supporting Fisher's side of the story, one sympathetic to the Buttafuocos, and one seen largely through the eyes of a *New York Post* columnist.

For an example of the claim that women have special wisdom, see DiPerna, "Truth vs. 'Facts' "; for a critical analysis of the argument, see Pollitt, "Are Women Superior?" Two teams of New York journalists have written books about the Tawana Brawley case: see *Times* reporters McFadden et al., *Outrage*; WCBS-TV's Taibbi and Sims-Phillips, *Unholy Alliance*.

On the 1992 PBS documentary "Liberators: Fighting on Two Fronts in World War II," see Goldberg, "Exaggerators"; Dubner, "Massaging History." Under pressure, New York's PBS station, WNET, withdrew the program for reevaluation. In an internal report completed in September 1993 — only a summary of which was made public — WNET concluded that "Liberators" did not meet its "standards of accuracy" and removed its name from the film.

The defender of the green pea was Joel Fierman, president of the Hunts Point Fresh Produce Cooperative in the South Bronx. The First Lady's spokesman responded that her statement had been taken out of context. "Mrs. Clinton doesn't dislike peas at all," he said. "Mrs. Clinton likes peas" (quoted in Eric Wilson, "Hillary Told: Mind Your Peas and Q's," *New York Newsday*, 16 October 1993, p. 2).

18. Carey, *Communication as Culture*, p. 43.

SOURCES

Manuscript Collections

Durham, North Carolina
William R. Perkins Library, Duke University
   Bedinger–Danske Family Papers
   Gallaher Family Papers
Little Rock, Arkansas
Arkansas Historical Commission
   William E. Woodruff Papers
New York, New York
Manuscripts and Archives Section, Astor, Lenox and Tilden Foundations, New
     York Public Library
   James Gordon Bennett Papers
   Horace Greeley Papers
Vincennes, Indiana
Lewis Historical Library, Vincennes University
   Vincennes Collection
Washington, D.C.
Library of Congress
   James Gordon Bennett Papers
   Horace Greeley Papers

Newspapers

Advocate of Moral Reform (New York)
Arkansas Gazette (Little Rock)
Eastern Argus (Portland, Maine)
Kennebec Journal (Augusta, Maine)
New York Commercial Advertiser
New York Courier and Enquirer
New York Evening Post
New York Herald
New York Journal of Commerce
New York Transcript
New York Tribune
Portland Courier and Family Reader (Maine)
Princeton Whig (New Jersey)

Sun (New York)
Vincennes Western Sun (Indiana)
Virginia Free Press (Charles Town, [West] Virginia)

Books, Articles, and Dissertations

Alterman, Eric. *Sound and Fury: The Washington Punditocracy and the Collapse of American Politics.* New York: HarperCollins, 1992.

Authentic Life of John C. Colt, Now Imprisoned for Killing Samuel Adams, in New York, on the Seventeenth of September, 1841. Boston: S. N. Dickinson, 1842.

Bagdikian, Ben H. *The Information Machines: Their Impact on Men and the Media.* New York: Harper and Row, 1971.

Baldasty, Gerald J. "The Nineteenth-Century Origins of Modern American Journalism." *Proceedings of the American Antiquarian Society* 100, pt. 2 (1990): 407–19.

Barker, Jacob. *Conspiracy Trials of 1826 and 1827: A Chapter in the Life of Jacob Barker.* Introduction by R. D. Turner. Philadelphia: G. W. Childs, 1864.

Barnes, James J. *Authors, Publishers, and Politicians: The Quest for an Anglo-American Copyright Agreement, 1815–1854.* Columbus: Ohio State University Press, 1974.

Barnouw, Erik. *A Tower of Babel: A History of Broadcasting in the United States to 1933.* New York: Oxford University Press, 1966.

Barnum, P. T. *Humbugs of the World.* New York: G. W. Carleton, 1865.

——. *Struggles and Triumphs of P. T. Barnum, Told by Himself.* Edited by John G. O'Leary. London: MacGibbon and Kee, 1967.

Bender, Thomas. *New York Intellect: A History of Intellectual Life in New York City, from 1750 to the Beginnings of Our Own Time.* New York: Knopf, 1987.

Berg, Barbara J. *The Remembered Gate: Origins of American Feminism: The Woman and the City, 1800–1860.* New York: Oxford University Press, 1978.

Bergmann, Johannes Dietrich. "The Original Confidence Man: The Development of the American Confidence Man in the Sources and Backgrounds of Herman Melville's *The Confidence-Man: His Masquerade.*" Ph.D. diss., University of Connecticut, 1968.

Bledstein, Burton J. *The Culture of Professionalism: The Middle Class and the Development of Higher Education in America.* New York: Norton, 1976.

Bliss, Edward, Jr. *Now the News: The Story of Broadcast Journalism.* New York: Columbia University Press, 1991.

Blumenthal, Sidney. "Letter from Washington: The Syndicated Presidency." *New Yorker,* 5 April 1993, pp. 42–47.

Blumin, Stuart. *The Emergence of the Middle Class: Social Experience in the American City, 1760–1900.* Cambridge: Cambridge University Press, 1989.

Bok, Sissela. *Lying: Moral Choice in Public and Private Life.* New York: Vintage, 1979.

Boyer, Paul. *Urban Masses and Moral Order in America, 1820–1920.* Cambridge, Mass.: Harvard University Press, 1978.

Braudy, Leo. *The Frenzy of Renown: Fame and Its History.* New York: Oxford University Press, 1986.

Briggs, Charles Frederick. *The Adventures of Harry Franco, a Tale of the Great Panic.* 2 vols. New York: Saunders, 1839.

Brooks, Peter. "The Mark of the Beast: Prostitution, Melodrama, and Narrative." *New York Literary Forum 7: Melodrama* (1980): 125–40. Daniel Gerould, guest editor.

Browder, Clifford. *The Wickedest Woman in New York: Madame Restell, the Abortionist.* Hamden, Conn.: Archon Books, 1988.

Brown, Charles H. *The Correspondents' War: Journalists in the Spanish-American War.* New York: Charles Scribner's Sons, 1967.

Browne, Junius Henri. *The Great Metropolis: A Mirror of New York.* Hartford, Conn.: American, 1869.

Buckley, Peter George. "To the Opera House: Culture and Society in New York City, 1820–1860." Ph.D. diss., State University of New York at Stony Brook, 1984.

Byrnes, Thomas. *1886 Professional Criminals of America.* 1886. Facsimile reprint. Introductions by Arthur M. Schlesinger, Jr., and S. J. Perelman. New York: Chelsea House, 1969.

Carey, James W. *Communication as Culture: Essays on Media and Society.* Boston: Unwin Hyman, 1989.

———. "The Dark Continent of American Journalism." In Robert Karl Manoff and Michael Schudson, eds., *Reading the News: A Pantheon Guide to Popular Culture,* pp. 146–96. New York: Pantheon, 1987.

———. "The Press and the Public Discourse." *Center Magazine,* March–April 1987, pp. 4–32.

Carlson, Oliver. *The Man Who Made News: James Gordon Bennett.* New York: Duell, Sloan and Pearce, 1942.

Charvat, William. *The Profession of Authorship in America, 1800–1870: The Papers of William Charvat.* Edited by Matthew J. Bruccoli; foreword by Howard Mumford Jones. Columbus: Ohio State University Press, 1968.

Clark, Clifford E., Jr. *Henry Ward Beecher: Spokesman for a Middle-Class America.* Urbana: University of Illinois Press, 1978.

Clark, Willis Gaylord, and Lewis Gaylord Clark. *Letters.* Edited by Leslie W. Dunlap. New York: New York Public Library, 1940.

Cohen, Anne B. *Poor Pearl, Poor Girl! The Murdered-Girl Stereotype in Ballad and Newspaper.* Publications of the American Folklore Society, memoir series, vol. 58. William Hugh Jansen, general editor. Austin: University of Texas Press, 1973.

Cohen, Patricia Cline. "The Helen Jewett Murder: Violence, Gender, and Sexual Licentiousness in Antebellum America." *NWSA Journal* 2 (Summer 1990): 374–89.

Comparato, Frank E. *Chronicles of Genius and Folly: R. Hoe and Company and the Printing Press as a Service to Democracy.* Culver City, Calif.: Labyrinthos, 1979.

Congdon, Charles. *Reminiscences of a Journalist.* Boston: Osgood, 1880.

Crouthamel, James L. *Bennett's "New York Herald" and the Rise of the Popular Press.* Syracuse, N.Y.: Syracuse University Press, 1989.

——. *James Watson Webb: A Biography.* Middletown, Conn.: Wesleyan University Press, 1969.

Czitrom, Daniel J. *Media and the American Mind: From Morse to McLuhan.* Chapel Hill: University of North Carolina Press, 1982.

Davidson, Cathy N. "The Life and Times of *Charlotte Temple*: The Biography of a Book." In Cathy N. Davidson, ed., *Reading in America: Literature and Social History*, pp. 157–79. Baltimore, Md.: Johns Hopkins University Press, 1989.

Davis, David Brion. *Homicide in American Fiction, 1798–1860: A Study in Social Values.* Ithaca, N.Y.: Cornell University Press, 1957.

DiPerna, Paula. "Truth vs. 'Facts.'" *Ms.*, September–October 1991, pp. 21–26.

Douglas, Ann. *The Feminization of American Culture.* New York: Avon, 1977.

Dubner, Stephen J. "Massaging History." *New York*, 8 March 1993, pp. 46–51.

Durkheim, Émile. *The Division of Labor in Society.* Translated by George Simpson. New York: Free Press, 1964.

Eberhard, Wallace B. "Mr. Bennett Covers a Murder Trial." *Journalism Quarterly* 47 (1970): 457–63.

Edwards, William B. *The Story of Colt's Revolver: The Biography of Col. Samuel Colt.* Harrisburg, Pa.: Stackpole, 1953.

Emerson, Ralph Waldo. *Letters.* Edited by Ralph L. Rusk. 6 vols. New York: Columbia University Press, 1939.

Ericson, Carolyn Reeves. *Nacogdoches—Gateway to Texas, a Biographical Directory, 1773–1849.* Fort Worth, Tex.: Arrow/Curtis, 1974.

——, ed. *The People of Nacogdoches County in 1850: An Edited Census.* Owensboro, Ky.: Cook and McDowell, 1980.

——, transcriber. *1847 Census, Nacogdoches County.* N.p., n.d.

Erikson, Kai T. *Wayward Puritans: A Study in the Sociology of Deviance.* New York: John Wiley, 1966.

Fowley, William Chauncey. *History of Durham, Connecticut, from the First Grant of Land in 1622 to 1866.* Hartford, Conn.: Wiley, Waterman and Eaton, 1866.

Fox, Stephen. *The Mirror Makers: A History of American Advertising and Its Creators.* New York: Morrow, 1984.

Francke, Warren Theodore. "Investigative Exposure in the Nineteenth Century: The Journalistic Heritage of the Muckrakers." Ph.D. diss., University of Minnesota, 1974.

——. "James Gordon Bennett." In Perry J. Ashley, ed., *American Newspaper Journalists, 1690–1872.* Vol. 43 of *Dictionary of Literary Biography*, pp. 31–43. Detroit, Mich.: Gale Research, 1986.

Friendly, Alfred, and Ronald L. Goldfarb. *Crime and Publicity: The Impact of News on the Administration of Justice.* New York: Vintage, 1968.

Gaskell, Philip. *A New Introduction to Bibliography*. Oxford: Oxford University Press, 1972.

Gilfoyle, Timothy J. *City of Eros: New York City, Prostitution, and the Commercialization of Sex, 1790–1920*. New York: Norton, 1992.

Godkin, E. L. *Life and Letters*. Edited by Rollo Ogden. 2 vols. New York: Macmillan, 1907.

Goldberg, Jeffrey. "The Exaggerators." *New Republic*, 8 February 1993, pp. 13–14.

Greeley, Horace. *Recollections of a Busy Life: Including Reminiscences of American Politics and Politicians*. New York: Ford, 1868.

Grossman, Lawrence K. "TV News: The Need for a New Spirit." *Columbia Journalism Review*, July–August 1990, pp. 47–48.

Hale, William Harlan. *Horace Greeley, Voice of the People*. New York: Harper and Brothers, 1950.

Hall, David D. "The Uses of Literacy in New England, 1600–1850." In William L. Joyce, David D. Hall, Richard D. Brown, and John B. Hench, eds., *Printing and Society in Early America*, pp. 1–47. Worcester, Mass.: American Antiquarian Society, 1983.

Halttunen, Karen. *Confidence Men and Painted Women: A Study of Middle-Class Culture in America, 1830–1870*. New Haven, Conn.: Yale University Press, 1982.

Harris, Neil. *Humbug: The Art of P. T. Barnum*. Chicago: University of Chicago Press, 1973.

Hart, James D. *The Popular Book: A History of America's Literary Taste*. Berkeley and Los Angeles: University of California Press, 1963.

Haswell, Charles H. *Reminiscences of an Octogenarian of the City of New York (1816 to 1860)*. New York: Harper, 1896.

Hofstadter, Richard, and Michael Wallace, eds. *American Violence: A Documentary History*. New York: Vintage, 1971.

Hone, Philip. *The Diary of Philip Hone, 1828–1851*. New enlarged ed. Edited and with an introduction by Allan Nevins. 2 vols. New York: Dodd, Mead, 1936.

Hudson, Frederic. *Journalism in the United States, from 1690 to 1872*. New York: Harper, 1872.

Hugins, Walter. *Jacksonian Democracy and the Working Class: A Study of the New York Workingmen's Movement, 1829–1837*. Stanford, Calif.: Stanford University Press, 1960.

Jackson, David K. "A Poe Hoax Comes before the U.S. Senate." *Poe Studies* 7 (1974): 47–48.

Jaffe, Steven Harold. "Unmasking the City: The Rise of the Urban Newspaper Reporter in New York City, 1800–1850." Ph.D. diss., Harvard University, 1989.

Johnson, Paul E. *A Shopkeeper's Millennium: Society and Revivals in Rochester, New York, 1815–1837*. New York: Hill and Wang, 1978.

Katz, Jon. "Rock, Rap, and Movies Bring You the News." *Rolling Stone*, 5 March 1992, pp. 33–40+.

Kluger, Richard. *The Paper: The Life and Death of the "New York Herald Tribune."* New York: Knopf, 1986.

Lawson, John D., ed. *American State Trials: A Collection of the Important and Interesting Criminal Trials That Have Taken Place in the United States.* 17 vols. St. Louis, Mo.: Thomas Law Book Company, 1914–36.

Lee, Alfred McClung. *The Daily Newspaper in America: The Evolution of a Social Instrument.* New York: Macmillan, 1937.

Leonard, Ira M. "New York City Politics, 1841–1844: Nativism and Reform." Ph.D. diss., New York University, 1965.

Leonard, Thomas C. *The Power of the Press: The Birth of American Political Reporting.* New York: Oxford University Press, 1986.

Life and Writings of James Gordon Bennett, Editor of the New York Herald. New York: By the Principal Booksellers, 1844.

Lippmann, Walter. *Public Opinion.* New York: Macmillan, 1961.

McDade, Thomas M. *Annals of Murder: A Bibliography of Books and Pamphlets on American Murders from Colonial Times to 1900.* Norman: University of Oklahoma Press, 1961.

McDonald, Archie P., comp. *Inventory of Court Records, Nacogdoches County Courthouse, Nacogdoches, Texas.* Austin: Center for Community Services, North Texas State University, and Archives Division, Texas State Library, 1975.

McFadden, Robert D., Ralph Blumenthal, M. A. Farber, E. R. Shipp, Charles Strum, and Craig Wolff. *Outrage: The Story behind the Tawana Brawley Hoax.* New York: Bantam, 1990.

Marryat, Frederick. *A Diary in America with Remarks on Its Institutions.* Edited by Sydney Jackman. New York: Knopf, 1962.

Mathews, Cornelius. *Puffer Hopkins.* New York: Appleton, 1842.

Maverick, Augustus. *Henry J. Raymond and the New York Press, for Thirty Years: Progress of American Journalism from 1840 to 1870.* Hartford, Conn.: Hale; Chicago: Rogers, 1870.

Mayhew, Henry. *London Labour and the London Poor: A Cyclopaedia of the Condition and Earnings of Those That Will Work, Those That Cannot Work, and Those That Will Not Work.* 4 vols. London: Griffin, Bohn, 1861–62.

Melville, Herman. "Bartleby the Scrivener: A Story of Wall-Street." In Harrison Hayford, Alma A. MacDougall, G. Thomas Tanselle, et al., eds., *The Writings of Herman Melville*, Northwestern-Newberry Edition, 9:13–45. Evanston, Ill.: Northwestern University Press and Newberry Library, 1987.

Miller, Perry. *Errand into the Wilderness.* Cambridge, Mass.: Belknap Press, 1956.

——. *The Raven and the Whale: The War of Words and Wits in the Era of Poe and Melville.* New York: Harcourt, Brace, 1956.

Minter, David. *The Interpreted Design as a Structural Principle in American Prose.* Yale Publications in American Studies, no. 15. New Haven, Conn.: Yale University Press, 1969.

Mintz, Max M. *Gouverneur Morris and the American Revolution.* Norman: University of Oklahoma Press, 1970.

Mollenkopf, John Hull, ed. *Power, Culture, and Place: Essays on New York City.* New York: Russell Sage Foundation, 1988.

Moran, James. *Printing Presses: History and Development from the Fifteenth Century to Modern Times.* Berkeley and Los Angeles: University of California Press, 1973.

Moss, Sidney P. *Poe's Literary Battles: The Critic in the Context of His Literary Milieu.* Durham, N.C.: Duke University Press, 1963.

Mott, Frank Luther. *American Journalism, a History: 1690–1960.* 3d ed. New York: Macmillan, 1962.

———. *A History of American Magazines, 1741–1850.* Cambridge, Mass.: Belknap Press, 1957.

Murrie, Pauline Shirley, comp. *Early Records of Nacogdoches County, Texas.* Waco, Tex.: n.p., n.d.

Newton, Edward C. "The Coming of the Telegraph to Arkansas." *Arkansas Gazette,* 20 November 1919, suppl. sec., p. 105.

New-York City Temperance Society. *First Annual Report . . . Presented May 11, 1830.* New York: Sleight and Robinson, 1830.

Nichols, Thomas Low. *Forty Years of American Life.* 2 vols. London: Maxwell, 1864.

Nord, David Paul. *The Evangelical Origins of Mass Media in America, 1815–1835.* Journalism Monographs no. 88. Columbus, Ohio: Association for Education in Journalism and Mass Communications, 1984.

Novick, Peter. *That Noble Dream: The "Objectivity Question" and the American Historical Profession.* Cambridge: Cambridge University Press, 1988.

O'Brien, Frank M. *The Story of the "Sun."* New ed. New York: Appleton, 1928.

Papke, David Ray. *Framing the Criminal: Crime, Cultural Work, and the Loss of Critical Perspective, 1830–1900.* Hamden, Conn.: Archon Books, 1987.

Park, Robert E. *The Crowd and the Public and Other Essays.* Edited with an introduction by Henry Elsner, Jr.; translated by Charlotte Elsner; notes by Donald N. Levine. Chicago: University of Chicago Press, 1972.

———. "The Natural History of the Newspaper." *American Journal of Sociology* 29 (November 1923): 273–89.

Parton, James. *The Life of Horace Greeley, Editor of the "New York Tribune."* New York: Mason, 1855.

Pessen, Edward. *Jacksonian America: Society, Personality, and Politics.* Rev. ed. Urbana: University of Illinois Press, 1985.

Pfaff, Daniel W. "Horace Greeley." In Perry J. Ashley, ed., *American Newspaper Journalists, 1690–1872.* Vol. 43 of *Dictionary of Literary Biography,* pp. 256–72. Detroit, Mich: Gale Research, 1986.

Poe, Edgar Allan. *Collected Works.* Edited by Thomas Ollive Mabbott. 3 vols. Cambridge, Mass.: Belknap Press, 1978.

——. *Essays and Reviews.* Library of America, no. 20. New York: Literary Classics of the United States, 1984.

Pollitt, Katha. "Are Women Morally Superior to Men?" *The Nation,* 28 December 1992, pp. 799–807.

[Pray, Isaac C.] *Memoirs of James Gordon Bennett and His Times.* By a Journalist. New York: Stringer and Townsend, 1855.

Pred, Allan R. *Urban Growth and the Circulation of Information: The United States System of Cities, 1790–1840.* Cambridge, Mass.: Harvard University Press, 1973.

Reynolds, David S. *Beneath the American Renaissance: The Subversive Imagination in the Age of Emerson and Melville.* New York: Knopf, 1988.

Richards, Leonard L. *"Gentlemen of Property and Standing": Anti-Abolition Mobs in Jacksonian America.* Oxford: Oxford University Press, 1970.

Riis, Jacob A. *The Making of an American.* Edited with an introduction by Roy Lubove. New York: Harper and Row, 1966.

Rohan, Jack. *Yankee Arms Maker: The Incredible Career of Samuel Colt.* New York: Harper, 1935.

Ross, Margaret. *"Arkansas Gazette," the Early Years, 1819–1866: A History.* Little Rock: Arkansas Gazette Foundation, 1969.

Rowson, Susanna Haswell. *Charlotte Temple.* Edited with an introduction by Cathy N. Davidson. Oxford: Oxford University Press, 1986.

Rush, Benjamin. *Selected Writings.* Edited by Dagobert D. Runes. New York: Philosophical Library, 1947.

Russo, David J. *The Origins of Local News in the U.S. Country Press, 1840s–1870s.* Journalism Monographs no. 65. Lexington, Ky.: Association for Education in Journalism, 1980.

Saxton, Alexander. "Problems of Class and Race in the Origins of the Mass Circulation Press." *American Quarterly* 36 (1984): 211–34.

Schiller, Dan. *Objectivity and the News: The Public and the Rise of Commercial Journalism.* Philadelphia: University of Pennsylvania Press, 1981.

Schudson, Michael. *Discovering the News: A Social History of American Newspapers.* New York: Basic Books, 1978.

Schwarzlose, Richard A. *The Nation's Newsbrokers.* 2 vols. Evanston, Ill.: Northwestern University Press, 1989–90.

Sennett, Richard. *The Fall of Public Man: On the Social Psychology of Capitalism.* New York: Vintage, 1978.

Seward, William H., and Frederick W. Seward. *Autobiography of William H. Seward from 1801 to 1834; with a Memoir of His Life, and Selections from His Letters from 1831 to 1846.* New York: Appleton, 1877.

Silver, Rollo G. *The American Printer, 1787–1825.* Charlottesville: University Press of Virginia, for the Bibliographical Society of the University of Virginia, 1967.

——. "The Power of the Press: Hand, Horse, Water, and Steam." *Printing History* 9 (vol. 5, no. 1, 1983): 5–16.

Silverman, Kenneth. *Edgar A. Poe: Mournful and Never-Ending Remembrance.* New York: HarperPerennial, 1992.

Smith-Rosenberg, Carroll. *Disorderly Conduct: Visions of Gender in Victorian America.* New York: Oxford University Press, 1985.

Spann, Edward K. *The New Metropolis: New York City, 1840–1857.* New York: Columbia University Press, 1981.

Sperber, A. M. *Murrow: His Life and Times.* New York: Freundlich Books, 1986.

Stanley, Henry Morton. *The Autobiography of Sir Henry Morton Stanley.* Edited by Dorothy Stanley. Boston: Houghton Mifflin, [1937].

Stansell, Christine. *City of Women: Sex and Class in New York, 1789–1860.* New York: Knopf, 1986.

Steffens, Lincoln. *The Autobiography of Lincoln Steffens.* New York: Grosset and Dunlap, 1931.

Stephens, Mitchell. *A History of News from the Drum to the Satellite.* New York: Viking, 1988.

Stevens, John D. *Sensationalism and the New York Press.* New York: Columbia University Press, 1991.

Strong, George Templeton. *The Diary of George Templeton Strong.* Edited by Allan Nevins and Milton Halsey Thomas. 4 vols. New York: Macmillan, 1952.

Sutton, Charles. *The New York Tombs: Its Secrets and Its Mysteries, Being a History of Noted Criminals, with Narratives of Their Crimes.* Edited by James B. Mix and Samuel A. MacKeever. New York: United States Publishing Company, 1874.

Swanberg, W. A. *Citizen Hearst.* New York: Bantam, 1971.

——. *Pulitzer.* New York: Charles Scribner's Sons, 1967.

Taibbi, Mike, and Anna Sims-Phillips. *Unholy Alliance: Working the Tawana Brawley Story.* New York: Harcourt Brace Jovanovich, 1989.

Talese, Gay. *The Kingdom and the Power.* Garden City, N.Y.: Anchor Doubleday, 1978.

Thompson, Lawrance. "The Printing and Publishing Activities of the American Tract Society from 1825 to 1850." *Papers of the Bibliographical Society of America* 35 (1941): 81–114.

Thoreau, Henry David. *Journal*, vol. 4, 1851–52. Edited by Leonard N. Neufeldt and Nancy Craig Simmons; general ed., Robert Sattelmeyer. The Writings of Henry D. Thoreau. Princeton, N.J.: Princeton University Press, 1992.

——. *Walden.* Edited by J. Lyndon Shanley. The Writings of Henry D. Thoreau. Princeton, N.J.: Princeton University Press, 1971.

Tilly, Charles. *Big Structures, Large Processes, Huge Comparisons.* New York: Russell Sage Foundation, 1984.

Times Mirror Center for The People and The Press. *The Press and Campaign '92: A Self-Assessment.* Washington, D.C.: Times Mirror Center, 1993.

Tocqueville, Alexis de. *Democracy in America.* Edited by J. P. Mayer; translated by George Lawrence. Garden City, N.Y.: Anchor Doubleday, 1969.

The Tribune, 1841–April 10, 1891: Fifty Years of Service, Crowned with a Golden Jubilee. New York: The Tribune, 1891.

Trollope, Mrs. Frances. *Domestic Manners of the Americans.* Edited with an introduction, new materials, and notes by Donald Smalley. New York: Vintage, 1949.

Tucker, Stephen D. "History of R. Hoe and Company, 1834–1885." Edited with an introduction by Rollo G. Silver. *Proceedings of the American Antiquarian Society* 82, pt. 2 (1973): 351–453.

Twain, Mark [Samuel L. Clemens]. *Roughing It.* Vol. 2 of *The Works of Mark Twain.* Introduction and notes by Franklin R. Rogers; text established by Paul Baender. Berkeley: University of California Press for the Iowa Center for Textual Studies, 1972.

U.S. Senate. "Immigration to the United States." Reprinted in Douglass C. North and Robert Paul Thomas, eds., *The Growth of the American Economy to 1860*, pp. 225–36. New York: Harper and Row, 1968.

Van Deusen, Glyndon G. *Horace Greeley, Nineteenth-Century Crusader.* New York: Hill and Wang, 1953.

Walling, George A. *Recollections of a New York Chief of Police: An Official Record of Thirty-Eight Years as Patrolman, Detective, Captain, Inspector, and Chief of the New York Police.* New York: Caxton, 1887.

Welter, Barbara. "The Cult of True Womanhood." *American Quarterly* 18 (1966): 151–74.

Whittington, Hiram Abiff. *Letters of Hiram Abiff Whittington, an Arkansas Pioneer from Massachusetts, 1827–1834.* Edited by Margaret Smith Ross. Pulaski County Historical Society Bulletin no. 3. Little Rock, Ark.: The Society, 1956.

Wilentz, Sean. *Chants Democratic: New York City and the Rise of the American Working Class, 1788–1850.* New York: Oxford University Press, 1984.

Williams, Daniel E. " 'Behold a Tragic Scene Strangely Changed into a Theater of Mercy': The Structure and Significance of Criminal Conversion Narratives in Early New England." *American Quarterly* 38 (1986): 827–48.

———. "Rogues, Rascals, and Scoundrels: The Underworld Literature of Early America." *American Studies* 24, no. 2 (Fall 1983): 5–19.

Wilmer, L. A. *Our Press Gang: Or, a Complete Exposition of the Corruptions and Crimes of the American Newspaper.* Philadelphia, Pa.: Lloyd, 1859.

Wolf, Marvin, and Katherine Mader. *Rotten Apples: True Stories of New York Crime and Mystery, 1689 to the Present.* New York: Ballantine, 1991.

Zboray, Ronald J. "Antebellum Reading and the Ironies of Technological Innovation." *American Quarterly* 40 (1988): 65–82.

INDEX

ABC, 202

Abolitionists, 126

Abortionists, 101, 132, 180, 181

Accuracy in Media, 233 (n. 13)

Adams, Emeline, 99, 150

Adams, John Quincy, 13

Adams, Samuel: murder described, 1, 101–2; disappearance of, 99; body found, 100, 140; body reported cut up, 157–58; character of, 163. *See also* Colt case

Advertising, 9, 15–16, 131, 132, 199–200

Advocate of Moral Reform, 65, 219–20 (n. 7)

Ainsworth, William, 125

Alamo, 88

Alcoa, 200

American Anti-Slavery Society, 126

American Bible Society, 126

American Female Moral Reform Society, 146

American Institute, 81

American Sunday School Union, 126, 146

American Tract Society, 126, 146

Amundsen, Roald, 43

Anthon, George, 174

Anthon, Reverend Henry, 106, 153, 155–56, 165, 174

Arcturus, 160

Arkansas, 92; crime in, 93–94, 96; provincialism of, 178; and telegraph, 193

Arkansas Gazette, 88, 90; local news in, 92–93; crime news in, 93–94, 96; on Jewett murder, 94–96; on New York crime, 147, 172; on Fort Sumter, 195

Associated Press, 115, 192, 200; and country press, 193–96; standardized language of, 194–96

AT&T, 200

Attree, William, 27, 32, 121, 169, 214–15 (n. 2)

Aunt Nelly, 53, 58, 60. *See also* Heth, Joice

Authority: country editor as, 89–90; in penny press, 187–89

Baltimore Patriot, 91

Balzac, Honoré de, 68, 212 (prologue, n. 1), 231 (n. 3)

Barnum, P. T., 59; establishes museum, 48; and Joice Heth, 48, 53; on humbug, 49, 52; and humbug as entertainment, 55–57; and idea of public, 58; and Jenny Lind, 58

Beach, Moses Y., 114–15, 189. *See also* New York *Sun*

Bedinger, Henry, 89

Benjamin, Park, 117

Bennett, James Gordon, 37, 109; starts *Herald*, 8, 18–19; covers Salem murder, 11, 93; background of, 16–18; self-assessment of, 19–20, 150–51; enduring reputation of, 20, 84, 186, 222 (n. 8); marriage of, 118–19; satirized by elite, 159–61; death of, 196; in *Sun*'s fake diary, 214–15 (n. 2). See also *New York Herald*

Bennett, James Gordon, Jr., 196

Blackwood's, 135